Championing Co-production in the Design of Inclusive Practices

This book brings together the voices of practitioners, researchers, parents, and children and young people themselves to explore innovative pedagogies where multiple voices have been actively engaged in co-producing the design of inclusive practices within education.

Each chapter focuses on how a particular approach, strategy, or project has included children and young people in the decisions that are made about them, their lives, and their education. These examples feature a mix of innovative, creative, and multisensory pedagogies that consider how to facilitate communication between children and the adults who work with them around the concept and application of inclusive education. Reflective questions are woven throughout, allowing the reader to engage with diverse voices and ensure everyone is involved in adapting teaching to create better learning opportunities for all. Practical takeaway activities are also included that can be discussed in schools and easily applied to a range of different settings.

Championing Co-production in the Design of Inclusive Practices champions teaching and learning pedagogies which not only reflect individuality and difference but also actively seek to position children, young people, and learners at the very heart of their own educational experience. It is valuable reading for SENCOs, practising and trainee teachers, and school inclusion managers.

Clare Woolhouse is Reader at Edge Hill University, and her research is based within school communities working directly with teachers, children, and young people. Clare explores marginalised identities, multi-modal methodologies, and pedagogies, with particular attention given to aspects of educational difference, inclusion, and social justice.

Virginia Kay is Senior Lecturer at Edge Hill University working with student teachers and postgraduate education students. Her research interests are rooted in social justice and perceptions of difference, particularly as this pertains to the policy and practice of inclusive education provision and the role of the SENCo.

nasen is a professional membership association that supports all those who work with or care for children and young people with special and additional educational needs. Members include SENCOs, school leaders, governors/trustees, teachers, teaching assistants, support workers, other educationalists, students and families.

nasen supports its members through policy documents, peer-reviewed academic journals, its membership magazine *nasen Connect*, publications, professional development courses, regional networks and newsletters. Its website contains more current information such as responses to government consultations.

nasen's published documents are held in very high regard both in the UK and internationally.

For a full list of titles see: https://www.routledge.com/nasen-spotlight/book-series/FULNASEN

Other titles published in association with the National Association for Special Educational Needs (nasen):

Championing Co-production in the Design of Inclusive Practices: Positioning Children and Young People's Voices at the Heart of Education
Clare Woolhouse and Virginia Kay
2025/pb: 978–1–032–60279–0

The Secret Life of SENCOs: Practical Insights on Inclusion and Specialist Provision
Adam Boddison and Maxine O'Neill
2025/pb: 978–1–032–63478–4

AAC and Aided Language in the Classroom: Breaking Down Barriers for Learners with Speech, Language and Communication Needs
Katy Leckenby and Meaghan Ebbage-Taylor
2025/pb: 978–1–032–53196–0

Supporting Children and Young People Through Loss and Trauma: Hands-On Strategies to Improve Mental Health and Wellbeing
Juliet Ann Taylor
2024/pb: 978–1–032–23023–8

Language for Learning in the Primary School: A Practical Guide for Supporting Pupils with Language and Communication Difficulties across the Curriculum, 3ed
Sue Hayden and Emma Jordan
2023/pb: 978–1–032–34259–7

Beating Bureaucracy in Special Educational Needs: Helping SENCOs Maintain a Work/Life Balance, 4ed
Jean Gross
2023/pb: 978–1–032–32239–1

Inclusive and Accessible Science for Students with Additional or Special Needs: How to Teach Science Effectively to Diverse Learners in Secondary Schools
Jane Essex
2023/pb: 978–0–367–76627–6

True Partnerships in SEND: Working Together to Give Children, Families and Professionals a Voice
Heather Green and Becky Edwards
2023/pb: 978–0–367–54494–2

Championing Co-production in the Design of Inclusive Practices

Positioning Children and Young People's Voices at the Heart of Education

Edited by Clare Woolhouse and Virginia Kay

LONDON AND NEW YORK

Designed cover image: © Clare Woolhouse and Robert Monfea, produced as part of the VOICES project. The image depicts origami cranes created as a 'wish for peace' made by children and other visitors who attended workshops as part of an exhibition at Tate Liverpool art gallery.

First published 2025
by Routledge
4 Park Square, Milton Park, Abingdon, Oxon OX14 4RN

and by Routledge
605 Third Avenue, New York, NY 10158

Routledge is an imprint of the Taylor & Francis Group, an informa business

© 2025 selection and editorial matter, Clare Woolhouse and Virginia Kay; individual chapters, the contributors

The right of Clare Woolhouse and Virginia Kay to be identified as the authors of the editorial material, and of the authors for their individual chapters, has been asserted in accordance with sections 77 and 78 of the Copyright, Designs and Patents Act 1988.

All rights reserved. No part of this book may be reprinted or reproduced or utilised in any form or by any electronic, mechanical, or other means, now known or hereafter invented, including photocopying and recording, or in any information storage or retrieval system, without permission in writing from the publishers.

Trademark notice: Product or corporate names may be trademarks or registered trademarks, and are used only for identification and explanation without intent to infringe.

British Library Cataloguing-in-Publication Data
A catalogue record for this book is available from the British Library

ISBN: 978-1-032-60280-6 (hbk)
ISBN: 978-1-032-60279-0 (pbk)
ISBN: 978-1-003-45965-1 (ebk)

DOI: 10.4324/9781003459651

Typeset in Helvetica
by Apex CoVantage, LLC

Clare: I dedicate this book to Rob, for his never-wavering belief in me, his constant support, and his encouragement. He makes me a better person, the person I want to be.

Virginia: I would like to dedicate this book to both my husband, Christian, and my parents, Linda and David. I wouldn't be the person I am without their never-ending support and encouragement.

Contents

List of figures and tables   ix
List of contributors   x
Foreword   xiii
Acknowledgements   xiv
List of abbreviations   xv
Glossary   xvi

Introduction   1
Clare Woolhouse and Virginia Kay

Section I   Listening to the voices of children and young people   5

1. **How inclusive is the school environment? The reality of implementing children's right to express their views**   7
   Carol Robinson

2. **Re-thinking inclusive practice within early years education**   17
   Naomi Jackson

3. **Enabling children to feel happier, heard, and connected: the Hamish & Milo well-being programme enabling primary school children to share their feelings and experience, develop their social and emotional skills, and improve their well-being**   27
   Clare Williams

4. **My school, my voice: development of an inclusive student council in a large special school for autism**   45
   Sara Muršić

5. **Sharing case studies of supporting SEND in schools drawing from three national contexts**   59
   Christine Sanders

6. **Reimagining inclusive education: power, status, and voice**   69
   Fiona Hallett and Graham Hallett

7. **Reimagining the role of children and young people's voices within the design of inclusive education**   77
   Clare Woolhouse and Virginia Kay

Section II Involving young people and adults in developing inclusive communities 87

8 **'Nothing about us without us': developing inclusive and meaningful research collaborations with autistic young people and peers** 89
Angela Wearn, Zoe Collier, Katie Jenkins, Lily Wearn, Niamh Carson, Catherine El Zerbi, Felicity Shenton, Liam Spencer, and Amy Pearson

9 **The inclusive design of a digital education programme – contribution and experiences of people with accessibility needs** 101
Esther Murphy, Daniela Bratković, and Alisa Vivoda

10 **Rooted in Nature: improving the involvement of young people as research advisors** 115
Elaf Alasi, Kacie Hodgson, Charley McFarlane-Troy, and Catherine El Zerbi

11 **Creating neuro-mixed learning environments in higher education** 125
Allison Moore and Paul Davies

Conclusion 139
Clare Woolhouse and Virginia Kay

Index 143

Figures and tables

Figures

3.1	Hamish & Milo sock puppets.	31
3.2	The four Ss model.	33
3.3	Examples of children's drawings prior to participating in the programme.	37
3.4	Examples of children's drawings prior to participating in the programme.	37
3.5	Examples of children's drawings prior to participating in the programme.	38
4.1	Student council application form.	53
7.1	In the art classroom.	79
7.2	Photograph and information card: 'Nowhere to Sit'.	81
7.3	Photograph and information card: 'Painting Trees'.	82
8.1	The Ladder of Participation – demonstrating ways in which children and young people may be involved in community activity.	91
9.1	James presenting his work	107

Table

4.1	Student voice system	52

Contributors

Elaf Alasi is a young advisor on the Rooted in Nature project.

Daniela Bratković is currently a full professor at the University of Zagreb, Faculty of Education and Rehabilitation Sciences, where she completed her formal education. She has also continuously participated in numerous study visits abroad and lifelong learning courses. She has worked in the Department of Inclusive Education and Rehabilitation since 1993. In two mandates, she was the vice dean for science. Daniela's undergraduate, master's, and postgraduate teaching and professional and public work are focused on community-based support, person-centred planning, lifelong learning, and improving public policy for adults with intellectual and other disabilities. She is also a guest lecturer at other university studies in Croatia and abroad. She supervises MRes and PhD students and mentors early career researchers. Her main scientific interest and research projects are related to inclusive education and training, self-advocacy, sexuality, supported employment, and independent living of people with intellectual and other developmental disabilities.

Niamh Carson is a member of ARC NENC's Young Person's Advisory Network.

Zoe Collier is a member of ARC NENC's Young Person's Advisory Network and has recently completed her MSc in psychological research methods at Sunderland University. She is interested in research focused on the stigmatisation and victim blaming of autistic people.

Paul Davies is an autistic autism trainer, positive support instructor, and trainee psychotherapist. He received his diagnosis late in life. He has spent 25 years working in a range of equality projects, now focusing on autism. Paul works with a human rights–based, least-restrictive, autism-positive approach to autistic human beings. He has delivered sessions on 'autism and trauma-informed care' for a wide range of organisations, including the NHS. As a visiting lecturer, Paul worked alongside Dr Allison Moore to co-create and co-deliver the 'cutting-edge' MA in critical autism studies. In 2020, Paul contributed a chapter to *The Neurodiversity Reader* and has another forthcoming (2025) about 'double empathy', both edited by Dr Damian Milton.

Catherine El Zerbi is a NIHR ARC NENC research fellow working with the "supporting children and families" research theme. Her research interests include implementation and improvement science to reduce health inequalities and improve outcomes for children and families, and she co-produced mixed methods working alongside children and young people to include their voices in the research process to improve science.

Fiona Hallett and Graham Hallett are the joint editors of the *British Journal of Special Education*. Between them, they have over 40 years of experience teaching in a range of special settings and have run undergraduate and postgraduate courses around inclusive and special education. They have used this style of teaching across a range of settings and continue to be fascinated by the responses of those who engage. Fiona and Graham have published books and articles around the role of the SENCO, exclusionary educational practices, inclusive education, and disability discrimination.

Kacie Hodgson is a young advisor on the Rooted in Nature project.

Naomi Jackson is a nursery manager with over 30 years' experience of working within nursery settings. Having completed an NNEB diploma in 1994, she has gone on to work in a variety of nursery settings and continued her professional development, gaining BA (Hons) in early years practice. She has been a SENDCO for over 15 years and has worked with a diverse range of children with additional needs while supporting her team in delivering inclusive practice.

Katie Jenkins is a member of ARC NENC's Young Person's Advisory Network.

Virginia Kay has been a senior lecturer in education at Edge Hill University since 2010, becoming the course leader for the National Award for SEN Co-ordination in 2013. She works with over 100 SENCos from across England per year as they create their own strategic vision for SEN provision in their settings and navigate ways in which they can meet the needs of both learners and other staff members in the development of inclusive practices. Her previous and professional experience includes 12 years teaching in a variety of settings across key stages 1, 2, and 3, including two years in the United States. Virginia has a strong professional interest in inclusion and SEN, in relation to both policy and practice, and is passionate about all aspects of social justice within education.

Charley McFarlane-Troy has worked as a secondary school teacher for two years in China, then England after acquiring her MA in Anthropology and her PGCE in secondary English. Charley recently completed a research assistant role on the Rooted in Nature project and now works in a secondary school in Newcastle as an English teacher.

Allison Moore is a reader in social sciences at Edge Hill University. Since graduating with a degree in applied social sciences in 1999, Allison has worked in a variety of settings, including higher education and the voluntary and community sector. Her approach to critical autism studies is largely underpinned by a constructionist perspective read through a feminist lens. However, she is also influenced by sociologists, especially Pierre Bourdieu and Norbert Elias, who have attempted to move beyond the binaries of micro/macro and individual/society. Her desire to look beyond either micro or macro explanations of social life in order to understand the complexity of autistic people's lived experiences also leads to her interest in ecological approaches that see individuals as active agents in a network of dynamic and interrelated relationships.

Esther Murphy is the principal investigator for the interdisciplinary European digital inclusion programme *Digi-ID Plus* based at Trinity College Dublin's (TCD) School of Engineering and an academic collaborator at the ADAPT Centre. She is also the founder of the TCD campus inclusive employer company *DigiAcademy*, which is a European Commission Award–winning accessible digital skills e-learning platform co-designed with and for people with intellectual disabilities, their education, health providers, and families/carers. Esther holds a PhD in disability studies and an MA in intercultural studies from Dublin City University, Ireland, with 15+ years' experience in social science disability, mental health, and inclusive technology research in academia, NGOs, and collaborations with industry. At the heart of Esther's work is a commitment to ensure the full inclusion of citizens with disabilities into all phases of the research innovation process via the development of innovative inclusive research methods, including citizen teaching training and video co-production.

Dr Sara Muršić is an advocate for inclusive education and a researcher in the field of learning technologies. She is currently a specialist study skills tutor for students with disabilities at Liverpool John Moores University. Previously, she served as the head of autism research and development at a local special school. Dr Muršić holds a PhD in education from Edge Hill University, where she also taught modules on special education, inclusion, and diversity. Her research interests focus on the application of innovative technologies, such as augmented reality, to support students with specific learning difficulties. She has presented her work at international conferences and published multiple papers on the topic. Dr Muršić is passionate about creating inclusive learning environments that leverage technology to empower students of all abilities.

Amy Pearson is an assistant professor in psychology and a chartered developmental psychologist at Durham University. Her research focuses on understanding factors that impact on well-being among autistic people across the lifespan. She is particularly interested in interpersonal relationships and victimisation, social identity and stigma, and increasing accessibility for neurodivergent people in higher education.

Carol Robinson is a professor of children's rights at the Institute of Education, University of Strathclyde. Carol started her career as a teacher and has taught in secondary schools, in pupil referral units, and in a college of further education. She completed her PhD at the University of Sussex in 1996 and then took up a post as a research fellow within the University of Sussex's Education Faculty. Carol joined the Education Research Centre within the School of Education at the University of Brighton in 2008 and became a professor of children's rights there in 2019.

Her research interests combine theoretical and empirical work focusing on the voices, experiences, rights, and empowerment of children and young people, and she has published widely in this area. A major focus of Carol's work has been around developing insights into issues relating to children's human rights education.

Christine Sanders is a primary school teacher with over 25 years of experience. She has taught across the primary age phases years 1 to 6 (ages 5–10) and has experience of working in the UK, Switzerland, and Australia. She has taught in a variety of schools, including an international school, an Islamic school, a Jewish school, and many Christian schools. She has taught a range of subjects, including English, mathematics, science, computing, history, geography, art, design and technology, PSHE, PE, RE, music, and French. Christine now enjoys working for Jam Coding, one of the largest providers of computing education in the UK. She delivers a multi-award-winning bespoke computing curriculum and after-school workshops to a variety of primary schools across Lancashire, reaching out to hundreds of pupils every week.

Felicity Shenton is the public involvement and engagement manager for the NIHR ARC NENC, based at Cumbria, Northumberland, Tyne, and Wear (CNTW) NHS Trust. She has a background in rights-based practice and participatory research, co-production, and youth-led peer research.

Liam Spencer is a mental health research fellow affiliated with the "health inequalities and marginalised communities" research theme for NIHR ARC NENC. He works within Newcastle University's Population Health Sciences Institute. His research interests include young people's mental health, early intervention and prevention, and whole-school-based mental health interventions.

Alisa Vivoda is a research assistant working on the EU project Digi-ID Plus at the Faculty of Education and Rehabilitation Sciences, University of Zagreb. Through project activities, she has gained experience in inclusive approach and teamwork with adults with ID. Before working at the Faculty, she was employed in an educational centre where she worked with preschool children with disabilities. Alisa is actively involved in organising social skills trainings and leisure activities for children and young adults with disabilities. She has also participated as a speaker in many national and international conferences. Her main interests are inclusive approach, mental health, and digital and social inclusion of people with ID.

Angela Wearn is a chartered psychologist (academic) specialising in health psychology and a research fellow in public involvement and community engagement for the NIHR Applied Research Collaboration (ARC) North East and North Cumbria (NENC). Within her current role, Angela often works as a lived experience researcher working alongside diverse, marginalised communities on a range of topics related to inclusion, improved access to care, and the accessibility and relevance of applied health research.

Lily Wearn is a member of ARC NENC's Young Person's Advisory Network. She is interested in research that focuses on the mental health and well-being of neurodivergent young people.

Clare Williams is an educational psychotherapist, primary teacher, and trauma-informed trainer. Clare has worked in primary schools, in mental health and education provision, and within Child and Adolescent Mental Health Services (CAMHS). She has led on national initiatives for local authorities as the social and emotional aspects of learning (SEAL) consultant, leading on training, curriculum implementation, and development, as well as the local coordination of the National PSHE CPD Programme. She was a consultant trainer for the Institute of Education, London, and a trainer for the Education Development Association at Homerton College, Cambridge, providing courses for overseas teachers. As the manager of a multi-agency service for vulnerable children at risk of exclusion, Clare also developed Thrive Education Zones, an alternative provision based on nurture and attachment-aware principles.

Clare Woolhouse is currently a reader at Edge Hill University. After completing her PGCE, Clare worked in two secondary schools and a further education college before moving into higher education. At Lancaster University, she taught undergraduate students for five years while studying for her PhD. In 2007, she moved to the Faculty of Education at Edge Hill University. Clare's teaching relates to sociological approaches to a range of educational subjects and concerns. She supervises MRes and PhD students and mentors early career researchers and academic colleagues new to teaching or research in higher education. She is a senior fellow of the Higher Education Academy. Clare's research adopts a feminist approach to exploring marginalised identities, multi-modal methodologies, and pedagogies, with particular attention given to aspects of educational difference, inclusion, and social justice.

Foreword

Welcome to this new collection of writings about ensuring the voices of children and young people are placed at the heart of school education policies and practices. The idea for this text arose following our presentation at the nasen conference in July 2022 and the conversations we had with other academics, teachers, and practitioners at the event. There was a sense that a text was needed that was a departure from the more usually seen texts which offer only an academic 'walk-through' of issues or a 'how-to' guide for current practitioners. Accordingly, this text offers a range of voices, from academics, practitioners, children, and young people themselves.

The text brings together 11 chapters to look broadly at inclusion, blending academic, professional, and personal perspectives and amplifying the voices of children and young people. Case studies are provided of innovative, creative, or multisensory pedagogies which have enabled the wide-ranging, diverse voices and experiences of children and young people to be actively engaged in the design of inclusive practices within education. The purpose here is not merely to demonstrate the value of particular approaches but to offer an exciting array of difference in both approaches and perspectives, which will allow for new ways of thinking around inclusion to emerge.

Each chapter concludes with a section containing guided reflective questions which can be used as prompt questions within taught higher education courses; as continuing professional development starting points for settings such as schools, youth groups, and healthcare facilities; or as part of a more individual journey towards a path of more inclusive practice. Each chapter will also include 'takeaway activities', with suggestions for adapting the approaches discussed in ways that can suit individuals' diverse settings. In doing so, this text offers a clear and unique approach to thinking about how inclusion can be enacted in ways that really actively engage with the children and young people, who are the reason for practitioners wanting to enhance school education policy and practice.

Clare Woolhouse and Virginia Kay
Faculty of Education, Edge Hill University, Ormskirk, UK

Acknowledgements

The authors would like to thank all the colleagues, parents, pupils, and students whose experiences and shared stories have contributed to the chapters included in this book.

Abbreviations

BA	bachelor of arts
BEd	bachelor of education
BERA	British Educational Research Association
CFET	certificate in further education and training
CPD	continuous professional development
DfE	Department for Education, England
EAL	English as an additional language
ECF	early career framework
ECR	early career researcher
EdD	doctorate in education
EERA	European Educational Research Association
EU	European Union
EYE	early years education
FTE	full-time equivalent
HE	higher education
HEFC	Higher Education Funding Council (England)
HEI	higher education institution
HESA	Higher Education Statistics Agency (UK)
ITE/ITT	initial teacher education/training
Key Stage 1–4	stages of the state education system (UK)
LEA	local education authority
LS	lesson study
MA	master of education
MRes	master of research
NSS	National Student Survey (UK)
NUS	National Union of Students (UK and various other countries)
Ofsted	Office for Standards in Education
PGCE	postgraduate certificate in education
PGDE	postgraduate diploma in education
PhD	doctor of philosophy
QAA	Quality Assurance Agency for Higher Education
QTS	qualified teacher status (England)
REF	research excellence framework (UK)
SCITT	school-centred initial teacher training (England)
SEND	special education needs and disabilities
SENCo	special education needs co-ordinator (England)
TA	teaching assistant
TEF	teaching excellence framework (UK)

Glossary

CPD	Continuing professional development. Of a practicing professional beyond the training period.
DfE	Department for Education. Government department responsible for all education policy in England.
ECF	Early career framework. A new programme of CPD for early career teachers in England in their first and second year of teaching, rolled out nationally as a statutory entitlement from 2021. This follows on from the ITT Core Content Framework (see definition).
ECR	Early career researcher. This term is usually used to refer to academic staff within an HEI who are either studying for a PhD or have recently (within five years) completed one. They would be evaluated in a different way when competing for funding with more experienced researchers, and/or they often have access to funding sources specific to ECRs.
EHCP	Education, health, and care plan.
epistemology	One of the core areas of philosophy. It is concerned with the nature, sources, and limits of knowledge.
epistemological	Research that studies what we know, and how we know what we know. It adds to and explores academic knowledge.
ethnography	Can be defined as 'social scientific writing about particular folk' (Silverman, 2001: 45). It is the study of individuals or groups in specific bounded settings, for example, mature students undertaking professional development in a university. Ethnography explores how individuals understand, or make sense of, their social world and how these understandings develop and change.
evaluative	Research that investigates the quality, importance, amount, or value of something, for example, research that studies how successfully a government policy, such as Every Child Matters or the Rose Review, has been implemented in a school.
examinations	In England, external school examinations consist of Standard Assessment Tests in primary education and General Certificates of Education (GCSEs) and Advanced Level qualifications (A-Level) at secondary level. All pupils undertake these examinations at the relevant point in their school careers.
FTE	Full-time equivalent.
HEFC	The Higher Education Funding Council for England was replaced by the UK Research and Innovation and Office for Students. The Higher Education Funding Council for England (HEFCE) distributed public money for teaching and research to universities and colleges.
HEI teacher educator	A university tutor who identifies a professional educator of teachers and training teachers. They are usually the personal supervisor of a group of trainee teachers.
higher education institution	The provider of tertiary education leading to award of an academic degree beyond formal/compulsory education.
ITE/ITT	Initial teacher education/training. The programme of learning undertaken by a professional student on a professional training programme for teaching. It is usually attached to gaining qualified teacher status.

ITE provider	An accredited provider of initial teacher education. To be accredited, a provider must have been graded at least a "good" (grade 2) in its most recent Ofsted ITE inspection report.
ITT core content framework	A core curriculum framework listing the entitlement of training for all training teachers. This precedes the early career framework (see definition).
in-service	Placement activity undertaken whilst being paid to qualify.
internally focused mentoring	Mentoring that takes account of only internal influences within the school they work within.
key stage	These are stages of the state education system in England, Wales, Northern Ireland, and the British Overseas Territory of Gibraltar setting the educational knowledge expected of students at various ages:
	Foundation (Reception/3- to 5-year-olds) – infant Key Stage 1 (Years 1–2/5- to 7-year-olds) – nursery Key Stage 2 (Years 3–6/7- to 11-year-olds) – primary Key Stage 3 (Years 7–9/11- to 14-year-olds) – lower secondary Key Stage 4/GCSE (Years 10–11) – upper secondary After GCSEs, students can opt to enter Key Stage 5 and take A-Levels (Years 12–13/16- to 18-year-olds).
local authority	A local political unit that controls education in state-funded schools that are not academies, private schools, or free schools in England.
methodology	A system of principles, practices, and procedures applied to a specific branch of knowledge. The way in which information is found or something is done. The methodology includes the approach taken to gather data, the methods, procedures, and techniques used to collect and analyse information, and might include the gathering of case study data via tests, interviews, or questionnaires. A *methodology* represents a package of practical ideas and proven practices for a given area of activity, such as the planning, design, development, or management of educational research in the area of primary teaching.
multi-academy trusts (MATs)	A group of schools/academies that work as one unit, independently funded separately from the local authority in any one jurisdiction (England).
Ofsted	Office for Standards in Education (in England). This organisation inspects all nurseries, schools, and all initial teacher training providers, as well as other relevant courses, for example, apprenticeships. All such learning organisations receive a quality grade for their provision from grade 1 (outstanding) to grade 4 (unsatisfactory).
partnership	A professional relationship between an HEI and an organisation (often a school) involved in training a professional student, usually based upon mutually agreed-upon professional principles relevant to that setting.
pedagogy	The study of the methods and activities of teaching.
PGCE	Postgraduate certificate in education (60 credits at master's level). The most common academic award attached to a teacher training course in the UK.
PGDE	Postgraduate diploma in education (120 credits at master's level). A less-common academic award attached to a teacher training course in the UK.
practitioner/action research	Research that can be based on your teaching and which can help inform and improve teaching practice.
pre-service	Status before qualification is awarded in a profession.
primary/secondary age phase	In England, *primary education* refers to ages 4–11, *secondary education* to 11–18.

QTS	Qualified teacher status is conferred when an individual has successfully completed an undergraduate or postgraduate degree in education and is required to undertake a teaching post within a school in England.
research	A detailed study of a subject, especially in order to discover (new) information or reach a (new) understanding.
research philosophy	The theoretical framework or school of 'thought' that research is grounded in, that is, interpretivism.
research school	A school with the designated status of being a research school undertaking pedagogic research and disseminating this in the region it is located in to other schools.
school-centred initial teacher training (SCITT)	A QTS training route which is based primarily in a school setting only.
university tutor	An HEI tutor who monitors the progress of a professional student both academically and in professional placement.

Introduction

Clare Woolhouse and Virginia Kay

For several decades, inclusion has been a priority for many professionals working with children and young people, but this is usually written about from a leadership or policy standpoint and, almost always, from the perspective of adults – school leaders, teachers, and academics. This book seeks to address two gaps: that which exists between adult-centric views of inclusion and those of learners and young people, and the contrast between the academic notions of inclusion and what this means in practice for children's real-life learning experiences (Allan, 2022). Both these identified gaps will be explored in different ways across the chapters of this book, with a focus on how children and young people's voices can be more effectively championed in practice. At this point, it is important to note that as a starting point for this book, *inclusion* is interpreted as widely as possible to cover a range of experiences and situations beyond special educational needs (SEN), whereas in the past it had been a narrower definition.

In 2014, the Code of Practice (DfE, 2014) categorised mental health difficulties as SEN; this is particularly important, given the rise of mental health difficulties following the Covid pandemic. Indeed, Young Minds (2022) noted that one in six children aged 5 to 16 was identified as having a probable mental health need, a huge increase from one in nine pre-pandemic in 2017. Yet the number of mental health nurses employed by the NHS has actually dropped between 2009 and 2022 (The Kings Fund, June 2023), so many children and young people are likely to still be unable to access the resources they need. It is recognised that risk factors for experiencing mental health needs include LGBTQIA+ identities, poverty, parental separation, financial crisis, being a carer, and being 'looked after' by the local authority. It is also acknowledged that those who experience mental health difficulties are more likely to be excluded from school.

Although inclusion covers a range of topics, from mental health, poverty, and social isolation to SEN, sexuality, gender, ethnicity, and race, a central focus for those involved with children and young people is around how to provide effective and efficient support to a growing number of increasingly diverse young people with a shrinking amount of money available. UK government proposals in the SEN Green Paper of March 2023 (DfE, 2023) laid out aims to offer better support for children and young people with special educational needs and disabilities, with a promise to spend £70 million of new money on SEN provision over the next three years. However, *The Guardian* noted in September 2023 that rising demand for SEN provision has coincided with a rise in complaints from parents and carers being upheld by the Local Government and Social Care Ombudsman (LGO). It is claimed that in many instances, this has been due to a lack of appropriate educational psychologists and other specialists, meaning, that children do not receive an education plan or must wait a considerable length of time before receiving one. As we write this introduction in July 2024, the UK is two weeks into a new Labour-led government; regardless of this, there is and will remain an urgent need to explore innovative and creative ways to engage children who are not supported appropriately or who may be at risk of exclusion. Education also needs to foster new and enterprising practice which makes best use of the financial resources available.

This book seeks to showcase new ways of thinking about inclusion and voice through case studies and reflective questions posed by children and young people themselves, and the professionals with whom they work. The various chapters involve academics and professionals, sometimes writing alongside the children and young people they work with, sharing first-hand knowledge about their experiences of teaching and learning within educational settings.

Each of the main chapters will discuss a case study of how a particular approach, strategy, pedagogy, or project has been used to include children, young people, and/or learners in the decisions that are made about them, their lives, and their education. There will be an indication of how various approaches to practice have enabled children and young people to be involved in the design and development of inclusive curricula and pedagogies within education. In doing so, each chapter will prompt reflection around how learners from all age phases can be both repositioned and empowered using multi-modal and innovative pedagogies which aim to increase the inclusivity of the educational offer.

Defining key terms and themes

Each of the chapters has addressed some key themes relating to inclusion, children's rights, and their voices relating to their own settings, experiences, and practice. This has inevitably meant that they have employed a range of definitions for key terms that, while similar, may have nuances that are specific for their area of study. We do not seek to homogenise such interpretations, since a key strength of this text is the opportunity to share and explore collegially diverse, although related, aspects of inclusive practice. However, we offer definitions in what follows of two central themes.

Inclusion

Inclusion as a term and practice is a central concept for policies and practice relating to children and young people across different national contexts (Engsig and Johnston 2015; Schneider 2015), yet what it actually means for individuals remains up for negotiation (Dunne et al. 2019). Inclusion can be associated with a sense of belonging or participation (Booth and Ainscow 2011), and perhaps a sense that every individual is welcomed and valued within a given situation. As a concept in practice, it will be informed by the multiple and fluid ways in which professionals such as teachers enact it (Woodcock and Hardy 2017). In the past (Dunne et al. 2019, p. 22), we have argued that inclusion does not exist in a vacuum and it cannot be viewed 'as independent from the notion of exclusion; they are not binary opposites'. To address this, we have used the term 'in(ex)clusion' to indicate how they partially co-exist and inform each other. At the same time, we acknowledge that there is a need for a practical and experiential understanding that can inform practice, and this is what is offered by the wide range of experiences shared within the chapters of this book.

Children's agency, rights, and voice

A central theme weaving throughout this text is the need to facilitate children in expressing themselves and for their views and opinions to be listened to and valued. As pointed out by Robinson in the first chapter, the United Nations states that

> parties shall assure to the child who is capable of forming his or her own views the right to express those views freely in all matters affecting the child, the views of the child being given due weight in accordance with the age and maturity of the child.
>
> (Article 12.1)

This view is reaffirmed by the UK government, which identifies a need for children to be consulted on practices that affect them (Section 2B of UK Children and Families Act, 2004). However, such a commitment is somewhat vague and provides minimal practical guidance on how teachers or other adults working with children can listen and respond to experiences shared by children. This text, while not claiming to offer any definitive answers, can start to address this gap by sharing examples of pedagogies that have been used to elicit the priorities of children, with an intention of positively impacting on health and well-being as well as their learning experiences.

Structure of the book

This book is divided into two sections. Section I (Chapters 1–7) considers the importance of involving children in their own education and enabling the sharing of their stories and experiences to better inform the (re)design of policy and practice. Section II (Chapters 8–11) develops the themes previously introduced, with a specific focus on developing the routes for communication between young people and adults to inform the development of inclusive communities.

In Chapter 1, Professor Carol Robinson introduces the underpinning principles for engaging with children and young people by adopting a 'children's rights' point of view focused on articles from the (UN) Convention on the Rights of the Child (CRC) (UN, 1989) and key principles inherent within these articles. Professor Robinson carefully examines key articles, with a particular emphasis on Article 12, to frame the importance of involving children's voices and experiences in the design of inclusive education. Following this discussion, eight factors are identified that can act as a starting point for practitioners to consider how children's voices can be facilitated. These factors are definitions, power, inclusivity, listening, time and space, approaches, processes, and purposes, all of which are aspects returned to within the other chapters of this book.

Rich case study examples from practice and useful questions and reflections for educators and SENCO staff form the basis for Chapter 2, which explores practice within an early years education setting. Concerns relating to child development, such as resilience, emotional safety, child voice, and independence, are explored, as are aspects relating to practitioner approaches, such as the use of reflective cycles and involvement with parents. These discussions bring to light some of the tensions and challenges within policy, theory, and practice which will greatly benefit practitioners and students considering working in early years settings.

Chapter 3 picks up on many of the themes from the previous two chapters, as it considers the experiences of children who have participated in the Hamish & Milo emotional and mental health well-being programme. The programme focuses upon core emotion themes and centres the voices of young people, as it encourages them to talk about their lives and their experiences from within their own emotional worlds. The chapter illuminates some of the key considerations when creating safe physical, emotional, and psychological environments for children to share their voices, and for adults to listen to them.

The focus for Chapter 4 is on exploring the introduction of an inclusive student voice programme in a school. Consideration is given to how opportunities for the voices of under-represented children can be advanced, with particular attention paid to autistic children and those with a range of associated communication, interaction, social, sensory, and learning differences. The intention is to initiate discussion around how more inclusive and democratic approaches can be put into practice.

Chapter 5 engages with Knowles's (2011, p. 9) criteria for identifying inclusivity to frame six case studies. The author tackles concerns relating to the negative impacts for children that can arise from the application of labels by sharing her reflections of striving to listen to, and understand, the children she has worked with in order to develop her inclusive classroom. Sanders considers examples drawn from different national contexts, highlighting how school policies and processes can create challenges, and shares with us some successful responses that can be transferred to different contexts.

A fictional child, Stephen, is the focus of Chapter 6, as decisions around his education become the centre of a problem-based learning activity given to students engaged in undergraduate education programmes. Discussion considers the content and positionality of information gathered as the chapter prompts us to reflect upon both the nature and the value of voice and the irony of a system which, on one hand, aims to support children and, on the other, actively marginalises their views.

In the seventh chapter, the 'Visualising Opportunities: Inclusion for Children, Education, and Society' (@VOICES_Ed) project is discussed. VOICES utilises photo elicitation and other visual methods to engage children and young people in discussing, and where possible, in redesigning, education in ways that can enable the development of more inclusive approaches, policies, and environments. In doing so, alternative strategies are shared for facilitating how children and young people's experiences and reflections are listened to.

Chapter 8 outlines the development of a collaborative research project, the design and delivery of which were guided by a group of autistic young people, who also contributed to the writing of the chapter. At points, the authors of the chapter reflect on their various experiences of being involved in the project and consider whether and how what has been learnt could be useful in forming future education policy and practice.

The subject of digital inclusion is the topic for Chapter 9, with discussion centring upon an innovative project taking place in Ireland and Croatia. DigiAcademy seeks to empower adults with intellectual disabilities to engage with technology in ways which enhance their own quality of life and independence, and then to go on and teach others with similar learning profiles to do the same. The discussion showcases the impact of the project and gives an overview of the journey taken to achieve this.

The work undertaken by the authors of Chapter 10 represents a collaborative and innovative piece of research around utilising nature-based activities to improve mental health. Young people in every stage of the project, they were able to access bespoke and interactive research training, tailored to their needs and priorities. These young people were then actively involved as peer advisors and on the research group in order that the *Rooted in Nature* project attended to their priorities.

Chapter 11 takes aim at the gap in research regarding the experiences, challenges, and support needs of learners with neurodivergence within higher education, drawing upon the author's own experiences of neuro-mixed spaces within the university education. The benefits of multi-modal methods of teaching and learning are considered, ending with some useful guidance and strategies which consider the needs of all students within this context.

Although each of the chapters described adopts different approaches and is framed in terms of different educational settings, the overarching aim is to champion teaching and learning pedagogies which not only respect and reflect individuality and difference but also actively seek to position children, young people, and learners at the very heart of shaping their own educational experience.

References

Allan, J. 2022. "Challenges and Dilemmas in Inclusive Education: What We Can Learn from Children." In *The Inclusion Dialogue* (pp. 23–35). Routledge.

Booth, T., and M. Ainscow. 2011. *Index for Inclusion: Developing Learning and Participation in Schools*. Bristol: Centre for Studies on Inclusive Education.

Department for Education (DfE). 2014. *Special Educational Needs and Disabilities Code of Practice: 0 to 25 Years*. DfE.

Department for Education (DfE) (Green paper). March 2023. *Special Educational Needs and Disabilities (SEND) and Alternative Provision (AP) Improvement Plan Right Support, Right Place, Right Time*. London: HM Government. Available at: https://assets.publishing.service.gov.uk/government/uploads/system/uploads/attachment_data/file/1139561/SEND_and_alternative_provision_improvement_plan.pdf

Dunne, L., F. Hallett, V. Kay, and C. Woolhouse. 2019. "Spaces of Inclusion: Investigating Place, Positioning and Perspective within Educational Settings through Photo-elicitation." *International Journal of Inclusive Education* 22 (1): 21–37.

Engsig, T., and C. J. Johnston. 2015. "Is There Something Rotten in the State of Denmark? The Paradoxical Policies of Inclusive Education – Lessons from Denmark." *International Journal of Inclusive Education* 19 (5): 469–486.

Knowles, G. 2011. *Supporting Inclusive Practice*. London: Routledge.

Schneider, C. 2015. "Social Participation of Children and Youth with Disabilities in Canada, France and Germany." *International Journal of Inclusive Education* 19 (10): 1068–1079.

The Guardian. September 2023. *England's Special Educational Needs Crisis 'Out of Control' Amid Record Complaints*. Available at: https://www.theguardian.com/education/2023/sep/03/special-educational-needs-provision-crisis-england-record-complaints [Accessed 15th September 2023]

The Kings Fund, June. 2023. *Workforce and Skills*. Available at: https://www.kingsfund.org.uk/projects/nhs-in-a-nutshell/nhs-workforce?gclid=CjwKCAjwgZCoBhBnEiwAz35RwkLYDYkl5Ow08pFp1QExgFlOgjnv5aBxyk4myPDJ4Qjcpzwic7ro9RoCHGkQAvD_BwE [Accessed 15th September 2023]

United Nations (UN). 1989. *United Nations Convention on the Rights of the Child (CRC)*. General Assembly Resolution 44/25, 20 November 1898. U.N. Doc. A/RES/44/25. Geneva: Unite Nations.

Woodcock, S., and I. Hardy. 2017. "Beyond the Binary: Rethinking Teachers' Understandings of and Engagement with Inclusion." *International Journal of Inclusive Education* 21 (6): 667–686.

Young Minds. 2022. *Coronavirus: Impact on Young People with Mental Health Needs*. Available at: https://www.youngminds.org.uk/about-us/reports-and-impact/ [Accessed 15th September 2023]

Section I

Listening to the voices of children and young people

1 How inclusive is the school environment?

The reality of implementing children's right to express their views

Carol Robinson

Key words

Children's rights, Children's voice, Inclusive practices, UNCRC

Children's right to express their views

Children's rights are outlined in the United Nations (UN) Convention on the Rights of the Child (CRC) (UN, 1989). This is an international document which sets out the rights to which all children should have access. The Convention applies to children up to the age of 18 and has been ratified by all countries across the world apart from the United States of America. Thus, the Convention is widely recognised by governments worldwide and provides a key reference point about how children should be treated. The Convention includes 54 articles which, between them, present a manifesto for how children should be treated, particularly in relation to (1) their welfare and protection, (2) the promotion of their agency, and (3) their participation in decisions on matters affecting them. The United Kingdom government ratified the Convention in 1991 and, by doing so, has indicated consent for the articles within it. All articles within the Convention are of equal importance; however, throughout this chapter, the focus will be on those articles which outline children's right to have their views heard, and the application of this right in school settings to support the development of inclusive environments.

In line with the wording in the CRC (UN, 1989), throughout the chapter, the term 'child' will be used to refer to children and young people up to the age of 18. When referring to adults who work in schools, to avoid the use of multiple terms depicting various roles, the generic term 'practitioners' will be used to refer to all adults in school settings who work with or for children.

Children's rights within Article 12 of the UNCRC

The CRC article most concerned with children's right to express their views, and on which this chapter will primarily focus, is Article 12. Part 1 of Article 12 states:

> The child who is capable of forming his or her own views [has] the right to express those views freely in all matters affecting the child, the views of the child being given due weight in accordance with the age and maturity of the chid.
>
> (UN, 1989)

An inclusive school environment is one in which the policies, the practices, and the whole school ethos support children's rights under Article 12 to be realised. To understand more fully the extent and the nuances of the rights that apply to children within Article 12, reference will be made to the UN General Comments on the Committee of the Rights of the Child (UN, 2009), which intentionally unpacked the principles inherent with this article. This will help shed light on the factors that need to be considered when translating Article 12 into policies and practices necessary for an inclusive school environment in which the rights of *all* children to voice their views are acknowledged. Within these comments, the UN Committee on the Rights of the Child (hereafter rereferred to as the Committee) affirmed there was 'a need for a better understanding of what article 12 entails and how to fully implement it for every chid' (UN, 2009, para. 4). The Committee also noted that realising children's rights under Article 12 is often hindered by established practices and attitudes which are counter-productive to supporting the full implementation of the Article with all children.

Article 12 begins with the phrase 'The child who is capable of forming his or her own views' (UN, 1989). This first phrase poses an initial challenge to interpretating the Article as there is no indication about how decisions regarding the capability of a child should be made. One of the obstacles to implementing Article 12 in practice is that adults can assume that children are not capable of forming their own views on any matter. The Committee addressed this potential barrier by stating:

> This phrase should not be seen as a limitation, but rather. . .should presume that a child has the capacity to form her or his own views and recognise that she or he has the right to express them; it is not up to the child to first prove her or his capacity.
> (UN, 2009, para. 20)

Thus, there is a requirement to start from the assumption that children *are* capable of forming their own views, and not starting from this premise is contravening the intentions of Article 12. Furthermore, the Committee specifically noted that young children are able to form views even when she or he may be unable to express them verbally, through stating:

> Consequently, full implementation of article 12 requires recognition of, and respect for, non-verbal forms of communication including play, body language, facial expression, drawing and painting, through which very young children demonstrate understanding, choices and preferences.
> (UN, 2009, para. 21)

The Committee, therefore, asserted that adults need to be receptive to multiple forms of communication which extend beyond that of the spoken word. The Committee also affirmed that

> it is not necessary that the child has comprehensive knowledge of all aspects of the matter affecting her or him, but . . . has sufficient understanding to be capable of appropriately forming his or her own view on the matter.
> (UN, 2099, para. 21)

The implication of this is that it is the responsibility of adults to equip children with the knowledge and understanding necessary to enable them to be able to form their own opinion on a matter. In schools, the onus for equipping children with such information, therefore, falls on practitioners. In situations where children experience 'difficulties in making their views heard' (UN, 2009, para. 21), the Committee explicitly stated that children

> should be equipped with, and enabled to use, any mode of communication necessary to facilitate the expression of their views. Efforts must also be made to recognize the right to expression of views for minority, indigenous and migrant and other children who do not speak the majority language.
> (UN, 2009, para. 21)

Thus, with regard to creating an inclusive school environment, it is clear that children, regardless of their age or circumstances, should be considered capable of forming their own views, and that policies and practices need to be developed which accommodate the needs of all children in supporting them to do so.

The second phrase within Article 12 states that the child has 'the right to express those view freely in all matters affecting the child' (UN, 1989). The Committee asserted that, in the context of Article 12,

> 'freely' means that the child can express her or his views without pressure and can choose whether or not she or he wants to exercise her or his rights to be heard . . . [and] the child must not be manipulated or subjected to undue influence or pressure.
> (UN, 2009, para. 22)

Children, therefore, have a right to feel at ease to speak openly about their views on matters, and to choose to remain silent if they wish to. The Committee further qualified the notion of 'free expression' and affirmed that adequate measures should be taken to assure to every child the right to freely express his or her view and to have those views duly taken into account without discrimination on grounds of race, colour, sex, disability, religion, political or other opinion, national, ethic or social origin, property, disability, birth or other status.

(UN, 2009, para. 75)

An inclusive school environment will, therefore, encourage such freedom of expression, regardless of whether or not children's views align with the dominant rhetoric the school aims to promote. The Committee expanded the explanation about the conditions necessary to realise this right and stated, 'The realization of the right of a child to express her or his own views requires that the child be informed about matters, opinions and possible decisions to be taken and their consequences' (UN, 2009, p. 10, para. 25). It is, therefore, up to adults to ensure that children are provided with the information they need in ways that are accessible and understandable to them, to ensure they are sufficiently knowledgeable to be able to form a view on a matter and to understand the consequences of any decisions. Within school contexts, a plethora of debates and discussions will, by nature, focus on 'on matters affecting the child'. Thus, if the right of all children to express their views is to be acknowledged in schools, practitioners need to effectuate inclusive ways of incorporating the diverse range of children's perspectives across the broad range of matters about which decisions are made on matters that affect children.

The final phrase of Article 12 states, '[T]he views of the child being given due weight in accordance with the age and maturity of the child'. In interpretating this phrase, the Committee affirmed that 'simply listening to the child is insufficient; the views of the child have to be seriously considered when the child is capable of forming her or his own views' (UN, 2009, para. 28), and as 'age alone cannot determine the significance of a child's views . . . the views of the child need to be assessed on a case-by-case examination' (UN, 2009, para. 29). The implication of embedding this right is significant and clearly reinforces the notion that if school policies and practices are to adopt an inclusive approach and acknowledge children's rights under Article 12, all children need to be considered as unique individuals whose opinions matter.

Following the Committee's examination of each of the phrases that make up Article 12 (UN, 2009), it outlined further expectations around how Article 12 should be translated into practice. The implications of these expectations emphasise the need for inclusive approaches to be adopted in schools and other settings. For example, the Committee reported that 'participation' should be interpreted

broadly in order to establish procedures not only for individual children and clearly defined groups of children, but also for groups of children such as indigenous children, children with disabilities, or children in general, who are affected directly or indirectly by social, economic or cultural conditions of living in their society.

(UN, 2009, para. 87)

The Committee also stated that participation must be inclusive, avoiding any existing and inbuilt discrimination, while also encouraging opportunities for the inclusion of marginalised children (UN, 2009, para. 134(f)). It noted that '[c]hildren are not a homogonous group and participation needs to provide for equality of opportunity for all, without discrimination on any grounds' (UN, 2009, para. 134(f)). Thus, a specific requirement was made for procedures to be inclusive, and the need to include children who may be at risk of marginalisation was emphasised. Furthermore, it was the Committee's intention that 'environments and working methods should be adapted to children's capacities . . . [and] Consideration needs to be given to the fact that children will need differing levels of support and forms of involvement according to their age and evolving capacities' (UN, 209, para. 134(e)). The implication of this for schools is that practitioners need to recognise that different children will require different strategies to be applied in order to create an inclusive environment in which they have equal opportunities to be involved. Moreover, focusing on ways of encouraging the participation of only mainstream groups of children is clearly working against the intention of Article 12.

Thus, the Committee's comments about how Article 12 should be implemented in practice (UN, 2009) make it abundantly clear that when translating Article 12 into policy and practice, the fundamental expectations are that children should be assumed to be capable of forming their own views, they should be provided with appropriate information to enable them to do so, and their views should be listened to and taken notice of. With regard to children's learning specifically, the Committee stated that in education and school contexts, including in early years settings, 'the active role of children in a participatory learning environment should be promoted' (UN,

2009, para. 107). Practitioners are, therefore, required to work in ways that encourage children to be active participants in their own learning. The Committee also explicitly articulated that policies and everyday practices should reflect the expectation that ways of working will promote the involvement of children's views, through stating: 'If participation is to be effective and meaningful, it needs to be understood as a process not as an individual one-off event' (UN, 2009, para. 133).

Within the CRC, many of the articles overlap and are interdependent; it is, therefore, often necessary to consider articles in conjunction with each other. Although Article 12 is the primary article focusing on children's right to express their views, three other articles within the Convention accentuate the requirements for schools to create an inclusive environment in which the views and needs of all children are equally valued and addressed. Firstly, Article 13, which complements Article 12 by requiring that:

> The child shall have the right to freedom of expression; this right shall include freedom to seek, receive and impart information and ideas of all kinds, regardless of frontiers, either orally, in writing or in print, in the form of art, or through any other media of the child's choice.
> (UN, 1989)

Thus, when implementing Article 12 and equipping children with the information they need to be able to form an opinion, consideration also needs to be given to Article 13. Practitioners need to recognise, and be accepting of the fact, that children have a right to receive information through a medium of their choice, and that children will express themselves in different ways.

Furthermore, when supporting children to voice their opinions, and fundamental to creating an inclusive environment in schools, Articles 2 and 3 of the CRC also need to be acknowledged. Article 2 states that children's rights apply 'without discrimination of any kind, irrespective of the child's or his or her parent's or legal guardian's race, colour, sex, language, religion, political or other opinion, national, ethnic or social origin, property, disability, birth or other status' (UN, 1989). Article 3 states, 'In all actions concerning children . . . the best interests of the child shall be a primary consideration' (UN, 1989). Articles 2 and 3, therefore, emphasise the need for schools to create an inclusive environment in which children's rights, including their right to voice opinion and have their opinions taken seriously, apply to all children, without 'discrimination of any kind', and for any decisions taken by practitioners to be taken with the 'best interests' of the child in mind.

Introduction

An inclusive school is one in which all children are considered to be of equal importance and the views of all children are equally valued. Children have a right to be listened to and for their views to be taken into consideration on matters affecting them; thus, inclusive practices within educational settings necessitate acknowledging and upholding children's rights in this respect. In reality, however, children's right to express their views and be heard is not always realised equally with all children in schools, with the outcome that the voices of certain children are favoured above those of others by adults in schools. For example, those who 'speak' the same language as the dominant school narrative and have opinions that coincide with school norms are often listened to, while the views of children with opinions that conflict with the dominant school narrative, or whose voices are more difficult to reach, are often marginalised or silenced. Not only does failing to place equal value on all children's voices lead to a non-inclusive environment; such an approach also contravenes children's right to express their views and have their views listened to and taken into account. This chapter aims to outline specific rights that apply to children in relation to expressing their views and having their opinions listened to and taken seriously. Setting out these rights, to which all children are entitled, provides a fundamental and non-negotiable platform on which further considerations about inclusive practices within educational settings should sit.

Factors which impact on adopting inclusive approaches to listening to children in schools

It will have become apparent in the previous section that practitioners play a major role in mobilising Article 12 into school policies and practices and, as an outcome, can strongly impact on how inclusive (or otherwise) an environment is. Lundy highlights this point and stated how, 'in practice, children's enjoyment of Article 12 is dependent on the cooperation of adults' (2007, p. 929). Thus, in educational settings, practitioners can, to a large extent, dictate whether or not a child's view is listened to and taken into account, and whether the viewpoints of some children are prioritised over others. One of the key factors that steers how practitioners implement Article 12 relates to their construction of childhood and how capable they view children. Very broadly, there are two opposing views of childhood. At one extreme, children can be perceived as social agents in their own right (Cassidy, 2017; Tisdall, 2018) and fully capable decision-makers, with childhood being seen as a complete and finished status and afforded the same status as adulthood (Lee, 1998; James, Jenks & Prout, 1998). An alternative viewpoint at the other extreme is that children are seen as lacking competence and not capable of forming their own views (Raby, 2014), with the 'mature and competent' adult being seen as a desirable end outcome (McDonald, 2009), and children positioned as having a lower status when compared with adults (Mayall, 2002). These two opposing viewpoints represent far ends on a continuum, and the position at which practitioners place children along the continuum will vary depending on both the children concerned and the context. For example, children may be seen as fully competent in one area of their lives but less competent in other areas. The point is, however, practitioners within educational settings have the power to decide where on the continuum to position different children, and this will impact on how much notice is taken of children's viewpoints. In situations where practitioners perceive children as not capable of forming a view on a matter, it is unlikely that they will adopt an approach that is inclusive of children's views. Moreover, there may be situations where practitioners perceive some individuals or groups of children as capable of forming a view and others as less capable, and in such cases, it is likely that the importance placed on the views offered by different children will reflect practitioners' perceptions of the child's capability within a particular context. Thus, the biases and prejudices held by practitioners about how capable they consider children to be in different situations will impact on which children they listen to and whose views they prioritise over others. The outcome being that practitioners in schools can significantly influence the aspects of school life about which children can have a say, whose views are listened to, and whose views are marginalised or ignored. When reflecting on issues of inclusions and exclusion within schools, Fielding (2012) poses some critical questions which practitioners can ask of their own practice: Who is allowed to speak? What are they allowed to speak about? What language is encouraged or allowed? Who is listening? Why are they listening? Who authorises the legitimacy of different voices?

Moving towards the development of inclusive school practices for listening to children

It is only through embracing the diverse range of children's voices and having measures in place to ensure that the views of all children are listened to and treated with equal respect and importance that schools can begin to develop an inclusive ethos. As part of building an inclusive school ethos, the dynamics of children's everyday lives need to be integrated into the school environment. The whole spectrum of cultural resources which children bring to school need to be acknowledged, celebrated, and taken into account, including children's various language, histories, experiences, and voices (Giroux, 1999). Thus, to achieve an inclusive approach to listening to children's perspectives, practitioners need to be receptive to incorporating children's different cultural and historical backgrounds. In this section, we will explore factors to support implementing and enacting practices for listening to the views of all children in school settings.

The section draws upon thinking which has emerged from an international seminar series funded by the University of Strathclyde and led by Professor Kate Wall in 2017. This brought together international researchers and practitioners to collaborate, debate, and enhance understandings on the affordances and constraints associated with implementing Article 12 (Wall et al., 2017, p. 3). The seminar series was aimed specifically at determining factors which support facilitating the voices of children from birth to 7 years; however, findings apply equally to supporting all children to voice their views, including older children up to the age of 18. Eight factors were identified as necessary for consideration when supporting children's voice (Wall et al., 2019). These eight factors are not intended to be interpreted as a finished or complete recipe which covers all aspects that need to be considered when supporting children to voice their views. Rather, they are intended as a starting point to promote discussions about policies, practices, and ways of working in different settings that support facilitating children's voices.

Each factor will be explored in turn to provide insights into areas to deliberate when seeking to promote an inclusive environment where the voices of all children are listened to equally. At the end of the discussion about each factor, reflective questions are posed. Practitioners can use these questions to reflect on their own practice, and/or they can be used as a basis for discussion when reviewing the inclusive (or otherwise) nature of policies and practices. It should be noted that there is no particular order in which the factors should be considered. Moreover, all factors are interdependent on one another, and as thinking shifts about one of the factors, this is likely to impact on understandings about the other factors.

The eight factors identified are as follows:

1. **Definition.** When embarking on building an inclusive environment in which all children's voices are heard, there needs to be a common understanding about what 'voice' means in a particular context. Drawing on principles underpinning Articles 12 and 13 of the CRC (UN, 1989), *voice* refers to far more than the spoken word and is more concerned with how an individual or group chooses to express themselves. The definition attributed to *voice* in a school setting, therefore, necessitates broad and inclusive modes of communication which extend beyond the use of words alone (Wall et al., 2019, p. 268). It is also necessary to recognise that any definition of *voice* will not remain static but will change over time as practitioners encounter new situations and develop a deeper understanding of how *voice* can be defined within different contexts.

    Suggested reflective questions when considering how to define *voice* include: What does voice look like/sound like in my setting? How do I tune into different types of voices? How do I listen to silences? (ibid., p. 269).

2. **Power.** Power imbalances are present within all relationships, particularly in school contexts, where practitioners are automatically placed in a position of power over children. Different groups of children in schools will also have differential access to power, with some having more privileged access over others. We also need to be mindful that power is a two-way process, with some children exerting power over their peers, and there will be situations where children exert power over adults. One of the challenges which presents itself as an outcome of power imbalances is that opportunities for equality of voice are curtailed for some due to the presence of unequal power relationships. When creating an inclusive environment, measures need to be taken to reduce power imbalances, particularly amongst children.

    Suggested reflective questions when considering power relations: How do I position myself in relation to children? What is the balance between collective and individual voices? Who decides what to ask? Who determines when individuals speak? Are some voices more important than others? Who decides? (ibid., p. 269).

3. **Inclusivity.** 'Inclusion assumes that everyone has an equal voice' (ibid., p. 270). However, as already discussed, the voices of all children are not equally encouraged or listened to, with the outcome that certain groups of children may be listened to more than others. For example, children who have additional support needs, who are from lower socio-economic backgrounds, and whose cultural and ethnic backgrounds differ to the dominant groups within a school are often less listened to than other groups of children (Wall et al., 2019, p. 271). An inclusive environment necessitates placing equal value on the voices of all individuals and, in adopting an inclusive approach, it is imperative to recognise both the agency and identity of all concerned (Cassidy et al., 2022, p. 8). Thus, the adoption of an inclusive approach in schools requires practitioners to be receptive to different forms of voice, both in terms of how voice is presented and in terms of being receptive to alternative viewpoints, including what could be considered by some to be non-conformist voices.

    Suggested reflective questions when considering issues of inclusivity: Do I marginalise some voices? Does everyone have an equal voice? Is there time and space for minority voices? How are different opinions and views included? (Wall et al., 2019, p. 269).

4. **Listening.** 'Listening is vital in endeavouring to support children's *voice*' (ibid., p. 271) and is a fundamental requirement when developing an inclusive environment. Fielding (2004) highlights the notion of 'active listening', which places importance on exchanges being based on respectful and attentive dialogue. Furthermore, Lundy (2007) stresses the importance of a 'listening audience', whereby those speaking know they are being listened to by an audience who can act on what has been said. To create an inclusive environment in which all children have the opportunity to voice their views, those listening need to be adaptive and able to tune into different types of voices and different ways children choose to communicate (Glazzard, 2012). Thus, in schools, consideration needs to be given to

whether there are any forms of communication which are actively discouraged and, if so, whether this closes down opportunities for certain individual or groups of children to voice their opinions.

Suggested reflective questions when considering how children are listened to: How do children know when they have been listened to? How do I interpret or translate voices? How do I hear quiet or silent voices? How do I react when I listen to uncomfortable or non-conforming voices? (Wall et al., 2019, p. 269).

5. *Time and space*. Within school environments, consideration needs to be given to which spaces support and which constrain the voices of different individuals and groups of children. A critical eye also needs to be cast over the different opportunities of time that are made available for children to share their opinions freely and whether particular times and spaces within school actively discourage children to voice their opinions. An inclusive school environment is one in which space and time for children's voices are enabled within the school's formal and informal structures (ibid., p. 272).

    Suggested reflective questions when considering issues of time and space: How does the space/place shape voice? Am I patient when listening to children? What is voice squeezed/enabled by? (ibid., p. 269).

6. *Approaches.* In school contexts, the approaches adopted by practitioners to support facilitating children to express their views are paramount to creating an inclusive environment. The creation of an inclusive school environment necessitates encouraging and welcoming a range of diverse voices. By implication, practitioners need to be receptive and adopt a flexible approach when listening to children's voices (ibid., p. 273).

    Suggested reflective questions when considering approaches: What are the dispositions needed by children/practitioners to have a voice/be a listener? What types of participation are supported in my setting? How do we work as a community to support voice? How do I build trust with different groups? (ibid., p. 269).

7. *Processes.* Processes conducive to facilitating children to express their views need to be established. Thus, as well as practitioners adopting approaches which support listening to children, an inclusive school environment also requires the development of processes that encourage opportunities for practitioners and children to collaborate and to embed children's voices and views into school structures (ibid., p. 273).

    Suggested reflective questions when considering processes: How do I create brave and safe spaces? What does it look like when someone is empowered? How do I encourage/discourage voice? What processes need to change? (ibid., p. 269).

8. *Purposes.* When creating an inclusive school ethos, in which the voices of all children are listened to, practitioners need to have a clear understanding of the purpose for wanting to listen to children's perspectives (ibid., p. 274). If the reason for listening to children's views is not based on a genuine desire to understand and act on these views, then there is a danger that the purpose of listening to children is purely tokenistic. For example, a tokenistic approach to listening to children is likely to be adopted where the views of children are sought solely for the purpose of confirming what is already known (Robinson & Taylor, 2007), or where seeking children's views is a tick box exercise and part of a requirement to fulfil school monitoring criteria. In such cases, it is highly unlikely that listening to children will lead to action taken to improve children's experiences in school.

    Suggested reflective questions when considering purposes: What is the link between voice and democracy? Who defines the goals (of voice work), and how are they refined over time? How will we evaluate what we have done? (Wall et al., 2019, p. 269).

To conclude

The act of listening to all children is paramount for creating an inclusive school environment and for realising children's rights under Article 12 of the CRC (UN, 1989). By considering each of the aforementioned eight factors, we can begin to reflect critically on policies, practices, and ways of working that support, and those that inhibit, all children to openly voice their opinions. In 1991, Michael Fullan asked, 'What would schools look like if we treated the student as someone who mattered?' (Fullan, 1991, p. 170). We could reframe this question to read, 'What would schools look like if every child were treated as though their views and opinions mattered?' If an inclusive school environment is to be developed, this question needs to be addressed at a whole-school level, as well as in individual classrooms and other contexts within schools. Practices in schools which result in greater importance being placed on the voices of some individuals or groups of children above others are fundamentally unethical. When seeking to create an inclusive school environment, established policies and practices need to be scrutinised to ensure the implementation and enactment of these incorporate listening to, and placing equal importance on, the views of all children. Such practices can only be developed effectively if there is a whole school's commitment to the inclusion of all children. Creating an inclusive school ethos requires practitioners to be open to listening to multiple voices and to be willing to engage with children in different ways, depending on the preferences of individual children. Moreover, practices and processes need to welcome children's multiple viewpoints and respect and celebrate their diversity of opinions.

Reflective questions

1. What factors do you need to consider for children's voices to be listened to within an inclusive environment?
2. What do you see as the challenges in developing an inclusive environment in which all children are listened to?
3. How are children's right to express their views on matters affecting them enabled and/or squeezed within a setting with which you are familiar?
4. When listening to conflicting views, how do you decide which views to take notice of? Why?

Takeaway activities

(i) Invite a group of children to identify (1) ways in which the school creates an inclusive environment and (2) any aspects of school life in which some children may feel excluded. Ask the children to draw/paint/write/act out their ideas. In cases where children may feel excluded, ask children to suggest ways of addressing these areas and co-create, with the children, an action plan that can be implemented.
(ii) Inform a group of children about their rights to express their views and have their views taken seriously. Invite the children to consider how this right is upheld in practice, both in and out of school. Discuss how children could respond and the action they could take in cases where this right is not upheld.

References

Cassidy, C. (2017) 'Philosophy with children: A rights-based approach to deliberative participation', *International Journal of Children's Rights*, 25(2), pp. 320–334.

Cassidy, C., Wall, K., Robinson, C., Arnott, L., Beaton, M., and Hall, E. (2022) 'Bridging the theory and practice of eliciting the voices of young children: Findings from the *Look Who's Talking* project', *European Early Childhood Education Research Journal*, 30(1), pp. 32–47. DOI: 10.1080/1350293X.2022.2026431

Fielding, M. (2004) '"New wave" student voice and the renewal of civic society', *London Review of Education*, 2(3), pp. 197–217.

Fielding, M. (2012) 'Interrogating student voice: Preoccupations, purposes and possibilities', in H. Daniels, H. Lauder and J. Porter (eds) *Educational Theories, Cultures and Learning*. London: Routledge, pp. 101–106.

Fullan, M. (1991) *The New Meaning of Educational Change*. New York: Teachers College Press.

Giroux, H. (1999) *Rage and Hope: What Is Critical Pedagogy?* Online: Rage & Hope: Giroux-Critical Pedagogy (perfectfit.org) (Accessed: 20 September 2023).

Glazzard, J. (2012) 'Tuning into children's voices: Exploring the perceptions of primary aged children about their education in one primary school in England', *International Journal of Education*, 4(3), pp. 49–66.

James, A., Jenks, C., and Prout, A. (1998) *Theorizing Childhood*. Cambridge: Polity Press.

Lee, N. (1998) 'Towards an immature sociology', *Sociology Review*, 46(3), pp. 458–481.

Lundy, L. (2007) '"Voice" in not enough: Conceptualising Article 12 of the United Nations Convention on the Rights of the Child', *British Educational Research Journal*, 33(6), pp. 927–942.

Mayall, B. (2002) *Towards a Sociology of Childhood: Thinking from Children's Lives*. Maidenhead: Open University Press.

McDonald, C. (2009) 'The importance of identify in policy: The Case for children', *Children and Society*, 23(4), pp. 241–251.

Raby (2014) 'Children's participation as neo-liberal governance?', *Discourse: Studies in the Cultural Politics of Education,* 35(1), pp. 77–89.

Robinson, C. and Taylor, C. (2007) 'Theorising student voice: Values and perspectives', *Improving Schools*, 10(1), pp. 5–17.

Tisdall, K. (2018) 'Challenging competency and capacity? Due weight to children's views in family law proceedings', *International Journal of Children's Rights*, 26(1), pp. 159–182.

United Nations (1989) *United Nations Convention on the Rights of the Child*. General Assembly Resolution 44/25, 20 November 1898. U.N. Doc. A/RES/44/25. Geneva: Unite Nations.

United Nations Committee on the Rights of the Child (2009) *General Comment No 12: The Rights of the Child to Be Heard*, 20 July 2009, CRC/C/GC/12.

Wall, K., Arnott, L., Cassidy, C., Beaton, M., Christensen, P., Dockett, S., Hall, E., I'Anson, J., Kenyal, M., McKernan, G., Pramling, I., and Robinson, C. (2017) 'Looks Who's Talking: Eliciting the voices of children from birth to seven', *International Journal of Student Voice,* pp. 1–9.

Wall, K., Cassidy, C., Robinson, C., Hall, E., Beaton, M., Kanyal, M., and Mitra, D. (2019) 'Look Who's Talking: Factors for considering the facilitation of very young children's voices', *Journal of Early Childhood Research*, 17(4), pp. 263–278.

2 Re-thinking inclusive practice within early years education

Naomi Jackson

> **Key words**
>
> Early years, Inclusive practices, Listening to children, SEND

The ethos of early years

Early years education in England is in a good position to be inclusive because of the overarching principles in the statutory guidance for the Early Years Foundation Stage (EYFS) (DfE, 2024). This guidance sets a standard for how early childhood practitioners should treat all children as individuals and respect their personalities, interests, and learning styles. This creates a different education ethos to more formalised stages of education; in the early years (EY) curriculum, practitioners do not need to teach set information but instead can focus on personal skills, independence, and a love of learning. Early years education is enabled to focus on each individual, and this should lead to practice being inclusive by nature.

Early childhood education and care have been the subject of political scrutiny with frequent politically driven changes to policy (Cheminais, 2009). Expectations of the EY curriculum have shifted from a child-initiated, play-based approach, viewing play as the work of the child, and pivotal to their development, towards more formal, adult-led teaching and learning. Despite this, the overarching principles of the EYFS have survived several reviews and remained a consistent part of EY policy since 2012, still framing the curriculum as based on ideas from a range of philosophies and theories of child development. However, Cameron and Moss (2020) discuss how EY education in England is still a fragmented system that needs real transformational change to meet the needs of children and families. Trevor, Ince, and Ling (2020) highlight the tensions in delivering a curriculum which can change depending on political discourse rather than new research or established good practice. Several reviews of EY qualifications have caused further confusion and never lived up to the ambitions to drive up standards by raising the professional status of the EY workforce. Osgood et al.'s (2017) review of early years qualifications highlights how EY practitioners, whether in the private, voluntary, or independent sector, do not have the same status as qualified teachers in schools. For too long, EY has been viewed as preschool or 'getting ready for education', rather than an important phase of a child's education in itself. The importance of the EY phase of learning is underpinned by four overarching principles outlined in the EYFS guidance:

1. Every child is a unique child, who is constantly learning and can be resilient, capable, confident, and self-assured.
2. Children learn to be strong and independent through positive relationships.
3. Children learn and develop well in enabling environments with teaching and support from adults who respond to their individual interests and needs and help them build their learning over time. Children benefit from a strong partnership between practitioners and parents and/or carers.
4. Children are individuals who develop and learn at different rates. (This is particularly relevant for EY, since the framework covers the education and care of all children, including children with special educational needs and disabilities (SEND) (DfE, 2024).

To explore early years inclusivity, the chapter will address how these principles form an atmosphere of inclusivity, before exploring the difficulties of putting principles into practice.

How the overarching principles are designed to be tools to support inclusion

Every child is unique

The first principle from the DfE (2024) is the importance of viewing each child as unique, and therefore the importance of getting to know every child as an individual. Children have a wide range of cultural and social experiences when they come into a nursery setting, so to support new learning, practitioners need to be confident that they have productive ways to record and assess children's ability (Cowan & Flewitt, 2020). Practitioners also need to be able to adapt how they assess a child's prior learning to plan next steps that are relevant and challenging to each individual.

Practice needs to be based on in-depth knowledge of the children in a setting, and to do this, practitioners need to be in tune to listening to children and aware of their life experiences. When exploring the voice of the child in early years, Wall et al. (2019) note how practitioners need to be open to many ways of listening. For the youngest children, and for many SEND children, this 'voice' is not an audible spoken voice but information that practitioners must gather by being tuned in to the children. Alongside this, they must work with parents, who are the experts on their children and their first and most enduring educators (Cottle & Alexander, 2014). This means that EY practitioners need to be versed in interpreting a child's needs and aware that they can get this wrong on occasion. For example, a child who every day chooses to play with a toy train may not be interested in trains at all but instead likes the texture of the wooden toy. Practitioners need to be careful to observe and spend time reflecting on what they know about a child to assess what they are communicating and be receptive to the child's voice (Wall et al., 2019).

Positive relationships

The key person approach in early years is statutory, and we need to ensure that all children can form secure attachments with the practitioners who are caring for them to develop positive relationships. Children often develop a dependency on their key person who gives them the confidence and security to explore the setting, so the key person also supports the emotional needs of the child and help build a positive emotional environment (Albin-Clark, Shirley, Webster & Woolhouse, 2018).

In many EY settings, it is usual for a 'buddy' key person to be nominated for a child so that holidays, sickness and professional development time can be covered without a negative impact on a child's well-being. For children with autistic spectrum conditions (ASC), this can be even more vital, as forming attachments can be more difficult for them, and early intensive educational and behavioural support may improve the long-term outcomes for them (Zwaigenbaum, Brian & Ip, 2019). A child in a preschool whom I was key person for would only speak to me and remained mute and behaved in a withdrawn manner if I was not in the classroom. For him to share his voice and be listened to, he needed the emotional safety net of his key person being there, and reflecting on this child reminds me how important the key person approach can be to young children. We can focus on the well-being of the child and ensure they feel settled in the setting before we begin to try to teach anything. Being emotionally ready to learn is the first step, which means having the resilience to be away from home and family, the ability to focus and concentrate, and the confidence to play. The key person needs to balance the need for support with providing challenge and encouraging independence, having high aspirations for what each child can achieve.

Finally, EY practitioners also need to consider that they may be dealing with challenging behaviour, such as meltdowns. In such circumstances, the well-being of the practitioner is also vital; they may need to step back and allow a buddy to step in and provide support to a child. This is particularly important, given that the majority of practitioners working with children report that they find their work stressful, so their mental health and well-being need to be given increased attention (Pre-school Learning Alliance, 2018).

Enabling environments

The third principle of the EYFS guidance focuses on an enabling environment. For the environment to be appropriate, it must be safe for all children, not just in a physical sense, but also as an emotionally safe space that provides children with the confidence to engage and explore. Practitioners need to consider the emotional environment first; a child who is not feeling safe and secure will not concentrate or engage in meaningful play, no matter how exciting the activities on offer are. The Reggio Emilio approach highly values the environment as an educating agentic space in itself, and consideration is given to the buildings in which children are cared for, as well as the furniture, sensory, and sound environment (Bruce, 2017). Complementing this, the Montessori approach uses the teacher's management of the environment to support the child's interest and engage with carefully planned learning activities that the practitioner is precisely taught to deliver (Aljabreen, 2020). From both points of view, the learning environment is key for EY practitioners; we manage a balancing act between keeping the rooms the same to provide stability and security for less-confident children and making enhancements to maintain the interests of the more confident explorers. Both can be judged as inclusive (Borkett, 2021).

Having access to the outside is also important; outdoor experiences can have a therapeutic and beneficial effect for children's well-being and development (Monti et al., 2019). For example, walking outdoors when comforting an anxious baby can help them settle more easily. The lighting, sounds, and smells inside a nursery room can be so unfamiliar that being outdoors can remove some of the additional stresses. Practitioners know the value of using the outdoors but cite bad weather or parental concerns about wet or muddy clothing as barriers to outdoor learning (Parsons & Traunter, 2020). Despite this, it is becoming more common for settings to offer forest school sessions or 'experiences', or outdoor nurseries, where children can spend the whole day outside, whatever the weather. Forest school provides opportunities to practice self-reliance, independence in risky play and curiosity-based learning, as well as taught skills, such as using tools and open-fire cooking, yet they can vary in quality (Garden & Downes, 2023). Balancing the therapeutic benefits of the outdoors, such as hands-on sensory learning, with ensuring the safety of neurodivergent children means EY practitioners must assess the potential risks against the learning experience and challenge that is on offer for the child to get the most from the environment.

Children are individuals

The fourth overarching principle that children are all capable and individual learners goes hand in hand with the SEND Code of Practice (Department for Education, 2014) in using a cycle of assess, plan, do, review for each individual child. All children in early years, not just those who need additional support, should have unique experiences designed by knowledgeable practitioners. The current EY curriculum in England is based on following children's interests and can be viewed as a curriculum of skills rather than knowledge. To enact this, settings can advocate for children to develop a love of books, understanding that print has meaning and encouraging children to recite refrains from a book that has resonance for them. There is no need to specify what book; it could be *The Gruffalo* or *The World of Tractors*, depending upon the interest of the child. Experiences should be tailored for each child to support their learning and development, irrespective of the fact that, often, *early years* is not understood as education but as playing or care, and unfortunately, little value may be given to the child's first learning experiences (Osgood, 2012). The knowledge of how children develop needs to be solid and ingrained to enable practitioners to teach by learning through play. Practitioners need to be able to plan in the moment, see what needs to be taught next, and devise an instant lesson plan whilst playing alongside the child. Children's play should be viewed as pivotal to their learning, and observations can be made in terms of schemas, sequences, and repeated behaviours. Always the key question is: What is the next step for this child?

The cycle of assess, plan, do, review

The four principles explored earlier have survived several reviews of the EYFS by successive governments, each having their own agenda for early education, which more recently has created a shift towards formal adult-led teaching away from child-led learning through 'hands-on' experiences. With these principles underpinning practice, EY education is in a strong legislative position for all settings to be inclusive by listening to the voices of children as individuals and making appropriate adapted provision for SEND children. The principles give us the basis for developing settings in which there is an ethos and strong commitment to inclusive pedagogies. EY should be an area of education where every child is educated at their own pace in a nurturing environment, but in reality, children may be unable to find a setting due to additional needs, and unhappy children will make poor progress. Support for children with complex needs is not always available, but settings can assess each child's needs and plan what is needed via a cycle of *assess*, *plan*, *do*, *review*, to include regular reflection on what is working and what needs adjusting.

Assess – admissions and early identification

Parents are children's first and most influential educators; they know their child as an individual and see all their little peculiarities. When parents choose to put their child in an EY setting, the child's key person becomes the professional who sees that child most often outside of the home. It can be months between appointments with professionals, such as health visitors, and then generally only to check a child's development at 2 years old, with the next statutory assessment scheduled when a child starts school. Therefore, EY practitioners have a vital role in identifying SEND children (Borkett, 2021), since they are often the only professionals working with families and the only people in a position to identify concerns about a child's development. EY practitioners have a responsibility to share any concerns with parents or carers as soon as they emerge. However, in my experience, this can be a difficult conversation to start and usually goes one of two ways: the parent says, 'Thank you, I have noticed that myself – what can we do about it?' or there may be a denial that there is a concern. In my role as a special educational needs and disabilities co-ordinator (SENDCO), I have had these conversations many times, and finding the right time to initiate them never gets easier. Parental permission is always needed to put any additional measures in place, although we can still implement strategies to target areas of development that are falling behind as part of our normal practice. This can allow parents the time that they need to consider what they feel is in their child's best interests, without overstepping any legal or ethical lines.

On very rare occasions, it may be necessary to consider at what point refusing to get help for a child becomes a safeguarding concern because the parents are not meeting the needs of the child. If this happens, a practitioner can refer to the local safeguarding procedures that guide the obligations of EY settings to ensure the needs of every child are being met alongside the parents' responsibility for the well-being of their children. If a family is struggling to meet these needs, a referral can be made to early help services, and a family support worker can work with the family in areas such as behaviour management and sleep routines. Not meeting a medical or educational need can be considered a form of neglect, so a referral to children's social care could be required if this meets the threshold of putting the child at risk of serious harm. At this point, the working together to safeguard children guidance (H.M. UK Government, 2023) can be used to clarify what services are to be involved at each level of concern.

Assessing a child's needs must start from the first moment of contact. When a parent wishes to enrol a child with a medical condition, special educational need, or disability (SEND) in a setting, the safety of the child must take precedence over the legal duty to be inclusive. The admissions process needs to work in tandem with the parents, and EY practitioners need to be open and honest about any potential barriers to accepting a child. An assessment of a child's needs should be conducted, and any need for adjustments made to ensure the child can attend safely. This involves writing detailed risk assessments and considering things such as: Is my garden secure, or will this child try to climb the fence? What level of supervision will this individual need to be kept safe? Does the child have specialist equipment which staff need to be trained on? If so, there may have to be a delay to the child's admission to an EY setting.

To offer an example, a child who had complex medical needs, including being fed through a gastric tube, applied to my setting. Following Lancashire County Council's procedure for early help assessment, a 'team around the family' meeting was set up by his specialist health visitor. First, this involved the outreach nursing team, a speech and language therapist from the feeding team, and Mum, which provided opportunities information to be shared. This assisted with identifying the training needed, and the outreach nurse was then able to arrange a date to come and deliver this. Unfortunately, more delays were caused due to a number of practical concerns, such as ensuring a comprehensive risk assessment was in place and that we had appropriate insurance cover to deliver the level of medical care required. This process dragged on for weeks and was complicated when his condition changed, meaning, a child who was already educationally behind because of frequent ill health and hospital stays was at risk of being excluded further because of delays in paperwork. Nursery provision that needed to be focused on narrowing the gap between him and his peers in preparation for school could not be accessed. We were able to get around this hurdle by offering stay-and-play sessions, where the child would attend the setting with Mum, who was required to stay on-site. We carried this on until all the training and adjustments were in place. This arrangement was not ideal for Mum, who could have made better use of her time, but worked well for the practitioners, who could ask any questions related to medication, feeding, or maintenance of the gastric tube. Most importantly, this approach worked for the child, and by the time Mum could leave the child, he was well settled. Mum, who had never left him anywhere except the hospital, was confident and relaxed, and the team were knowledgeable about his medical conditions. The admissions process, prioritising the training of the team and safety of the child, was difficult and long, but working in partnership with the family had a positive outcome.

Listening to children

Even the youngest children are capable communicators, able to express their needs, preferences, and enjoyment; we just need to know how to listen. And this is the start of inclusive EY practice. Loris Malaguzzi, who founded the Reggio Emilia approach, cites the '100 languages of children' to demonstrate how children express themselves in many diverse ways, and so we must have access to opportunities for creative play if we want to engage children's voices (Aljabreen, 2020). In settings that employ Reggio Emilio approaches, adults play alongside the children in creative activities, and a high value is placed on the children's drawing and what they are expressing through art and play (Teaching and Learning Scotland, 2006). Children are not regarded as having additional needs, but additional rights and more staff are allocated to classes to provide for children, but not to work on a specific, one-to-one basis. This chimes with the Mosaic approach (Clark & Moss, 2011), which encourages practitioners to build up an understanding of the children in their setting by pulling together many snippets of information from a wide range of observations, conversations, creative plays, and technologies, such as children's photographs. Any setting can apply such an approach by assessing children's preferences through observing where and how they play and trying to understand what children are expressing through their art, role-play, and interactions.

For example, a child who attended my setting came in and went straight to the sofa in the book area, lay down, and stayed there. We described his demeanour as like a rag doll just on the sofa, not engaging. The practitioners were concerned that although he was watching what was going on, he showed no interest in joining in. So the practitioners began to play next to him, modelling how to use toys and equipment, noting if any caught his attention. From this we were able to slowly engage him in the setting and get him playing and exploring. Knowing that the sofa was his safe space, we took the play to him rather than expecting him to engage elsewhere. By observing, we looked for a next step that would scaffold his learning, giving him the support to engage more.

As identified by Wall et al. (2019), when we talk about listening to a child's voice in EY, we very rarely mean an actual spoken voice but all the ways that children communicate with us, including behaviours that come from frustration and anger. Using a key person approach which really builds a relationship with the child means we can become experts on their individual needs, and our knowledge is key in ensuring children are supported in response to the SEND Code of Practice (DfE, 2014), which highlights the need for early identification and support.

Planning to be inclusive

Accessing additional support

EY educator qualifications focus on building a knowledge of typical child development and what milestones should be observed when. Knowledge, experience, and intuition often syndicate when a child is not developing typically. The graduated response set out in the SEND Code of Practice (DfE, 2014) means that practitioners intervene straight away by providing additional targeted support. This is then evidenced through targeted learning plans that take into account local policies, practices, and provisions. In Lancashire, one full cycle of 'assess, plan, do, review' needs to be evidenced before requests for support are submitted to the local authority specialist team, although where a child has an urgent need, I send evidence of the first stages with a cover letter to get the process of applying for support started. The local authority makes known what services are available in the area on their local offer website. On many occasions, I have contacted the service a child has been referred to, directly, to ask about the referral and ensure that the child's needs have been triaged appropriately.

As EY practitioners, we become specialists in child development, yet there is concern that often our voices seem to be ignored (Osgood, 2012). EY practitioners can be viewed as 'babysitters'. Despite that attempts to professionalise the workforce have been legislated for by successive government policies, Osgood et al. (2017) discuss how little progress has been made and note how EY practitioners are treated relatively poorly in comparison to the pay or status of qualified teachers in primary and secondary settings. Yet the care and emotional labour that is part of the EY cannot be separated from the educational aspects, and so practitioners need to be emotionally responsive to children (Osgood, 2012). As noted by Page (2016), the relationship between practitioner and child is 'professional love', giving value to the emotional labour in early education. Indeed, EY offers value like no other educational setting. Many services for children with additional needs do not take referrals for children under the age of 2 years, so we, as a workforce, need to have the confidence to challenge when we do not feel our voices are heard. We are the professionals spending the most time with young children, so we can be the people who have an impact on the provision they receive, ensuring they transition to an appropriate school at 5 with the skills to continue their educational journey. If EY practitioners are not supported to work with children with additional needs, there is the risk that the attainment gap widens before these children even start formal schooling.

Experiences of multi-agency working

Given the importance of the EY practitioner's role, it is essential that our voices are not sidelined in multi-agency meetings. I recall attending a 'child in need' review meeting chaired by social services, and the discussion focused on an older sibling's need for the opportunity to socialise in school due to only attending half days and his aggressive behaviour due to sensory overloads indoors. The discussion seemed to be taking a long time and going around in circles. When I spoke up, saying what I thought was obvious – to provide time for him to socialise outdoors – the school teacher rolled her eyes and completely dismissed my idea, as if spending time outdoors was a ridiculous idea, despite evidence to the contrary (Davies & Hamilton, 2018; Frost & Sutterby, 2017). I repeated the idea and was again dismissed. When I chatted to the foster parent the next week, she said she had arranged a play date for the child, wrapped him up as it was winter, and taken him to a local park to play and all had gone well. She then thanked me for the suggestion. Having the confidence to be a member of a professional team, to draw on our – often extensive – experience, and to feel that we are experts on our children can be very difficult, but our status as professionals cannot be imposed through changing qualifications or policy; instead, it needs to be constructed and respected by professionals' behaviour (Osgood, 2012).

Access to an inclusive environment

When planning inclusive environments, we need to consider if it meets the needs of the cohort of children we currently have. We need to plan for individual need and give consideration to children with sensory needs. For example, the lighting in a room can be impactful; bright strip lighting may be triggering for a child, yet dim lighting may cause a child with a visual impairment (VI) to struggle to engage. Whereas bright, defined colours can help a child with VI navigate the environment but may be distracting for a child with sensory overload. For the environment to be effective, we should acknowledge that no one size fits all; we must evaluate children's learning needs and continually adjust our environment to meet these.

Such concerns extend to planning outdoor provision carefully. Outdoor play is often undervalued, and the rich learning experiences offered need to be celebrated (Parsons & Traunter, 2020). Children who enjoy kinaesthetic learning, children with ADHD, or energetic children can often be best taught in a well-planned outdoor environment with space to move. Practitioners need to consider how teaching and learning can be made inclusive for these children. As examples, storytelling does not need to be a stationary activity, a bear hunt can cover the whole garden, and superhero play can be amazing for introducing new vocabulary and conversation about morals. A child with a sensory need who does not really engage with other children but loves the feeling of wind on his face can be encouraged to work with another child to get a lift in the back of a bike trailer. When we support the beginnings of communication in such a context, we teach a skill that will later be transferable.

Developing communication is an essential skill, and this can be impacted by the noise levels in EY environments. My setting has high ceilings and can be echoey and loud. We have supplied ear defenders for a child who found this too much. I had reservations about doing this, as the child needed to focus on developing language – and how would this develop if we closed him off to our language-rich environment? I went back to the concept of the emotional environment and realised that if the child did not feel safe and secure, no learning would have the chance to happen. Jarman's (2009) work on communication-friendly spaces argues for planning an auditory environment carefully to encourage spaces that are enclosed, such as cosy dens using natural fabrics that soften noise. Planning EY classrooms so that we can encourage the quieter voices in the class to be heard can be very beneficial and again focuses on the emotional environment as well as the physical.

Do – strategies for inclusive practice

Once the planning has taken place, the next stage of the cycle is 'doing', turning plans into action, and I will outline two examples that focus on aspects of communication to build on the previous section.

Enhancing language

When EY practitioners identify a delay in understanding spoken language, they can draw upon a range of strategies to develop language, and this is often very necessary, because waiting lists for speech and language therapy assessment can be many months, if not more than a year, which is too much of a delay to do nothing. To make sure we are doing as much as we can without specialist input, we can put in place ways to make our language more accessible by using a total communication approach (Jones, 2000; Meadow, 2023). For example, we will implement a range of visual clues alongside spoken language to draw the child's attention to the words we are using, which can include using pictures and Makaton sign language. These are in no way intended to replace spoken language, but to increase accessibility. This approach can have clear benefits; in one case, a change was noted in the behaviour of a child around his third birthday – he was in the initial stages of being assessed by the community paediatrician, and a referral had been made to speech and language therapy. He was using no spoken words, just vocalisations, and was unable to follow simple oral instructions, showing little or no understanding of spoken language. By observing him, we were able to see his vocalisations were anger and frustration at not being understood. We needed support in finding a way to 'hear his voice' in a different way, because being able to make a choice and express a preference does not take an understanding of language (Wearmouth, 2013). His key person introduced him to picture cards of his favourite activities, beginning with just two images to set up the concept that he could ask for something himself; we added more over time. These were attached to an area of the wall so they could be removed and stuck back easily; the child could go and get the image of what he wanted and could direct his own communication, but practitioners continued to model language alongside the pictures, not replacing spoken language, but enhancing it. Giving him control over his voice had a massive impact on his levels of well-being and calmed the frustration and anger at not being listened to, and when calm, he was able to begin to use single words alongside the photographs.

When introducing pictures for communication in my nursery, we use photographs of the actual staff and objects in the setting. Cartoon-style images can be purchased or found online, but when first introduced to pictures for communication, a young child may not understand what they are intended to represent. For some children, even photographs are too abstract, and we use the object to enable the child to make choices, or two objects, such as a paintbrush and a coat, to represent outdoor play.

In implementing inclusive practice, it is important to work with colleagues as a team to tailor practice to individual children by trying out ideas to find out what works best. When my team were having difficulty with a child who had become very unsettled and frustrated because he was not able to express himself, we found we were each responding in our own way as individual practitioners using the same strategies, but each in a slightly different way. For instance, at mealtimes, we wanted the child to come to the table to eat. I was showing the food to him and then guiding him to the table, while another practitioner was putting his food on the table then leading him to it, offering him the chair. We decided at a team meeting to sit together and design an individual provision map. A document that covered each part of our routine and how we were going to be consistent in our approach. By designing a simple map, we were able to pull together an approach that ensured he understood what was expected of him from all of us, and this consistency encouraged his engagement.

Review – reflecting on practice

Being able to reflect on our provision to assess how we are planning and implementing practice to meet every individual child's need can be difficult, particularly when our children may be non-verbal. We cannot always know if our aspirations for each child are high enough, so we need to revisit what we do. To explore this, I want to provide one contextually specific example that led to a significant change in how EY practitioners can reflect upon practice.

As previously mentioned, the key person approach is ingrained in everything we do; all the practitioners in the setting really value these relationships. If a child develops a special bond with a particular person, then this is respected, and they become the key person. During the first lockdown during the Covid pandemic, I had cause to reflect on if this practice was always appropriate. My setting closed, and I decided to transfer to another setting that was staying open to support the children of key workers working at a large NHS hospital. When I arrived in the setting, several of the usual staff had been told to shield and were not at work, and others had developed symptoms and were required to self-isolate. This was not a normal time for us, and all our normal expectations went out of the window. I began my week going into the pre-school, working with another practitioner who had volunteered from another setting. Neither of us knew the children we were to work with so set about playing alongside the children to get to know their abilities, in the hope we could extend their learning. Later in the week, I had time to catch up with reading about the children and found out that one child in the group was undergoing assessment for ASC and was noted as having aggressive behaviours that were considered difficult to manage in the group. I had no knowledge of this, so I had treated him in the same manner as all the other children, as an individual, but as able to meet the same expectations as other children without any adjustments. The child carried on engaging in the routine throughout the months I was in the setting; however, when his key person was told she no longer needed to shield and popped in for a return-to-work well-being chat, he saw her, ran, and hugged her, showing obvious affection, but then a couple of minutes later demonstrated aggressive behaviour and began to shout at her, which had been his usual pattern of behaviour with her. Removing all the team that work in a room and replacing them with strangers should not happen, but this enforced process enabled me to see how a key person relationship could be negative for a child. The child had the ability to function as part of the group, but the learnt behaviour with the key person did not support involvement.

Experiences such as the one just described have caused me to reflect on how EY practitioners can question if our expectations are appropriate and high enough for the children in our care. We are never going to intentionally take away all the familiar adults, but someone else stepping in to offer different opportunities or challenges can sometimes be appropriate. Making a judgement of when this should happen returns to the idea that the key person is an expert for a child and so will know when to step back, although listening to and assessing a child's voice is not down to just one key person, and sharing observations and perspectives can contribute to a more holistic, shared approach to knowledge.

Reflection is not always this dramatic; often, the type of reflection that makes the most difference is ongoing refection in practice (Schon, 1983; Pendrey, 2022). Our children who are non-verbal cannot express their moods and may react differently from day to day, or even hour to hour, so we cannot become creatures of habit and instead need to respond when something is not going well by stepping back and reviewing what is happening, what the child is communicating to us, and how to interpret their voice. As part of this, peer observations, where the practitioners observe each other's interactions, can be a revelation. One practitioner may have a different interpretation of a child's actions than another. By having these discussions, we widen our knowledge of a child's voice and learn new ways to interpret their communications.

Conclusion: getting it right

Early years has an emphasis on the individual, which puts us in a position where the child's voice should be central to everything we do, as noted by Robinson in Chapter 1 of this text (see also UNCRC Article 12.1, 1989; Wall et al., 2019). We can never be sure we are getting it right for all the individual children in the setting and that every child's voice is heard. Knowing each child as an individual and taking the time to really observe our children's many forms of expression give us the best chance of making the right decisions. Constant reflection in practice also helps us evaluate what we are getting right and ensures that we never stagnate in our practice and our routines need to remain flexible.

Reflective questions

1. How well can we listen to a child's voice when they are non-verbal?
2. Are we following the overarching principles, or are day-to-day practicalities getting in the way?

Takeaway activity

Take time to stand back and really observe a child in their play with a colleague. Follow them for as long as possible, noting what they do, how they play, and what seems to be important to them.

- Does your colleague observe the same as you?
- Are there any differences in how you interpret the child's play?
- Are we really listening to the child's voice or filtering it through our own preferences?

References

Albin-Clark, J., Shirley, I., Webster, M., and Woolhouse, C. 2018. Relationships in early childhood education – beyond the professional into the personal within the teacher–child dyad: Relationships 'that ripple in the pond'. *Early Child Development and Care*, 188(2), 88–101.

Aljabreen, H. 2020. Montessori, Waldorf, and Reggio Emilia: A comparative analysis of alternative models of early childhood education. *International Journal of Early Childhood*, 52, 337–353.

Borkett, P. 2021. *Special educational needs in the early years: A guide to inclusive practice*. London: SAGE Publications.

Bruce, T. 2017. *Early childhood education* (5th edition). Hodder Education.

Cameron, C. and Moss, P. 2020. *Transforming early childhood in England*. London: UCL Press.

Cheminais, R. 2009. *Effective multi-agency partnerships: Putting every child matters into practice*. London: Sage.

Clark, A., and Moss, P. 2011. *Listening to young children: The mosaic approach* (2nd edition). London: National Children's Bureau.

Cottle, M., and Alexander, E. 2014. Parent partnership and 'quality' early years services: Practitioners' perspectives. *European Early Childhood Education Research Journal*, 22, 637–659.

Cowan, K., and Flewitt, R. 2020. Towards valuing children's signs of learning. In Cameron, C., and Moss, P., *Transforming early childhood in England*. London: UCL Press.

Davies, R., and Hamilton, P. 2018. Assessing learning in the early years' outdoor classroom: Examining challenges in practice. *Education 3–13*, 46(1), 117–129.

Department for Education. (2024). *Early Years Foundation Stage (EYFS) Statutory Framework*. Available at: https://www.gov.uk/government/publications/early-years-foundation-stage-framework--2

Department for Education (DfE). 2014. *Special educational needs and disability code of practice: 0 to 25 years*. Available at: https://www.gov.uk/government/publications/send-code-of-practice-0-to-25

Frost, J.L., and Sutterby, J.A. 2017. Outdoor play is essential to whole child development. *Young Children*, 72(3), 82–85. Available at: https://www.naeyc.org/resources/pubs/yc/jul2017/outdoor-play-child-development

Garden, A., and Downes, G. 2023. A systematic review of forest schools' literature in England, Education. *International Journal of Primary, Elementary and Early Years Education*, 51, 10.1080/03004279.2021.1971275

H.M. UK Government. 2023. *Working together to safeguard children*. Available at: https://assets.publishing.service.gov.uk/media/65cb4349a7ded0000c79e4e1/Working_together_to_safeguard_children_2023_-_statutory_guidance.pdf

Jarman, E. 2009. *The communication friendly spaces approach*. Bethersden Kent, England: Elizabeth Jarman.

Jones, J. 2000. A total communication approach towards meeting the communication need of people with learning disability. *Tizard Learning Disability Review*, 5(1), 20–30.

Lancashire County Council. *Early help assessment*. Available at: https://www.lancashire.gov.uk/practitioners/supporting-children-and-families/early-help-assessment/

Meadow, K.P. 2023. *Deafness and child development*. University of California Press.

Monti, F., Farné, R., Crudeli, F., Agostini, F., Minelli, M., and Ceciliani, A. 2019. The role of Outdoor Education in child development in Italian nursery schools. *Early Child Development and Care*, 189(6), 867–882.

Osgood, J. 2012. *Narratives from the nursery: Negotiating professional identities in early childhood*. Abingdon: Routledge.

Osgood, J., Elwick, A., Robertson, L., Sakr, M., and Wilson, D. 2017. *Early years teacher and early years educator: A scoping study of the impact, experiences and associated issues of recent early years qualifications and training in England*. Middlesex University.

Page, J. 2016. *Characterising the principles of professional love in early childhood care and education*. University of Brighton.

Parsons, K.J., and Traunter, J. 2020. Muddy knees and muddy needs: Parents perceptions of outdoor learning. *Children's Geographies*, 18(6), 699–711.

Pendrey, A. 2022. *The little book of reflective practice: A practical guide to the early years*. Routledge.

Pre-school Learning Alliance. June 2018. *Minds matter: The impact of working in the early years sector on practitioner health and wellbeing*. Available at: https://www.eyalliance.org.uk/sites/default/files/minds_matter_report_pre-school_learning_alliance.pdf

Schon, D.A. 1983. *The reflective practitioner*. New York: Basic Books.

Teaching and Learning Scotland. 2006. *The Reggio Emilia approach to early years education*. Glasgow Scotland.

Trevor, G., Ince, A., and Ling, A. 2020. Towards a child centred curriculum. In Cameron, C., and Moss, P., *Transforming early childhood in England*. London: UCL Press.

United Nations Convention on the Rights of the Child (UNCRC). 1989. Available at: http://www.ohchr.org/EN/ProfessionalInterest/Pages/CRC.aspx

Wall, K., Cassidy, C., Robinson, C., Hall, E., Beaton, M., Kanyal, M., and Mitra, D. 2019. Look who's talking: Factors for considering the facilitation of very young children's voices. *Journal of Early childhood Research ECR*, 17(4), 263–278.

Wearmouth, J. 2013. *Special educational provision in the context of inclusion: Policy and practice in schools*. David Fulton Publishers.

Zwaigenbaum, L., Brian, J.A., and Ip, A. 2019. Early detection for autism spectrum disorder in young children. *Paediatrics & Child Health*, 24(7), 424–432.

3 Enabling children to feel happier, heard, and connected

The Hamish & Milo well-being programme enabling primary school children to share their feelings and experience, develop their social and emotional skills, and improve their well-being

Clare Williams

Key words

Emotional well-being, Children's voice, Relationship, Psychoeducation, Belonging, Emotional safety, Trust, connection, Co-regulation, Social and emotional skills, Self-regulation, SEMH

Introduction

A recent survey conducted by the NHS reported that one in six children currently has a probable mental disorder (NHS Digital, 2022). The increase in referrals and the long waiting times for children to be assessed and treated by Child and Adolescent Mental Health Services (CAMHS) have been linked to poorer outcomes for those seeking care (Stafford et al., 2020), with only 25% of young people needing treatment receiving it (Public Health England, 2016). These reports reflect the mounting concern within the schools and education sector about the prevalence of children's mental health issues and how this is affecting children and young people's engagement with learning. It can be argued that there is significant need for targeted social, emotional, and mental health (SEMH) interventions for children with emerging mental health needs as a proactive and preventative measure – particularly children who have experienced adverse risk factors, those that have specific social and emotional learning needs, and those who may be struggling to feel included within the school culture (Department of Health and Department for Education, 2017) may need additional targeted support to alleviate impact on long-term mental health and emotional development (Public Health England and Department for Education, 2021).

In this chapter, we describe Hamish & Milo, a SEMH well-being programme ('the programme') used in primary schools across the United Kingdom to develop pupils' social and emotional skills and improve well-being. The programme is delivered as an individual and/or small group intervention by a pastoral staff member within a school setting and addresses key areas of emotional development, such as self-esteem, friendship, resilience, and anxiety.

The impacts and outcomes of the programme are currently being evaluated in a collaborative research project with the University of Bath's Psychology Department (Joiner et al., 2023). The initial phase of the project involved 478 children and 250 education practitioners from over 90 schools across the UK currently using the programme, consisting of a series of ten-week well-being sessions. The programme acknowledges and values the concept of 'child's voice', which it describes as being the child's experience of being valued and of belonging as part of a group, wherein the child feels heard, feels safe to talk about their emotions and lived experiences, and is able to share their views and ideas. Along with measures for pre- and post-intervention to measure impact, the initial phase of the research project also captured the thoughts, feelings, and reflections of the children participating in the programme through the completion of child's voice questionnaires.

DOI: 10.4324/9781003459651-5

Data collected from participating schools during the initial phase of the collaborative project was captured using a unique digital impact measurement platform called 'Navigator'. The platform has become a pivotal tool in measuring the impact of children's experiences, showing shifts and changes in the development of social and emotional skills, and capturing the children's experiences through both quantitative and qualitative data collection. We shall explore this in more detail through the voices of children and the adults that work with them. Emerging evidence from the data collection in the initial phase will also be presented, and in sharing the rationale and approach for the research project, we will also consider the vital role of the pastoral staff in creating a safe base for the children involved in the programme, enabling them to feel included, valued, and heard, and the importance of ensuring that the child's voice is prioritised at the centre of practice in order to make a real difference in children's lives and learning.

The Hamish & Milo intervention programme

Hamish & Milo is a comprehensive emotions curriculum and SEMH intervention for primary-aged children. The programme provides an explicit framework to enhance PSHE delivery through ten modules, or 'emotions themes': friendship; resilience; anxiety; diversity; strong and angry feelings; transition and change; conflict resolution; loss, bereavement, and grief; sadness; and self-esteem. Each of the ten-week themes is facilitated by school teaching assistants (TAs), emotional literacy support assistants (ELSAs), or pastoral staff through detailed session plans containing opportunities for creative activities, discussion, and reflection about situations, emotions, and experiences that may be occurring in the children's lives. Each theme provides the opportunity for social and emotional skills development, psychoeducation, and gaining understanding of emotional experiences.

Opportunities for psychoeducation include learning about simple brain structure and what is happening inside their body and brain when they are feeling sad, angry, or worried, for example. Each theme focuses on the development of the five emotional literacy skills that constitute emotional intelligence, including self-awareness and strategies to regulate emotions. The programme promotes a nurturing group experience in that it allows for structured and predictable sessions facilitated by an empathic, caring, and nurturing adult who enables the children to feel emotionally and psychologically safe, included, valued, and heard. In this way, the children may feel that they are not alone with big, and sometimes overwhelming, feelings but instead are supported to experience the full range of emotional experience, allowing them to grow, learn, and thrive.

The Hamish & Milo programme has been designed within the context of the theoretical landscape of relational-cultural theory (Miller, 1986), which acknowledges the inherently social nature of human beings that drives an individual to grow through and toward connection throughout the lifespan. These interpersonal connections, built on mutual empathy, allow us to feel safe, be comforted, and have a sense of belonging, which supports our well-being and creates a desire in us for more connection (Jordan, 2017). A large and growing body of literature emphasises that nurturing, reliable, and responsive relationships are fundamental to optimal development and well-being (National Scientific Council on the Developing Child, 2004). Through these loving and trusted relationships, children learn how to think, understand, communicate, express emotions, and develop social skills (National Scientific Council on the Developing Child, 2020). At the heart of the programme is the understanding that these nurturing relationships are crucial for the child's development of healthy brain and body functioning, which, in turn, lays the foundation for later outcomes, such as physical and mental well-being, academic performance, and interpersonal skills.

The framework for the Hamish & Milo programme is structured around a range of theoretical contexts, models, and research evidence, all of which place the significance of relationships at the core of optimal human development, including attachment theory (Bowlby, 1978; Ainsworth et al., 1978), emotional regulation theory (Schore, 2015), psychosocial development theory (Erikson, 1980), Maslow's theory of motivation (1943), adaptive brain theory (Steffen et al., 2022), social brain hypothesis (Dunbar, 2009; Adolphs, 2009), ecological systems theory (Bronfenbrenner, 2005), adverse childhood experiences model (Felitti et al., 1998), positive childhood experiences model (Bethell et al., 2019), group development theory (Tuckman and Jensen, 1977), emotional intelligence model (Goleman, 1996), and emotional literacy model (Faupel, 2003). The programme also acknowledges the importance of co-regulation in establishing biological and emotional safety as a key factor in supporting children to develop their emotional vocabulary and in navigating their emotional experiences (Schore, 2015). Consistent experiences of co-regulation allow children to develop increasingly complex emotional literacy skills – learning to identify emotions, connect emotions to experiences, and respond adaptively to their emotional experiences – alongside the growth of their cognitive and language skills (Payley and Hajal, 2022).

Addressing social and emotional learning at school

Social and emotional learning (SEL) is described as

> the process through which all young people and adults acquire and apply the knowledge, skills, and attitudes to develop healthy identities, manage emotions and achieve personal and collective goals, feel and show empathy for others, establish and maintain supportive relationships and make responsible and caring decisions.
>
> (CASEL, 2023)

There is extensive evidence associating social and emotional skills development in childhood with school readiness, improved academic outcomes, and in relation to physical and mental health, crime, employment, and income level later in life (Domitrovich et al., 2017; Heckman and Kautz, 2013; Goodman et al., 2015). There is also compelling evidence that teaching SEL through planned programmes can have a positive impact on children's attitudes to learning, relationships in school, academic attainment, and a range of other outcomes (Education Endowment Foundation and Early Intervention Foundation, 2019). Research undertaken by Panayiotou et al. (2019) draws a correlation between having social and emotional skills (SES) and academic achievement by protecting individuals from poor mental health, which would otherwise reduce their ability to learn. Further evidence from this study also shows that having good SES enables students to build relationships with both teachers and peers, helps children manage their emotions, navigate challenges, and demonstrate resilience in the event of failure (Panayiotou et al., 2019). A study conducted recently by the Centre for Education and Youth concluded that because schools are influential social environments in the lives of children and young people, they can play a definitive role in helping them develop SES through good relational practice and targeted intervention (Granada et al., 2022).

All children, and especially those most disadvantaged, need to have their SES nurtured, supported, and encouraged and should be equipped with social and emotional skills to be able to live life well and to have long-term mental wellness. The evidence is clear that if schools are able to successfully address SES deficits, then children and young people who are at risk, including those from socio-economically disadvantaged backgrounds, the resulting benefits would be a reduction in the attainment gap and reduced inequality in later life (Feinstein, 2015).

The importance of pupil voice

Children's right to be heard and to have their views taken seriously was established through Article 12 of the United Nations Convention of the Rights of the Child (UNCRC, 1989). The UK government has since committed to the promotion and protection of children's rights in this country, in line with the Convention, and has stated its belief that all children and young people should have opportunities to express their opinion in matters that affect their lives (Department for Education, 2014). For all children, and particularly those living with adversity and/or those with specific SEMH needs, the importance of feeling heard and having their thoughts and experiences validated, is paramount to their well-being (Porter, 2014). Providing and facilitating meaningful opportunities where children feel safe, protected, and included, and where they are met with empathy, compassion. and care, is vital for developing emotional resilience and emotional regulation (Conkbayir, 2023). All children have the right to feel safe, heard, and valued, and it is necessary to create regular opportunities for children to share their ideas, thoughts, and aspirations – both on a personal and at whole-school level – to

- understand a child's thoughts, wishes, and feelings;
- build trust and emotional safety;
- gain perspective from the child's point of view;
- establish meaningful connection for collaborative meaning-making;
- enable shared understanding; and
- enable a felt sense of mattering and belonging.

With a national focus on mental health and well-being (Department for Education, 2018; NHS Digital, 2022) and the subsequent promotion of 'Mentally Healthy Schools' (Anna Freud, 2024), a recognition of the need for whole school cultures, including policy and practice, that support and promote positive mental health has been acknowledged (Public Health England, 2016). A key element of this approach is the commitment from schools in hearing and valuing each child's view of their ideas, desires, and experiences, with the evidence showing that schools that embed this practice within their culture report many positive outcomes (Flutter and Rudduck, 2004), including a reduction in exclusions, increased pro-social behaviour, and better relationships across the whole school community (Rudduck and McIntyre, 2007), which is reflected in improved academic attainment and pupil attendance (Department for Education, 2014). But despite the growing awareness and recognition of this necessity, all too often children feel unable to share their feelings and what matters most to them (Weare, 1999). This oversight can be attributed to a number of factors, including limited time and opportunities for connection due to curriculum pressures, overwhelming demand, funding cuts (Hayes, 2022), and a lack of knowledge and training amongst teachers (Early Intervention Foundation, 2021). Additionally, there may be several factors that prevent children from being able to voice what matters to them and how their experiences are affecting them, including the fear of not being listened to or truly understood, the lack of opportunities to talk about their lived experiences, their need to fulfil adult expectations by approval-seeking and compliance, the lack of confidence or belief in themselves, and unconscious or emotionally painful feelings due to adverse childhood experiences (Dolton et al., 2020; Keenan, 2022).

The Hamish & Milo programme ensures that the child's voice is discerned through various processes included in each session, including the use of puppets for emotional expression, open discussion, engagement in creative expression activities, and active reflection. The programme acknowledges that the concept of child's voice is not just about affording children the opportunity to express their feelings, thoughts, and opinions but, additionally, encompasses their ability to freely express their uniqueness in this world and to be fully accepted and celebrated for who they are.

Creating an environment of emotional safety through trusted relationships

A foundational element of the Hamish & Milo programme is the establishment of an emotionally and psychologically safe learning environment, where the child has the physical and emotional sense of being accepted for who they are, what they need, and what they feel. Having this sense of emotional safety enables the child to express themselves freely and allows them to collaborate and share experiences with others. The latest research in neurobiology shows that emotional safety is one of the most important aspects of a satisfying connection in social relationships (Porges, 2017). In order to establish a place of safety for both adults and children, it is essential to ensure that the school's safeguarding principles and practice are robust and adhered to, and that staff know the relevant processes to ensure all children are kept safe as a matter of the highest priority.

> *'I don't feel safe at home, but I feel safe here.'*
> *'I wish the group went on longer.'*
> *'I feel listened to.'*
> *'Telling others how you feel, and talking, feels good to me.'*
> *'It helps with my depression and makes me calmer in the day. The classroom gets too loud for me, and I feel relief in this group.'*
> *'It's helped me think and not worry and just relax. I worry about learning, and I don't have to when I'm in here.'*

Comments from children participating in the Hamish & Milo programme from a primary school in Lancashire

One of the key methods used within the programme to establish emotional safety is the use of sock puppets as 'pets' for each of the children participating. The use of puppets has long been practiced as a tool to animate and communicate key ideas and needs as part of human culture and oral tradition (Fourie, 2009). Using puppets as a tool for developing social and emotional learning can bolster confidence and communication skills, foster relationships, build connections, and develop a community of learners who are respectful and inclusive (Kröger and Nupponen, 2019). Puppets are a powerful tool for helping children talk about difficult experiences, feelings, and ideas without them feeling exposed or vulnerable (Renfro, 1984). Puppets can have experiences that children can relate to, understand, and be able to think about at a safe emotional distance, while beginning to reflect on, think about, and heal through their own experiences (Potgieter and Van Der Walt, 2021). Puppets can tell a story, express a situation, or portray an emotional reaction to something that has happened, which enables the child to feel empathy or resonance with it. By attributing their thoughts, feelings, and experiences to the puppet and not themselves directly, the child can explore and test out their thinking in a way that will elicit responses that exclude fear, blame, or judgement (Korošec, 2012). By talking as a puppet or to a puppet, children can explore emotional responses and actions and can name feelings that may otherwise be too scary or powerful to name, and in so doing, they can begin to recognise deeper feelings within themselves and gain a sense of self-awareness that comes as they feel heard and understood (Korošec, 2012).

Sock puppets are intrinsic to the delivery of the Hamish & Milo programme, as they are used to introduce emotional themes whilst creating an atmosphere that is safe and nurturing, thereby allowing children to explore sensitive emotional themes in a way that is supported and emotionally and psychologically safe. The sock-puppet-making activity at the start of the programme allows both the children and the adults to be playful, creative, imaginative, and expressive in a fun and relaxed way. Donald Winnicott, the British paediatrician and psychoanalyst, first described the significance and importance of *transitional objects* in the development of children (Litt, 1986). *Transitional objects* are described as chosen possessions that offer security and comfort to a child whilst they are learning and gaining independence (Winnicott, 1953). Sock puppet pets can be seen as an example of a transitional object for children participating in the programme, in that they provide a sense of security, comfort, and consistency whilst they are working through the Hamish & Milo themes. Once they have completed the ten-week theme, the children are able to take the sock puppet home with them to keep as a 'special pet' or 'friend', as a reminder of the work they have undertaken during the course of the programme.

Figure 3.1 Hamish & Milo sock puppets.

Puppets have been identified as an effective mediating tool in communication between children and adults, as the use of them can liberate the adult from their traditional role in the classroom, enabling them to become more playful, allowing for more freedom in interactions and exploration (Forsberg Ahlcrona, 2012). A playful approach to learning adopted by the adult helps create a safe learning environment, allowing children to take risks, make mistakes, and rectify them without fearing the 'traditional authority' of a teacher (Hensberry et al., 2018).

The following comments and quotes were collected from schools using the Hamish & Milo programme with their pupils and demonstrate the significance the use of puppets had in helping the children feel safe enough to talk about and share their feelings and describe experiences that are important to them:

> Whilst there was initially some reluctance from some of the adults leading the programmes about using the puppets, it soon became clear from the feedback from schools that the puppets were powerful in enabling children to talk about their experiences, develop relationships, and build a sense of connection within the group. . . . [T]he children are verbalising things they wouldn't have verbalised before.
> SENCO for a primary school, Dorset

> We have one looked after child who is having a really hard time at the moment. He often comes in to see his puppet, even on days when we don't have the group. Yesterday he came in and he wouldn't talk to us, but he sat in his safe space and told his puppet. The eye contact between him and the sock puppet is amazing, as he doesn't usually give eye contact.
> pastoral assistant for a primary school, Kent

> His sock puppet pet helps him feel not so alone and scared at night. He keeps his whole pack under his pillow and every night takes his puppet out to talk to. It has become his friend.
> emotional literacy support assistant for a primary school, Dorset

> She loved her sock puppet and wanted to take it with her to her new home. It was so brilliant, as this was a sense of safety for her. She was just able to be herself in the group, not the girl who is being fostered. She excelled in making her sock puppet; it helped her to distance herself from everything. There was a real sense of safety and acceptance, and she just felt part of the group.
> learning support assistant for a junior school, Gloucestershire

The importance of the trusted adult in SEMH outcomes for children

> If children feel safe, they can take risks, ask questions, make mistakes, learn to trust, share their feelings, and grow. If they are taken seriously, they can respect others. If their emotional needs are met, they have the luxury of being able to meet other people's needs. Deprived of these things, however, they may spend their lives doing psychological damage control.
> (Kohn, 2018, p. 239)

The experiences children have in their early years have a significant impact on how they grow and develop, their physical and mental health, and their thoughts, feelings, and behaviour (Manchester University NHS Trust, 2024). Two important factors affecting mental well-being and the development of social and emotional skills are the quality of children's early attachment relationships and their history of adversity. Attachment theory (Bretherton, 1992) emphasises that the child's first safe base is created through a close relationship with a sensitive and responsive attachment figure who meets the child's needs and to whom the child can turn as a safe haven when upset, anxious or, dysregulated (Purnell, 2004). When children develop trust in the availability and reliability of this relationship, their anxiety is reduced, and they can then explore and enjoy their world independently, safe in the knowledge that they can return to their secure base whenever needed (Cassidy, 1999). It is often assumed that children naturally possess the foundational skills to regulate their own emotions, or that these skills can be taught and learned by instruction (Delahooke, 2022). However, it is not possible to teach emotional self-regulation skills; in order for children to develop them, they must first experience them through caring, consistent, and attuned relationships with adults (Delahooke, 2022).

Adverse childhood experiences (ACEs) are described as 'highly stressful, and potentially traumatic, events or situations that occur during childhood and/or adolescence; they can be a single event, or prolonged threats to, and breaches of, the child's safety, security, trust or bodily integrity' (Young Minds, 2018). ACEs were identified in a groundbreaking study by Felitti et al. (1998) and include traumatic experiences, such as domestic violence, parental abandonment through separation or divorce, a parent with a mental health condition, being the victim of abuse (physical, sexual, and/or emotional), being the victim of neglect (physical and emotional), a member of the household being in prison, and growing up in a household in which there are adults experiencing alcohol and drug use problems (Public Health Scotland, 2021). Trauma and stress caused by these experiences can change a child's brain structure and function and can severely impact their ability to emotionally self-regulate (Lackner et al., 2021).

Children who have experienced ACEs in their early years, children in care, and neurodivergent children, and those children that may have missed out of some of the early experiences of good-enough attachment and felt emotional safety, may be more vulnerable and, therefore, in need of greater support within the school (Delahooke, 2022). Having a trusted adult who is empathic, emotionally aware, and containing has been identified as a significant protective factor in reducing harmful outcomes for children and young people who had been subjected to ACEs (Frederick et al., 2023). A recent review by the Welsh government (2021) highlighted that having at least one trusted, stable, and supportive relationship with an adult is emerging as one of the most important aspects of childhood resilience. The same review emphasised the importance and effectiveness of targeted support provision in school, including nurture groups and other evidence-based SEMH programmes (Welsh Government, 2021).

The renowned neuropsychiatrist Dr Dan Siegel and paediatric psychotherapist Dr Tina Bryson introduced 'the four Ss' model of fostering secure attachment in children (Siegel and Payne Bryson, 2020). Their model asserts that adults who 'show up' and provide consistent, attuned, and emotionally responsive care and support enable children to feel safe, seen, soothed, and secure, enabling them to form trusting relationships with their carers and with others. Siegel and Bryson's model is depicted in graphic form in Figure 3.2.

The role of the trusted adult leading the Hamish & Milo programme is vital in creating a sense of belonging for each child participating, which enables the children to feel safe enough to express themselves, talk about their experiences, and feel emotionally validated and responded to. The emotionally responsive, warm, and nurturing adult is the core element to the whole approach of the programme, as these qualities allow the children to develop a sense of being safe, seen, soothed, and secure. Many social and emotional interventions focus on children developing skills of self-regulation (Delahooke, 2023), but what is little recognised is that before a child is able to regulate their own feelings and behaviour, they require repeated experiences of being co-regulated by and with attuned and nurturing adults who can meet their needs (Delahooke, 2022). Interventions and programmes that focus on teaching emotional self-regulation should emphasise that emotional co-regulation is a pre-requisite to successful self-regulation (Delahooke, 2023).

> The children have learnt to trust me, so they even come and find me between sessions, just to check in and for reassurance.
>
> from an emotional literacy support assistant using the Hamish & Milo programme in a primary school, Southampton

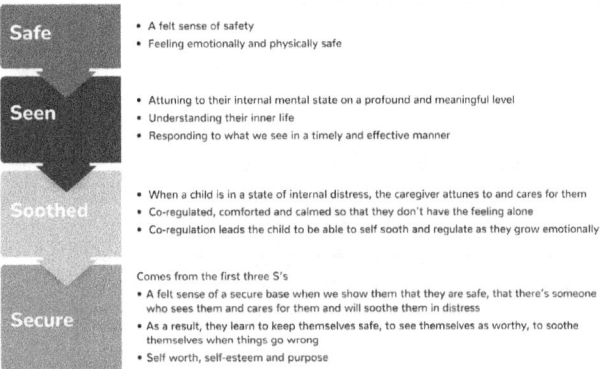

Figure 3.2 The four Ss model.
Source: Adapted from Siegel and Payne Bryson (2020, p. 6).

The Hamish & Milo programme has been designed with the awareness that some of the children participating may have gaps in their experience of being adequately co-regulated, and therefore, it may be more difficult for them to develop the social and emotional skills expected of them. Dr Mona Delahooke (2023) explains that for these children who have not experienced consistent nurturing and soothing co-regulation, they may not have the 'neural architecture in place' to develop the ability to self-regulate. The emotionally attuned and available adult leading the Hamish & Milo programme takes on the role of an emotional co-regulator and offers the child a safe, emotionally attuned structure in which to explore the activities and experiences within the programme that allow them to develop the full range of social and emotional skills.

> Hamish & Milo has been a remarkable new resource for [our school], which has changed the school provision in meeting the SEMH needs within the school. Moving forward, we are training more staff and increasing the number of groups we are running so that we can target even more children's needs.
>
> from an ELSA and mental health lead for a primary school in Southampton

Social connection in the Hamish & Milo programme

Social connectedness, or 'belongingness', is described as 'a feeling of being happy or comfortable as part of a particular group and having a good relationship with the other members of the group because they welcome you and accept you' (McIntosh, 2013). Maslow (1968) asserts that a sense of belonging is one of humanity's most fundamental needs and desires, since when we feel accepted, included, and welcomed, we experience positive emotions, including happiness, contentment, and calm (Baumeister and Leary, 1995). Research into the physical and psychological implications of belongingness has demonstrated that humans have a universal drive to form 'lasting, positive, and significant interpersonal relationships' (Baumeister and Leary, 1995, p. 497), and if we are not able to do this, our well-being is significantly adversely affected.

The structure and delivery of the Hamish & Milo programme allow for the establishment of social connections between the adult leading the programme and amongst the children participating. The small group structure of the programme facilitates and promotes a sense of belongingness amongst all the participants. The creative activities, discussions, and tasks enable opportunities for children to feel recognised and valued, and for connections and friendships to develop within the group. Children are given the opportunity to explore similarities and differences in feelings and experiences with their peers in a protected, nurturing, empathetic environment, allowing them to feel validated and to develop self-confidence. Anecdotal evidence shared by schools using the programme demonstrate that it may be easily adapted and successfully delivered on a one-to-one basis with an adult and one child.

> I've been doing memories and me [one-to-one] with a 13-year-old girl whose Mum died a year ago, and she is now living with her aunt and sees her Dad at weekends. She has written some beautiful things in our sessions about her Mum and the memories she has. She is autistic and has learning difficulties, and for her to open up has been amazing. She loves the sessions and keeps asking to come.
>
> from a teaching assistant from a special school in Dorset

The research psychologist Bruce Tuckman developed a model of group formation (Tuckman, 1965) which describes the stages observed in the development of a social group, namely, forming, storming, norming, performing, and transforming (Tuckman and Jensen, 1977). The format and structure of the sessions comprising the Hamish & Milo programme are designed around Tuckman's model, with each of the stages of group development recognised. Although Tuckman presented his phases as a linear model, it is important to recognise that, in practice, the phases are more fluid and group formation is not always a linear process, but it is a helpful model in seeing how the group process develops and highlights the importance of being within a group context for the intervention.

During the course of the programme, it is possible to observe all the stages of Tuckman's model of group development: In the initial *forming* stage, the group may a bit wary of each other and what to expect, but through the facilitation of the adult leading the group, they are able to embrace the possibility of what the experience may offer and form connections with each other. At this stage, the adult will establish clear and simple boundaries and outline straightforward expectations for working.

The *storming* phase follows as children feel more empowered to voice their ideas and feelings and may begin to test the boundaries or to check out the safety of the group. At this point, it is necessary for the adult to co-regulate, contain, and reassure the group, thereby establishing a safe structure for the dynamics that are being played out. The *norming* stage then comes into play as the group begins to settle and trust begins to form with the adult and amongst the children, facilitated by the familiarity of structure, relationships, and friendships that have been formed.

> A breakthrough moment was, a selective mute child with English as their second language, who rarely joins in, began speaking. He didn't speak at all until the fourth session of the 'Amazing Me' programme, when the children were asked to say one good thing as the 'welcome and check in' part of the session. The child spoke for the first time and said 'here', as in 'being here' in the group was what was good for him. It was a very special moment for the group, as the first time this child had spoken. Incredibly, the child went on to speak in the other sessions and has since been in a second intervention group and has spoken from the outset. He now has a big beam on his face.
>
> from a PSHE and intervention lead for a primary school in Lancashire

The *performing* stage evolves from the cohesiveness of the group, where a sense of belongingness allows for greater collaboration and confidence among the participants, and they are able to put into action the skills and strategies they are learning. Finally, the *transforming* stage may be observed where the children begin to use the skills learned within the group in other environments, including the classroom and at home. This stage signals the optimal time of closure and ending of the group, with children feeling confident to move on with the skills they have gained.

> What I like is that I can put children together that the teachers wouldn't necessarily, and it works within the small group experience because they can talk about things in different ways to being in the classroom. I had a group of children where one of them often just runs around school, another one is a selective mute, and they have really accepted each other and look after each other in the group, and they come every week!
>
> from an ELSA and mental health champion for a primary school in Southampton

Measuring the impact of the Hamish & Milo programme

The research framework for the impact study in collaboration with the University of Bath involved a single sample of 478 children who participated in the Hamish & Milo programme by completing ten sessions of a selected emotional theme, according to their assessed SEMH needs. To establish if the children's SEMH needs were impacted by the programme, pre- and post-intervention data was captured through the collection of the following impact measurement tools:

- The **strengths and difficulties questionnaire (SDQ)** is a standardised clinical measure widely used by clinical professionals in clinical work, in educational settings, and in research. SDQ can indicate changes in children's presenting behaviours through five subscale measures: emotional symptoms, conduct problems, hyperactivity/inattention, peer problems, and pro-social behaviours.
- The **child well-being profile (CWP)** is the primary impact measurement tool for the Hamish & Milo programme. CWP provides a descriptive indicator of underlying needs and presenting behaviours in the form of a quick and comprehensive checklist.
- The **child's voice questionnaire (CVQ)** is the impact measurement tool for the *child's voice*. CVQ is a child-friendly survey form that captures the child's experience of participating in the programme from their own perspective.

Participating schools were able to upload pre- and post-intervention data collected from the measurement tools directly to the Hamish & Milo Navigator digital development platform, which also enabled them to track children's progress, observe emerging patterns, and gather vital insight and reporting to support their SEMH intervention strategies. Preliminary results for the initial stage of the research project demonstrate statistically significant differences across all the impact measures:

- **SDQ** – overall improvement for children across all subscales
- **CWP** – improvement on all behaviour and protective factors scales
- **CVQ** – improvement across all measures

Emerging data shows statistically significant differences in observations about the emotional and behavioural presentation of children pre- and post-intervention.
October 2023, Professor Richard Joiner, University of Bath, Department of Psychology

Measuring the impact through children's voices

The Hamish & Milo child's voice questionnaires (CVQ) provides a child-friendly pre- and post-intervention measure of a child's perception of their experiences of the programme. The CVQ allows the child to self-identify their feelings (worry, sadness, feeling bad about abilities, friendship struggles, talking about feelings, anger and frustration, and asking for help), the frequency of their feelings, what they like/do not like about being in the group, their favourite parts of the group, and what they have learned about themselves. CVQs were completed by children themselves, supported by the adult group leader before and after the ten-week programme. The CVQ data shows that children experienced changes by an improvement in the following areas: worry (51%), difficulty in asking for help (51%), feeling bad about their own abilities (51%), talking about their feelings (51%), anger and frustration (50%), sadness (48%), and friendship struggles (44%).

In addition to the collection of quantitative data, it has been important to capture the children's opinions and thoughts of their experiences of the Hamish & Milo programme through the means of a qualitative method of data capture. The CVQ gives means to the children's representation of their feelings and perceptions in the form of drawings. Children's self-portrait drawings are routinely used by clinicians to generate information about things that are important to the child and have been described as an accessible and reliable screening tool technique used to evaluate emotional well-being, anxiety, and depression in school-aged children (Cohman and Timney, 2021; Tielsch and Allen, 2005). Children drew pictures depicting how they felt and perceived themselves prior to beginning the programme, and what they felt they would like help with. Following the completion of the programme, children gave their view of what they felt they had gained from the experience of participating in the programme. The information gathered from these questionnaires is informative and immensely impactful and provides a means to hear about what matters to each child.

The examples of children's drawings depicted in Figures 3.3–3.5 are a representative of many drawings amongst the study sample that provide a powerful and instructive insight into the children's inner emotional world.

> *'I want someone to talk to.'*
> *'I need help with being worried.'*
> *'My anger and sadness.'*
> *'To become braver.'*
> *'Controlling my emotions.'*
> *'Stress, feeling lonely, and the bullying.'*
> *'To say my feelings to other people.'*
> *'When I feel sad but no one notices, and what to say if someone is rude about my noises.'*
> *'I want help with feelings like anger, sadness, and worry.'*
> *'Saying my feelings when me and my friend fall out.'*
> *'I want people to listen to me. I want my social worker to let me have a voice.'*
> *'People understanding me.'*
> *'Feeling positive and confident about myself.'*
> *'I want help with saying how I feel without offending anyone.'*
> *'Getting friends.'*
> *'Making friends and being confident.'*
> *'To be able to say why I was sad.'*

Enabling children to feel happier, heard, and connected 37

Figures 3.3, 3.4, 3.5 Examples of children's drawings prior to participating in the programme.

'School stress, emotions, and anger.'
'Finding friends, being different to others, and sharing my feelings.'
'To control my anger.'
'To overcome nervousness.'
'Making friends, not feeling anxious, sad, lonely, and worried.'
　　'Feelings. I hide how I feel. I would like people to know.'

Quotations from children captured in the pre-intervention CVQ in response to the question 'What would you like help with?':

'I can talk to people about my bereavement.'
'I have got better by not bottling things up.'

Figures 3.3, 3.4, 3.5 (Continued)

'I am able to cry now and know that's OK.'
'I have learnt all about my feelings and techniques to manage my anxiety better.'
'That I can be brave when I want to and that I do have friends.'
'I'm perfect just the way I am.'
'I need to talk about my feelings, and it is OK to cry.'
'It is OK to have feelings.'
'I learnt about loss about Daddy.'
'I have empathy.'
'I don't have to deal with things on my own.'
'I am not the only one.'
'I am great at pushing myself through a challenge.'
'I have learned that I tense my fists when I get angry. This is a warning sign.'
'I have learned to let my mum know when I am feeling angry, and I ask for paper to rip up to help me.'
'That my brain is actually functional'
'I recognise that I start to make growling noises when I am getting angry.'
'I can believe in myself.'
'Talking to others helps me feel better.'
'Learning how I am able to say no.'
'I can stand up for myself!'
'I can be who I want to be.'
'It is OK to let your anger out.'
'That I will become happy again and that you never have to feel ashamed because of your feelings.'
'I have a voice.'

Quotations from children captured in the post-intervention CVQ in response to the question 'What have I learnt about myself?'

Impact

The self-reported improvement indicators relating to how children felt before and after participating in the Hamish & Milo programme demonstrate that they feel more able to express their feelings. Whilst this data represents only initial findings, it is very promising to see the positive impact reflected in the CVQs.

The emerging evidence shows significant statistical changes across all the CVQ initial impact measures in a positive direction. These positive findings have also been captured by the staff implementing and delivering the programme and highlights the potential longer-term impact as children are able to implement the positive outcomes gained during their participation in the programme back in the classroom and their wider world.

> Every child has made progress. We can see the children using the strategies. . . . [I]t is transferring back into class as well as during the intervention itself.
> from a pastoral support teaching assistant from an infant school in Cheltenham

Conclusion

From this initial research and experiences shared in using the Hamish & Milo programme, it is evident that enabling children's voice has multiple benefits in enabling children to speak about their experiences and to share what is happening in their lives. It is powerful in terms of supporting children to develop a sense of agency and empowerment and supports the fundamental right to feel heard and have their thoughts, ideas, and experiences taken seriously. The development of trust in relationships, feeling valued and heard, and having something to contribute promote inclusivity and recognition of the importance of different viewpoints, empathy for others' beliefs and opinions, and prepares children for life in the wider world beyond education.

Giving children a voice and opportunities to feel heard and valued is essential in creating well-being cultures in our schools, as well as being vital for mental health, relationships, and social and emotional development. It is therefore of paramount importance to provide a range of opportunities and ways for children to feel listened to and heard as they learn about the world and advocate for their own futures.

Reflective questions

1. What do you feel is the greatest impact for children's emotional well-being within this chapter?
2. What aspects of this approach do you feel would work well within your own setting?
3. Can you identify any challenges?
4. The voices of children are central to this approach, and parents' voices are a key element too. Can you think of how gathering both the voices of children and their parents' would support children's experience in school?
5. How do you think a small group experience that builds children's sense of safety and emotional literacy would impact back in the classroom and promote inclusion?

Takeaway activities

- Throughout the Hamish & Milo intervention programme, we use sock puppet pets as a therapeutic and engagement tool. Talking with and through a puppet can be fun and engaging, but it also serves to put a distance between uncomfortable feelings and enables a child to talk about experiences safely. Give a group of children the opportunity to create their own sock puppet pet and to create a story or fact file about them.
- Choose an emotion theme relevant for a small group of children, for example, friendship, conflict, sadness, angry feelings, loss. Ask the children to create a collage of what that theme looks like to them. They may want to create a banner or poster to depict their representation. Encourage them to identify expressive words within that theme, draw or find pictures that are representative, and then create a collage display. This could then lead on to further work around this emotion theme.

Acknowledgements

We would like to thank everyone within our Hamish & Milo team who are dedicated to make a real difference to children's emotional health and well-being. We would like to thank the University of Bath research team, led by Professor Richard Joiner and including Philip Clarke, Samantha Harris, and Melissa Ellis, who have given their time, expertise, and commitment to the impact study; to Anne Waddicor, who has contributed hugely to the data collation, analysis, and emerging impact report; and to Andrea Middleton, whose expertise in research, in the underpinning theoretical models, and as editor is invaluable.

We would like to give special thanks to all the schools within our Hamish & Milo community, and particularly those who have taken part in our research project and, especially, all the Hamish & Milo champions – the pastoral staff, ELSAs, and teaching assistants, who have given the children in their care the opportunity to be heard, valued, and recognised. We acknowledge, too, the children who have been brave enough to share their voices, to share their experiences, and who have given us such valuable insight into their inner worlds and their experiences of participating in the Hamish & Milo programme. This work continues to be vital in championing children's voices, their well-being, and placing these at the heart of education.

References

Adolphs, R. 2009. The Social Brain: Neural Basis of Social Knowledge. *Annual Review of Psychology*, 60, pp. 693–716. Available at: https://www.ncbi.nlm.nih.gov/pmc/articles/PMC2588649/

Ainsworth, M. D. S., Blehar, M. C., Waters, E., and Wall, S. 1978. *Patterns of Attachment: A Psychological Study of the Strange Situation*. New York: Lawrence Erlbaum.

Anna Freud Centre. 2024. *Mentally Healthy Schools*. Available at: https://mentallyhealthyschools.org.uk/

Baumeister, R. F., and Leary, M. R. 1995. The Need to Belong: Desire for Interpersonal Attachments as a Fundamental Human Motivation. *Psychological Bulletin*, 117(3), pp. 497–529. Available at: https://www.researchgate.net/profile/Mark-Leary-2/publication/15420847_The_Need_to_Belong_Desire_for_Interpersonal_Attachments_as_a_Fundamental_Human_Motivation/links/5b647053aca272e3b6af9211/The-Need-to-Belong-Desire-for-Interpersonal-Attachments-as-a-Fundamental-Human-Motivation.pdf

Bethell, C., Jones, J., Gombojav, N., Linkenbach, J., and Sege, R. 2019. Positive Childhood Experiences and Adult Mental and Relational Health in a Statewide Sample: Associations Across Adverse Childhood Experiences Levels. *JAMA Pediatrics*, 173(11). Available at: https://pubmed.ncbi.nlm.nih.gov/31498386/

Bowlby, J. 1978. Attachment Theory and Its Therapeutic Implications. *Adolescent Psychiatry*, 6, pp. 5–33. Available at: https://psycnet.apa.org/record/1982-00026-001

Bretherton, I. 1992. The Origins of Attachment Theory: John Bowlby and Mary Ainsworth. *Developmental Psychology*, 28(5), pp. 759–775. Available at: https://www.researchgate.net/publication/232490779_The_Origins_of_Attachment_Theory_John_Bowlby_and_Mary_Ainsworth

Bronfenbrenner, U. 2005. *Making Human Beings Human: Bioecological Perspectives on Human Development*. London: Sage Publications.

CASEL. 2023. *Fundamentals of SEL*. Available at: https://casel.org/fundamentals-of-sel/

Cassidy, J. 1999. The Nature of the Child's Ties. In: J. Cassidy and P. Shaver (Eds.), *Handbook of Attachment Theory, Research and Clinical Applications*, pp. 3–20. New York: Guildford Press.

Cohman, A., and Timney, C. 2021. *Developing a New Assessment Resource for EPs: The Children's Exploratory Drawings (CEDs)*. Available at: https://edpsy.org.uk/blog/2021/developing-a-new-assessment-resource-for-eps-the-childrens-exploratory-drawings-ceds/

Conkbayir, M. 2023. *The Neuroscience of the Developing Child: Self-Regulation for Wellbeing and a Sustainable Future*. London: Routledge.

Delahooke, M. 2022. *Brain-Body Parenting*. London: Sheldon Press.

Delahooke, M. 2023. *What to Know before We Teach Children Self-Regulation Skills*. Available at: https://monadelahooke.com/what-to-know-before-we-teach-children-self-regulation-skills/

Department for Education. 2014. *Listening to and Involving Young People: Statutory Guidance from the Department for Education*. Available at: https://dera.ioe.ac.uk/id/eprint/19522/1/Listening_to_and_involving_chidren_and_young_people.pdf

Department for Education. 2018. *Mental Health and Behaviour in Schools*. Available at: https://assets.publishing.service.gov.uk/government/uploads/system/uploads/attachment_data/file/1069687/Mental_health_and_behaviour_in_schools.pdf

Department of Health and Department for Education. 2017. *Transforming Children and Young People's Mental Health Provision: A Green Paper*. Available at: https://assets.publishing.service.gov.uk/media/5a823518e5274a2e87dc1b56/Transforming_children_and_young_people_s_mental_health_provision.pdf

Dolton, A., Adams, S., and O'Reilly, M. 2020. In the Child's Voice: The Experiences of Primary School Children with Social, Emotional and Mental Health Difficulties. *Clinical Psychology and Psychiatry*, 25(2), pp. 419–439. Available at: file:///C:/Users/middl/Downloads/Paper_InTheChildsVoice_%20FINAL%20CCPP%20-%20REVISED%20submitted.pdf

Domitrovich, C. E., Durlak, J. A., Staley, K. C., and Weissberg, R. P. 2017. Social Emotional Competence: An Essential Factor for Promoting Positive Adjustment and Reducing Risk in School Children. *Child Development*, 88(2), pp. 408–416. Available at: https://pubmed.ncbi.nlm.nih.gov/28213889/

Dunbar, R. I. M. 2009. The Social Brain Hypothesis and Its Implications for Social Evolution. *Annals of Human Biology*, 36(5), pp. 562–572. Available at: https://www.psy.ox.ac.uk/publications/295994

Early Intervention Foundation. 2021. *Adolescent Mental Health: A Systematic Review on the Effectiveness of School-based Interventions*. Available at: https://www.eif.org.uk/report/adolescent-mental-health-a-systematic-review-on-the-effectiveness-of-school-based-interventions

Education Endowment Foundation and Early Intervention Foundation. 2019. *Improving Social & Emotional Learning in Primary Schools: Guidance Report*. Available at: https://d2tic4wvo1iusb.cloudfront.net/production/eef-guidance-reports/primary-sel/EEF_Social_and_Emotional_Learning.pdf?v=1710933957

Erikson, E. 1980. *Identity and the Life Cycle*. New York: W. W. Norton & Company.

Faupel, A. 2003. *Emotional Literacy Assessment and Intervention Ages 11–16*. Southampton: Nfer-Nelson Publishing.

Feinstein, L. 2015. *Social and Emotional Learning: Skills for Life and Work*. Early Intervention Foundation. Available at: https://assets.publishing.service.gov.uk/media/5a80dc7240f0b62305b8d8ff/Overview_of_research_findings.pdf

Felitti, V. J., Anda, R. F., Nordenberg, D., Williamson, D. F., Spitz, A. M., Edwards, V., Koss, M. P., and Marks, J. S. 1998. Relationship of Childhood Abuse and Household Dysfunction to Many of the Leading Causes of Death in Adults: The Adverse Childhood Experiences (ACE) Study. *American Journal of Preventive Medicine*, 14(4), pp. 245–258. Available at: https://www.sciencedirect.com/science/article/abs/pii/S0749379798000178

Flutter, J., and Rudduck, J. 2004. *Consulting Pupils: What's In It for Schools?* London: Routledge.

Forsberg Ahlcrona, M. 2012. The Puppet's Communicative Potential as a Mediating Tool in Preschool Education. *International Journal of Early Childhood*, 44(2). Available at: https://www.researchgate.net/publication/257797309_The_Puppet's_Communicative_Potential_as_a_Mediating_Tool_in_Preschool_Education

Fourie, A. 2009. *Puppetry as an Educational Tool: An Explanatory Study On the Perceptions of Foundation Phase Educators and Learners*. Available at: https://www.researchgate.net/publication/313881429_PUPPETRY_AS_AN_EDUCATIONAL_TOOL_AN_EXPLORATORY_STUDY_ON_THE_PERCEPTIONS_OF_FOUNDATION_PHASE_EDUCATORS_AND_LEARNERS

Frederick, J., Spratt, T., and Devaney, J. 2023. Supportive Relationships with Trusted Adults for Children and Young People Who Have Experienced Adversities: Implications for Social Work Service Provision. *The British Journal of Social Work*, 53(6), pp. 3129–3145. Available at: https://academic.oup.com/bjsw/article/53/6/3129/7091809

Goleman, D. 1996. *Emotional Intelligence: Why It Can Matter More Than IQ*. London: Bloomsbury.

Goodman, A., Joshi, H., Nasim, B., and Tyler, C. 2015. *Social and Emotional Skills in Childhood and Their Long-term Effects on Adult Life: A Review for the Early Intervention Foundation*. Available at: https://www.eif.org.uk/report/social-and-emotional-skills-in-childhood-and-their-long-term-effects-on-adult-life

Granada, A., Hallgarten, J., and Hasset, A. 2022. *Catalysing Social and Emotional Learning in Schools in England: A Policy and Practice Review*. The Centre for Education & Youth. Available at: https://cfey.org/wp-content/uploads/2022/12/Catalysing-SEL-Report.pdf

Hayes, D. 2022. *Policy Context: Social, Emotional and Mental Health Needs*. Children and Young People Now. Available at: https://www.cypnow.co.uk/other/article/policy-context-social-emotional-and-mental-health-needs

Heckman, J. J., and Kautz, T. D. 2013. *Fostering and Measuring Skills: Interventions That Improve Character and Cognition*. Working Paper 19656. Cambridge, MA: National Bureau of Economic Research. Available at: https://www.nber.org/system/files/working_papers/w19656/w19656.pdf

Hensberry, K. K, Whitacre, I., Findley, K., Schellinger, J., and Wheeler, M. B. 2018. Engaging Students with Mathematics through Play. *Mathematics Teaching in the Middle School*, 24(3), pp. 179–183. Available at: https://www.researchgate.net/publication/328678375_Engaging_Students_with_Mathematics_through_Play

Joiner, R., Waddicor, A., Williams, C., Middleton, A., Clarke, P., Harris, S., and Ellis, M. 2023. *University of Bath Research Study with Hamish & Milo: The Emerging Evidence*. Available at: https://hamishandmilo.org/wp-content/uploads/Hamish-Milo-University-of-Bath-Wellbeing-Intervention-Imapct-Report.pdf

Jordan, J. V. 2017. Relational–Cultural Theory: The Power of Connection to Transform Our Lives. *Journal of Humanistic Counseling*, 56(3), pp. 228–243. Available at: https://doi.org/10.1002/johc.12055

Keenan, E. 2022. *Enhancing the Experiences of Children with Social Emotional and Mental Health Difficulties in a Primary Class*. Master thesis, National University of Ireland Maynooth. Available at: https://mural.maynoothuniversity.ie/17309/

Kohn, A. 2018. *Punished By Rewards: Twenty-Fifth Anniversary Edition: The Trouble with Gold Stars, Incentive Plans, A's, Praise, and Other Bribes*. San Francisco: Harper One.

Korošec, H. 2012. Playing with Puppets in Class – Teaching and Learning with Pleasure. In: L. Kroflin (Ed.), *The Power of the Puppet*, pp. 29–45. Zagreb: Union Internationale de la Marionette.

Kröger, T., and Nupponen, A-M. 2019. Puppet as a Pedagogical Tool: A Literature Review. *International Electric Journal of Elementary Education*, 11(4), pp. 393–401. Available at: https://files.eric.ed.gov/fulltext/EJ1212334.pdf

Lackner, C. L., Santesso, D. L., Dywan, J., O'Leary, D. D., Wade, T. J., and Segalowitz, S. J. 2021. Adverse Childhood Experiences Are Associated with Self-regulation and the Magnitude of the Error-related Negativity Difference. *Biological Psychology*, 132, pp. 244–251. Available at: https://www.sciencedirect.com/science/article/abs/pii/S0301051118300127?via%3Dihub

Litt, C. J. 1986. Theories of Transitional Object Attachment: An Overview. *International Journal of Behavioral Management*, 9(3). Available at: https://journals.sagepub.com/doi/abs/10.1177/016502548600900308

Manchester University NHS Foundation Trust. 2024. *Adverse Childhood Experiences (ACEs) and Attachment*. Available at: https://mft.nhs.uk/rmch/services/camhs/young-people/adverse-childhood-experiences-aces-and-attachment/

Maslow, A. H. 1943. A Theory of Human Motivation. *Psychological Review*, 50, pp. 370–396. Available at: http://www.ir.harambeeuniversity.edu.et/bitstream/handle/123456789/606/A%20Theory%20Of%20Human%20Motivation.pdf?sequence=1&isAllowed=y

Maslow, A. H. 1968. *Toward a Psychology of Being*. New York: Van Nostrand.

McIntosh, C. 2013. *Cambridge Advanced Learner's Dictionary*. 4th ed. Cambridge: Cambridge University Press.

Miller, J. 1986. *Toward a New Psychology of Women*. 2nd ed. Boston: Beacon Press.

National Scientific Council on the Developing Child. 2004. *Young Children Develop in an Environment of Relationships: Working Paper No. 1*. Available at: https://developingchild.harvard.edu/resources/wp1/

National Scientific Council on the Developing Child. 2020. *Connecting the Brain to the Rest of the Body: Early Childhood Development and Lifelong Health Are Deeply Intertwined: Working Paper No. 15*. Available at: https://developingchild.harvard.edu/resources/connecting-the-brain-to-the-rest-of-the-body-early-childhood-development-and-lifelong-health-are-deeply-intertwined/

NHS Digital. 2022. *Mental Health of Children and Young People Surveys: Mental Health of Children and Young People in England, 2022: Wave 3 Follow Up to the 2017 Survey*. Available at: https://digital.nhs.uk/data-and-information/publications/statistical/mental-health-of-children-and-young-people-in-england/2022-follow-up-to-the-2017-survey

Panayiotou, M., Humphrey, N., and Wigelsworth, M. 2019. An Empirical Basis for Linking Social and Emotional Learning to Academic Performance. *Contemporary Educational Psychology*, 56, pp. 193–204. Available at: https://psycnet.apa.org/record/2019-13089-018

Payley, B., and Hajal, N. J. 2022. Conceptualizing Emotion Regulation and Coregulation as Family-Level Phenomena. *Clinical Child and Family Psychology Review*, 1, pp. 19–43. Available at: https://www.ncbi.nlm.nih.gov/pmc/articles/PMC8801237/#CR166

Porges, S. W. 2017. *The Pocket Guide to Polyvagal Theory: The Transformative Power of Feeling Safe*. New York: W. W. Norton & Company, Inc.

Porter, J. 2014. Research and Pupil Voice. In: L. Florian (Ed.), *The SAGE Handbook of Special Education*, Vol. 2, 2nd ed. Los Angeles: SAGE Publications.

Potgieter, E., and Van Der Walt, M. 2021. Puppetry as a Pedagogy of Play in the Intermediate Phase Mathematics Classroom: A Case Study. *Perspectives in Education*, 39(3), pp. 121–137. Available at: https://www.researchgate.net/publication/346096801_Potgieter_E_Van_Der_Walt_M_2021_Puppetry_as_a_Pedagogy_of_Play_in_the_Intermediate_Phase_Mathematics_classroom_A_case_study_Perspectives_in_Education

Public Health England. 2016. *The Mental Health of Children and Young People in England*. Available at: https://assets.publishing.service.gov.uk/government/uploads/system/uploads/attachment_data/file/575632/Mental_health_of_children_in_England.pdf

Public Health England and Department for Education. 2021. *Promoting Children and Young People's Mental Health and Wellbeing*. Available at: https://www.gov.uk/government/publications/promoting-children-and-young-peoples-emotional-health-and-wellbeing

Public Health Scotland. 2021. *Adverse Childhood Experiences (ACEs) and Attachment*. Available at: https://mft.nhs.uk/rmch/services/camhs/young-people/adverse-childhood-experiences-aces-and-attachment/

Purnell, C. 2004. Attachment Theory and Attachment Based Theory. In M. Green and S. Scholes (Eds.), *Attachment and Human Survival*. Oxford: Routledge.

Renfro, N. 1984. *Puppetry, Language, and the Special Child: Discovering Alternate Languages*. Austin: Nancy Renfro Studios.

Rudduck, J., and McIntyre, D. 2007. *Improving Learning Through Consulting Pupils*. London: Routledge.

Schore, A. N. 2015. *Affect Regulation and the Origin of the Self: The Neurobiology of Emotional Development*. New York: Routledge.

Siegel, D., and Payne Bryson, T. 2020. *The Power of Showing Up*. London: Scribe Publications.

Stafford, J., Aurelio, M., and Shah, A. 2020. Improving Access and Flow within Child and Adolescent Mental Health Services: A Collaborative Learning System Approach. *BMJ Open Quality*, 9(4). Available at: https://www.ncbi.nlm.nih.gov/pmc/articles/PMC7677356/

Steffen, P. R., Hedges, D., and Matheson, R. 2022. The Brain Is Adaptive Not Triune: How the Brain Responds to Threat, Challenge, and Change. *Frontiers in Psychiatry*. Available at: https://www.frontiersin.org/journals/psychiatry/articles/10.3389/fpsyt.2022.802606/full

Tielsch, A. H., and Allen, P. J. 2005. Listen to Them Draw: Screening Children in Primary Care through the Use of Human Figure Drawings. *Pediatric Nursing*, 31(4), pp. 320–327. Available at: https://pubmed.ncbi.nlm.nih.gov/16229131/

Tuckman, B. 1965. Developmental Sequence in Small Groups. *Psychological Bulletin*, 63(6), pp. 384–399. Available at: https://psycnet.apa.org/record/1965-12187-001

Tuckman, B. W., and Jensen, M. C. 1977. Stages of Small-Group Development Revisited. *Group & Organization Management*, 2(4), pp. 419–427. Available at: https://www.proquest.com/openview/7a631d0ce4dd732776cd6ebec074105f/1?pq-origsite=gscholar&cbl=43244

United Nations. 1989. *Convention on the Rights of the Child*. Available at: http://www.ohchr.org/EN/ProfessionalInterest/Pages/CRC.aspx

Weare, K. 1999. *Promoting Mental, Emotional and Social Health: A Whole School Approach*. 1st ed. Oxford: Routledge.

Welsh Government. 2021. *Review of Adverse Childhood Experiences (ACE) Policy: Report: How the ACE Policy Has Performed and How It Can Be Developed in the Future*. Available at: https://www.gov.wales/sites/default/files/pdf-versions/2024/1/2/1705404494/review-adverse-childhood-experiences-ace-policy-report.pdf

Winnicott, D. W. 1953. Transitional Objects and Transitional Phenomena. *International Journal of Psychoanalysis*, 34, pp. 89–97. Available at: https://cir.nii.ac.jp/crid/1573668924523657472

Young Minds. 2018. *Supporting a Young Person with Trauma and Adversity: Understanding Trauma and Adversity*. Available at: https://www.youngminds.org.uk/professional/resources/understanding-trauma-and-adversity/

4 My school, my voice

Development of an inclusive student council in a large special school for autism

Sara Muršić

Key words

Autism, Student voice, Inclusive education

Introduction

Traditionally, student voice activities in schools (student council, class representatives, prefects) would gather opinions from the top-performing and often most popular students. Those students would naturally be voted for by peers through election processes that mimic political structures of the adult world. However, in most cases, neither the elected students nor their voters would be supported in developing skills to make the decision about representation, or represent others with respect and responsibility (Wyness, 2009; Biesta, 2011). Through that inaccessible process, somewhere in the background, the young minds of disabled or disadvantaged students are receiving a clear message that leadership and politics are not made for them.

The purpose of this chapter is to shed light onto this problem and offer solutions identified in research and practice which could influence future student voice programmes for all students. Following the introduction, which sets out the legal framework from a human rights perspective, I will discuss the challenges of traditional student council approaches and the importance of co-production in developing more inclusive systems. The population in focus are autistic students, who are often marginalised in these practices. In order to present these ideas as practically useful in a school context, I will share a case study of a special school for autism and the process of developing their inclusive student voice system, including lessons learned and recommendations for the future.

Legal framework

In the context of inclusive practices in education, the significance of student voice cannot be overstated. This key message stems from the foundations of our laws and policies as laid out in the Universal Declaration of Human Rights (Assembly, 1948) and later amplified by the Convention on the Rights of the Child (CRC) (Assembly, 1989). Articles of specific relevance to this chapter state that children have the right to express their views on all matters affecting them (Article 12), to maximum participation regardless of disability (Article 23), and to an education that prepares them for responsible life in a free society (Article 29).

In accordance with the Convention, various national policy and organisational guidance documents (National College of School Leaders, NASUWT Teachers' Union, specialist schools, and academies trust) now encourage schools to involve students as stakeholders in the decision-making process. Furthermore, the statutory guidance 'Listening to and involving children and young people' (DfE, 2014) states that schools are 'strongly encouraged to pay due regard to the convention' and that school leaders should use the guidance when 'considering how best to provide opportunities for pupils to be consulted on matters affecting them or contribute to decision-making in the school'.

In the field of special educational needs (SEN), the revised SEN Code of Practice (Department for Education & Department of Health, 2015) and the Children and Families Act (2014) further reinforce these views by placing children at the very heart of provision, emphasising the importance of listening to the views of children and young people and providing them with opportunities to participate in developing their individual educational plans. Additionally, the Code of Practice goes further than previous regulations by requiring local authorities to ensure that children and young people are involved in discussions and decisions about their individual support and local provision. This acknowledgement marks a paradigm shift, recognising students, including those who are autistic, as competent individuals 'playing an active part in a search for meanings' (Clark, 2017, p. 23).

In contrast, some reports from practice indicate that, even though the Convention was ratified in the UK more than three decades ago, a considerable amount of work is still needed to implement the Convention in its intended form. One example is the study by Castro and Palikara (2016), who reviewed educational, health, and care plans (EHCP) from different local boroughs in England and found that parents often described their child's views in the plans, which suggests that students are likely to be excluded from important decision-making processes that affect their lives. This practice was found to be significantly more prominent when supported children have identified communication difficulties. While most parents understand the needs of their children and actively advocate for their support, it is crucial to involve the children's voices in every instance. This can be achieved through various available accommodations, which will empower children and young people to expect active participation as a rule rather than an exception. Furthermore, with opportunities for regular practice, children will develop self-advocacy skills and confidence (Flutter and Rudduck, 2006).

In addressing children's needs, an added difficulty in reforming supportive practices comes from the complex and multifaceted nature of the concept of voice. It is understood as more than just speech in its literal meaning, with McLeod (2011, p. 179) defining it as

> an ideal, a political agenda, and a basis for political reform and action; it can declare difference and it can homogenise it; it has methodological and pedagogical dimensions and is rarely – if ever – simply a matter of creating opportunities for unfettered expression.

The key point for reflection is whether we attribute these powers and dimensions equally to students who are confident, verbal, and mature as we do to students who access education with greater difficulties.

The voice of the autistic population

Autism is a spectrum condition that affects people in different ways, mainly affecting how people communicate and interact with the world (National Autistic Society, 2023). Autistic individuals often exhibit unique strengths and preferences, with communication styles that may diverge from neurotypical norms. Many autistic individuals require support to communicate, which can include visual supports, symbols, signs, augmentative and alternative communication, or other, more specific strategies (Howard and Sedgewick, 2021). Additionally, sensory processing differences are common, influencing how individuals experience and respond to stimuli in their environment. In embracing a neuroaffirming perspective, it is essential to recognise these differences as valid expressions of neurodiversity rather than framing them as disorders or deficiencies.

However, these characteristic differences may pose challenges in the context of student voice activities designed based on neurotypical preferences. Neurotypical-centric approaches may inadvertently create barriers for autistic students, impacting their ability to fully engage in conventional student voice initiatives. Autistic students are found to be particularly vulnerable to exclusion from decision-making, with researchers noting this group to be less likely to participate in student voice than students with other forms of disabilities (Griffin et al., 2014; Wei et al., 2016; Shogren and Plotner, 2012). Challenges may arise in communication and sensory aspects, potentially hindering the expression of their perspectives within frameworks not attuned to neurodivergent preferences. To foster an inclusive environment for student voice, it becomes imperative to adopt an approach that acknowledges and accommodates the unique communication styles and sensory preferences of autistic students, ensuring their voices are valued and heard in a way that aligns with their neurodiversity.

Dimensions of the student voice and frameworks that are used to amplify it

The concept of 'student voice' is broad and encompasses a wide range of approaches. Researchers and practitioners have defined and operationalised *student voice* in different ways, depending on their perspectives and goals. One way to categorise student voice approaches is based on how students are viewed as participants in a research process. Fielding (2001) identified four types of student engagement, each of which positions students in a different way in relation to their active contribution:

- *Data sources.* Students are seen as providers of information, but they do not have a meaningful role in shaping the research or decision-making process.
- *Active respondents.* Students are involved in the research or decision-making process, but they are primarily seen as respondents to questions or prompts from adults.
- *Co-researchers.* Students are partners in the research or decision-making process, and they have a meaningful role in shaping the process and its outcomes.
- *Full independent researchers.* Students conduct their own research or make their own decisions, with minimal guidance from adults.

Another way to categorise student engagement within decision-making processes is based on determining who is the main driver of the process: adults or children. Larson, Walker, and Pearce (2005) identified two types of activities: adult-driven and child-driven. In adult-driven activities, adults initiate and structure the activity, and they have a significant degree of control over how it is conducted. In child-driven activities, children have a primary role in designing, implementing, and evaluating the activity. When reflecting on impact for the students, activities that position them as data sources or that are adult-driven are likely to be more limited in scope and impact than student voice activities that position students as co-researchers or that are student-driven.

Lundy (2013), in her insightful exploration of Article 12 of the CRC, identifies four essential dimensions of student engagement in decision-making: space, voice, audience, and influence.

This framework describes how authentic engagement with student perspectives extends beyond mere listening and goes towards actionable and genuine interest in lived experiences, feelings, and aspirations for the future. When their voice and lived experiences are active ingredients in leading organisational change, young people experience the transformative power of active citizenship, belonging, and validation within the group (Thomson, 2013).

Introduced by Roger Hart in 1992, the Ladder of Children's Participation applies Sherry Arnstein's citizen participation framework to children's involvement in projects. The ladder features eight rungs, illustrating varying levels of decision-making authority given to children. Initial rungs, like 'manipulation' and 'tokenism', indicate limited influence, progressing to 'consulted' and 'informed' levels, where children serve as consultants. The highest rungs, 'child-initiated and child-directed' and 'child-initiated shared decisions with adults', signify scenarios where children lead projects collaboratively.

Most frameworks and models relating to student voice refer to the concept of power or power dynamic in the context of the teacher–student relationship. It is necessary to explore the meaning attributed to this concept, as it serves as a fundamental principle in designing accessible and meaningful student voice activities. Reflecting on the work of Foucault (1980) enables a consideration of power as an entity that is not possessed or given away, or as inherently negative and solely vertical. Instead, Foucault (1980) views power as a dynamic force shaped by relationships, context, ongoing negotiation, and construction. Building upon this perspective, de los Reyes and Gozemba (2002) challenge the misconception of students' powerlessness by asserting that the absence of opportunities for students to experience and exercise their power prevents them from reclaiming an active role as social actors in their schools and broader communities.

Advantages of amplifying the voice of students

An increasing number of research studies focusing on the benefits of engaging students in the decision-making process reveal the significant advantages in nurturing student voice in all levels of education. According to research from the Quaglia Institute for School Voice and Aspirations (2016), students who feel their voices matter in school are seven times more likely to find academic motivation compared to those who do not feel included. Their study, conducted in USA across 239 schools in 14 states, finds that embracing student voice correlates with increased feelings of self-worth, engagement, and a sense of purpose in the school community.

The various advantages of developing student voice are recognised beyond academic success or retention, aligning seamlessly with the foundational principles of self-determination theory (Ryan and Deci, 2000). This theory highlights three student needs that fuel positive learning: competence (feeling capable), autonomy (having control), and relatedness (connecting with others). While self-determination theory focuses on beliefs, self-regulation theory (Zimmerman, 2002) explains the actions students take to stay engaged. It builds on the idea of active learning, where students construct knowledge rather than passively absorbing it.

Motivation, engagement, and voice are the essential elements of student-centred learning. Without motivation, students have no drive to learn; without engagement, they are unable to learn; and without voice, their learning is not authentic (Toshalis and Nakkula, 2012). Students need all three of these experiences to create new knowledge, succeed academically, and develop into healthy, independent, and successful adults.

The benefits of student voice also extend beyond an individual and impact the relationships across the whole school community. In research literature, we find voice-as-right and voice-as-participation being described through the importance of problem sharing for students (Mitra, 2004), students as researchers of the schooling experience (Fielding and Bragg, 2003), students helping other students with their learning (Topping, 2001), approaches to improving assessment practices (Flutter, 2007), and further, as informing and supporting teachers' professional development (Rudduck and Flutter, 2003). Voice has been an especially influential concept within schools-based projects that address empowerment and equality (Biesta et al., 2009).

The power of student voice to cultivate stronger relationships within the school community cannot be overstated. Multiprofessional partnerships thrive when relationships are of high quality, fostering an environment where individuals feel comfortable expressing diverse views and valuing differing perspectives (Lasker et al., 2001). This aligns with the idea that student–staff relationships serve as the cornerstone for increased student participation in decision-making, empowering their expression and opening access for all (Mannion, 2007). The reciprocal link between student voice and robust relationships becomes even more apparent when considering the 'partnership approach' to decision-making advocated by May (2004). In May's approach, strong relationships act as a catalyst for collaborative decision-making, where staff and students jointly share power through negotiation, joint goals, and reciprocal feedback. This illustrates the symbiotic nature of student voice and relationship-building within the school community, where meaningful relationships amplify the impact of student voice activities and, conversely, that engagement with student voice initiatives helps develop strong relationships and belonging.

Communication styles and preferences

The autistic population is diverse in terms of communication styles and preferences. Some autistic people communicate verbally, while others communicate non-verbally, using symbols or assistive technology. It is important to remember that the purpose, interest, pattern, or target audience of autistic communication can also be varied (Brown et al., 2022). Following are examples of diverse needs and preferences (in dimensions of voice and audience) for engaging with student council, all of which are derived from working directly with students in the case study school:

- **Verbal communication.** Autistic students who communicate verbally may want to participate in student council meetings, give speeches, or lead discussions.
- **Non-verbal communication.** Autistic students who communicate non-verbally may want to create artwork, posters, videos; use signs; or give presentations using visual supports (with or without the support of trusted adults).
- **Written-only communication.** Autistic students who prefer writing because it gives them time to think before they speak, making it easier to organise their thoughts without the pressure of quick responses needed in verbal communication. This way, students can process

information at their own pace and take the time they want to think thoroughly about the question (Howard and Sedgewick, 2021).
- **Supported communication.** Autistic students who prefer to communicate through a trusted person, without direct social engagement with others.
- **Assistive technology.** Autistic students who use assistive technology may prefer to participate in student council meetings, complete surveys, or join remotely. This is because written internet-mediated communication provides more control, thinking time, clarity, and fewer sensory issues (Benford and Standen, 2009; Gillespie-Lynch et al., 2014).
- **Individual communication.** Autistic students who prefer to communicate individually may want to meet with student council representatives one-on-one to share their ideas or suggestions but may not wish to join a group meeting or event.
- **Small group communication.** Autistic students who prefer to communicate in small groups may want to join a student council committee or participate in a focus group, sometimes if the group only includes familiar people and friends.
- **Large group communication.** Autistic students who are comfortable communicating in large groups may want to lead the meetings, give presentations to the student body, or participate in public events.

In order to enable and amplify the voices of autistic children and young people, options for expression must be just as diverse and flexible. This means providing a variety of ways for autistic students to engage with the student voice activities, such as through verbal communication, written communication, drawings, pictures, and assistive technology. It also means being mindful of the different ways in which autistic students may communicate and interacting with them in a way that is respectful of their individual needs and preferences.

Flexibility and choice in regard to space, voice, audience, and influence should always be present because students continuously change and develop. A student with a specific interest in art might choose to join a large group discussion on student artwork exhibition but, when discussing school lunch provision, only share their views through an online forum. As facilitators, adults should not assume the preferences of young people but instead allow them to choose the medium that represents their voice in the current situation, context, and group in the way they see fit (Sigafoos, 2006). This is similar to the respect given to international delegates in global political discussions, who can choose to speak in their native language and ensure that the message is not lost in the language barriers.

Traditional student council approaches: limitations and challenges

Traditional student council methodologies typically adhere to inflexible structures and rules that lack the adaptability required for inclusive participation by all students (Beattie, 2012). Such approaches undermine the fundamental purpose of representation within a council, potentially relegating students with disabilities to advising solely on matters related to their disabilities, rather than allowing them to participate fully in discussions that span all facets of school life. This limitation becomes particularly pronounced when students with disabilities are perceived primarily as experts in the field of disability, rather than as active contributors capable of influencing diverse aspects of education, such as discussions on the school canteen or field trips.

One of the consequences of traditional student council systems is the lack of diversity in representation. The emphasis on popularity or social skills in the selection process can marginalise students with autism, who may face difficulties conforming to conventional expectations of leadership or student council membership. The tendency to overlook quieter students (Finneran et al., 2021), who may actively avoid participating in voice activities (Perry-Hazan, 2021), exacerbates this imbalance. However, it is important to be mindful of the risks associated with the opposite scenario, where students with autism might be encouraged or pushed into joining the student council merely to fulfil a perception of diversity. While fostering inclusivity is essential, the activities must remain voluntary and student-led. An encouraging approach without adequate accommodations or support can inadvertently create a power dynamic that undermines the genuine efforts and potential benefits for the students involved. Achieving a balance between encouragement and respecting individual choices is crucial to maintaining the authenticity and effectiveness of student voice participation for students with autism. Tokenistic or symbolic participation, as identified by Alderson (2000), not only violates the CRC (particularly Article 12) but can also be detrimental to students, having a negative impact equal to or greater than having no council at all.

Another consequence of traditional approaches is the focus on verbal communication and confidence (Finneran et al., 2021). Students with autism, who may experience challenges in these areas, may struggle to effectively participate in the conventional student council setting. Difficulty accommodating students with communication and social needs perpetuates an environment that does not cater to the diverse strengths and contributions that students with autism can offer. Addressing these challenges requires a shift towards democratic approaches that are intentionally designed to be inclusive and equitable, providing diverse and flexible options for engaging with the student council. This ensures that all students, including those with autism, have an equal opportunity to participate meaningfully in decision-making processes.

Case study: development of an inclusive student council in a large special school for autism

School context

The school examined in this case study is situated within the urban area of northern England, providing education and support to students aged 3 to 19 living with autism and additional complex learning difficulties. The school embraces a diverse student body reflective of the intricate realities within the neurodivergent spectrum. While adhering to formal admission criteria, the school acknowledges and accommodates the varied characteristics within this group, encompassing additional speech and language difficulties, sensory processing disorders, and an increasing prevalence of mental health challenges.

Currently, the school has capacity for nearly 300 students, a result of the continuous expansion, which reflects the increasing demand for its specialised services. The holistic educational approach within this school incorporates diverse strategies, ranging from visual supports for communication and emotional regulation to personalised support delivered by a dedicated therapeutic team, including specialists in positive behaviour support (PBS), speech and language therapists, occupational therapists, and child and adolescent psychotherapists.

The commitment to a curriculum aligned with the ASD model (academic progress, specialist therapeutic support, and development of life skills) highlights the school's dedication to a comprehensive approach. Operating within small group settings, the institution emphasises personalised learning, high aspirations, and choices, equipping students for a meaningful and independent future. Positioned as a community, this case study school seeks to value the perspectives of students, parents, and staff, fostering an inclusive environment where all voices are not only heard but also valued. The curriculum, spanning a broad range of subjects and life skills, is tailored to individual needs, promoting emotional well-being, mental health, and the exploration of beliefs and morals.

Committed to being a centre of excellence for autism education, research, and professional development, this school cultivates an environment where staff engage in regular training to remain informed about the latest developments in autism education. The ethos revolves around acquiring specific and up-to-date knowledge to support students with both respect and expertise. The school's vision extends beyond its physical boundaries, aiming to raise awareness of the autistic population through collaboration with local schools and the wider community. This collaborative effort facilitates the inclusion of students' voices in decision-making processes at both local and national levels.

Initial challenges

The journey towards the reform of the student council at the case study school encountered a set of initial challenges rooted in traditional views and expectations of the system. Prevailing norms centred on the process of voting, a method familiar to both students and staff, albeit one that inadvertently favoured more vocal and confident students. This preference was often justified by the sentiment that it aligns with the established norm, 'because that is how it is done everywhere'. Consequently, students elected into the student council were often those deemed most popular, irrespective of their demonstration of fair representation, negotiation, or leadership skills. These reflections are echoed in research which reports on students often facing the perception that they lack the necessary sensibility or maturity (Gunter and Thomson, 2007; Lodge, 2005). Furthermore, a considerable number of teachers reportedly view student voice as peripheral, irrelevant, and not a priority in their beliefs or considerations (Fielding, 2001). The electoral process itself posed difficulties, with a majority of students struggling to grasp the responsibilities associated with the voter role, the choices available, and the consequential power bestowed upon them.

Reforming this approach involved challenging the perspectives of adults regarding the purpose of the student council system. Some held deeply ingrained beliefs that the student council should mimic the political structures of the country, complete with its often-convoluted and inaccessible rules. While many staff members were receptive to the proposed changes, concerns loomed regarding the additional time required to explain the changes and teach students about their new roles, responsibilities, and rights within the redesigned system. The new, more supportive system, designed to empower students in their roles, carried the risk of exposing gaps in available support for some students, as reflected in sentiments like, 'It is quicker and easier if I just do it for them'. Navigating these challenges required not only challenging traditional values but also addressing concerns about the practical implications and resource allocation associated with the reformed student council.

In the context of student voice within the field of autism, the phenomenon of masking emerges as a noteworthy barrier to meaningful engagement, particularly when discussing engagement with traditional student councils. Masking, or camouflaging, involves individuals concealing autistic behaviours to navigate communication and social challenges (Hull et al., 2019). This intricate process is often driven by a desire to 'fit in' and establish connections, as described by the work of Howard and Sedgewick (2021). The qualitative responses in the Howard and Sedgewick study highlight the prevalence of masking and 'performing neurotypicality' among autistic individuals. This theme, however, was not as pronounced in the presented case study, where the entire student body comprised autistic individuals. It is essential to note that this aspect of the autistic experience might not be as conspicuous in settings where everyone shares neurodivergent characteristics, such as in the case study. Nonetheless, it holds paramount importance for those utilising the case study to develop inclusive student voice practices in mainstream schools.

Strategies and activities for widening participation and ensuring accessibility for all students

Presenting an extensive range of activities, the school's new student voice system is designed to champion inclusivity and encourage active participation, recognising and accommodating diverse student characteristics. Each activity is purposefully designed to provide unique opportunities, ensuring students with varying communication preferences, age groups, interests, and other characteristics find a fitting platform to engage, express their opinions, and contribute meaningfully to the school community. This deliberate strategy not only encourages active engagement but also promotes a culture where every student feels valued and represented.

The **big question** stands as a cornerstone of the school's student voice system, constituting the most frequent and democratic activity engaging all students. This initiative places a paramount focus on regular, fully participative discussions concerning themes such as school dynamics, learning, safety, and enjoyment. These dialogues provide valuable insights into diverse perspectives and cultivate self-advocacy skills. Designed to align with Blank's levels of questioning (Blank and Sheila, 1986), the questions span varying levels of complexity, allowing staff to tailor discussions to the appropriate depth for their groups or individuals. Functioning as a versatile tool, the 'big question' can initiate conversations for settling or extending activities, foster relationship building, and enhance communication skills. While the theme/question is set, the modality of answering is open for the class to decide – some students use symbols or floor mats for expression of choice, while others enjoy a written activity or an open discussion or a debate. The continuous development of this activity promotes a culture of respectful listening and discussion at the heart of the school day.

The **ambassadors** activity welcomes applications from all students aspiring to become advocates for specific causes. Open year-round, this initiative attracts students with special interests

Table 4.1 Student voice system

Activity	Description	Participants	Frequency	Joining
The Big Question	Weekly class discussions about themes related to school, learning, safety, and enjoyment in order to learn about different perspectives and self-advocacy	All students	Weekly	All students can join and share their views in a discussion (answers recorded in an online survey).
Ambassadors	Raising awareness of a specific group or cause through blogs, leaflets, talks, research projects, and events	All students	Bespoke schedule	Filling in an application form ('student voice' box). Applications are open all year.
Young Student Leaders Club	Development of communication and leadership skills through a series of short sessions led by the student council	Primary department (age 5 to 11)	Termly (6 times per year)	Simply attending the sessions organised.
Student council	Leading students' experience through termly observations and discussions with peers and school leaders	Secondary department (age 12 to 19)	Termly (6 times per year)	Filling in the application form and sharing with the class. There can be more interested students in a class. Students can decide to participate in some or all activities, based on interest and preference.
Head student	Representation of the school in internal and external events (including participation in a regional schools' parliament)	Final year students	Bespoke schedule	Expressing interest to the head teacher via the application form.

Note: Table designed using five distinct activities.

seeking to contribute to the development of the school community in specific areas, such as climate change, trans rights, allergies, and more. To integrate this activity into the student voice system, a key emphasis is placed on guiding students to frame their applications around a specific problem or cause, fostering the creation of action plans that involve the wider school community. Adult facilitators support initially in screening applications to ensure they align with safe and inclusive principles, screening for potentially offensive, extremist, or unsafe ideas.

The **Young Student Leaders Club** is aimed for students aged 5–11, concentrating on skill development in communication, negotiation, representation, and advocacy. Serving as a version of the student council tailored for younger students, this group is facilitated jointly by student council members and supporting staff. It aims to prepare students for potential future roles in the student council, whilst creating a space for current student council members to hear views and problems of younger students in the school and contributing to their growth and understanding of leadership principles.

The **student council**, in alignment with the school's evolving ethos, has transformed to meet some of the traditional expectations while allowing space for experimentation in purpose, structure, and organisation. Comprising of class representatives, often perceived as messengers (see application form example in Figure 4.1), this activity facilitates group forums for sharing students' views and discussing broader issues. The student council retains its formal role in leading students' experiences through termly observations and discussions with peers and school

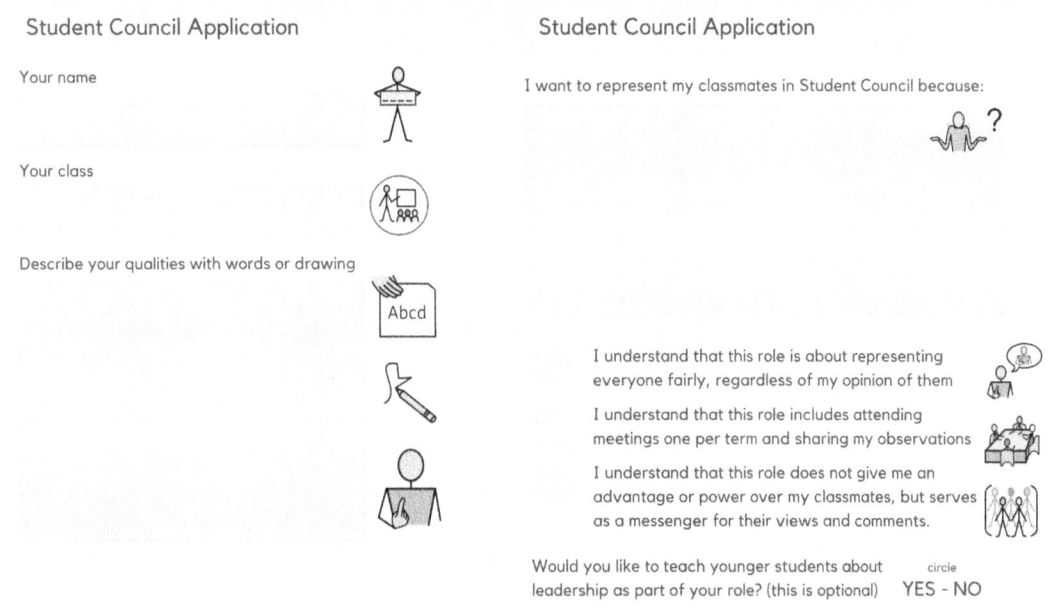

Figure 4.1 Student council application form (example).

leaders. Additionally, this activity is recognised by students as a valuable opportunity to socialise with students from other year groups and offer support for transition into new classes. As an ever-evolving structure, this activity may further adapt to reflect the school culture or be replaced by more specific activities covering various aspects of the multifaceted role of a school council, providing opportunities for more students to engage.

The **head student** role is designed for the oldest students, particularly those who enjoy representing others and demonstrate leadership in its traditional sense. The head student, along with their deputy, represents the student body and supports the head teacher in promoting the school. Duties encompass welcoming new students and staff, guiding prospective families through the school, answering questions about school life, and representing the school at local, national, and international events.

Offering a wide range of activities can help not only ensure that all students have an opportunity to access but also a chance to enjoy the process of providing their feedback without feeling self-conscious or intimidated. The fundamental idea behind this system is to provide a multitude of activities to attract a broader spectrum of diverse students, rather than attempting to adapt the methodology of a singular student voice activity to accommodate everyone.

Lessons learnt

Skills needed to facilitate, and skills needed to participate meaningfully

The case study school reflects on the vital significance of ensuring that both staff and students possess the necessary skills for meaningful engagement in the student voice system. Identifying a gap in awareness and skills, the school acknowledges that providing training could have improved confidence on both ends, potentially mitigating certain challenges.

In the process of developing student voice, students' self-advocacy emerges as a critical skill that requires deliberate practice, particularly among students with communication difficulties. The aim of these activities to involve students in decisions regarding their education is commendable; however, the practical implementation of it is not always straightforward. Staff feedback from the school suggests that making choices might be an unfamiliar and even daunting territory for some students. Similar comments are found in research literature, with Zilli et al. (2020) reporting on a comment by a teacher noting that their student 'felt scared at first' about the prospect of deciding on the topic for a lesson. Many similar studies emphasise that navigating decision-making processes can induce anxiety and apprehension in students (Rix et al., 2009), particularly those on the autism spectrum (Fayette and Bond, 2017; Hatfield et al., 2017;

Pellicano et al., 2014). The study by Hatfield et al. (2017), for instance, reports that autistic students expressed concerns about making decisions related to their transition to post-secondary education. This illustrates the reality seen in many educational contexts and points out that adults cannot assume that children and young people inherently have skills required to make informed decisions.

The anxieties expressed by students in these studies should not be used as grounds to sideline autistic students from opportunities to express their voice and impact change. On the contrary, they highlight the need for a more proactive approach in ensuring the necessary scaffolds, additional time, and targeted support to empower all students, especially those with autism, in making decisions about their education.

Transitioning the control and power to students was (and still is) very difficult for some adults. As the project developed, students in the school were introduced into taking more responsibility in leading their meetings more gradually, with adults supporting only when that was asked for or needed. The issue with power dynamics between staff and students in student council meeting is not unique to this school and is recognised in research literature. Some teachers are found to resist student empowerment initiatives due to concerns about relinquishing control (Lewis and Burman, 2008; MacBeath, 2006; Sellman, 2009). However, when given such opportunity, students often surprise their teachers by providing fair and realistic feedback (MacBeath, 2006). Moreover, the concept of student voice is occasionally interpreted as seeking input from students on predominately less-relevant, 'comfort issues', including matters like lockers, food, uniforms, and toilets (Lodge, 2005). Following the theme of lack of trust, Lundy (2013) highlights complaints from students about the fact that the issues they are allowed to influence are already decided by adults. While most adults suggest discussion points guided by the best intentions, it is detrimental to students' confidence and ownership of the work they do, for example, within a school council. Additionally, as Hummerstone (2018) points out, student responses often differ from responses given by their teachers when acting as a proxy, which makes it crucial to seek views directly from students whenever possible. As a starting point, students should be asked which matters they feel have an impact on them, and how (or, indeed, whether) they would like to be involved in influencing the outcome of the decision on that matter. By developing their self-advocacy skills, students become more empowered to ask for suggestions from adults when those are welcome, as well as disagree with suggestions that do not represent their thinking.

Authenticity

The challenge of genuine engagement in student voice initiatives extends to the problem of translating student suggestions into actionable change. Efforts to engage students in developing student voice activities can quickly become tokenistic if school leaders and teachers are not genuine and committed in their approach (Quinn and Owen, 2014). This commitment and value towards student voice, as well as school staff acting on student opinions, has been termed 'teacher authenticity' (Rudduck and Fielding, 2006, p. 226). Teacher authenticity is considered crucial for the success of student voice initiatives, as even in schools that promote student voice opportunities, students often remain passive rather than acting as leaders for change (Mitra and Gross, 2009).

Building upon the importance of teacher authenticity, the challenge lies not only in school leaders and teachers being genuine but also in their willingness to act on students' suggestions. Kehoe (2015) suggests that proposed change from a student perspective involves offering voice while accepting that the actions to create these changes are only legitimately made by school leaders and adults in power. Tokenistic approaches, where the inclusion of student opinions is superficial and lacks genuine commitment to change, risk perpetuating power imbalances (Quinn and Owen, 2014). This issue is further complicated by the tendency to inadvertently marginalise certain voices and reinforce existing hierarchies within the school community (Fielding, 2004; Whitty and Wisby, 2007). The danger lies in the potential appropriation of student voices to maintain control, rather than fostering genuine empowerment (Fielding, 2004). In this context, fostering authentic student voice requires a commitment to dismantling power imbalances, recognising and valuing the diversity of student experiences, and ensuring that students are active participants rather than passive recipients of decision-making processes.

In the case study school, the challenge of maintaining authenticity in student voice initiatives is acknowledged, but limitations arise due to constrained resources and conflicting priorities between school leaders and students. Balancing legal obligations and the need for transparency, school leaders grapple with the tension between genuine interest in student input and the practical constraints imposed by external regulations. The proposed solution involves fostering honest communication with students about the realistic extent of their influence, which, while pragmatic, contrasts with the research literature advocating a critical and progressive approach to power dynamics in student–teacher relationships.

Time

The case study school has gained valuable insights into the demands of implementing an inclusive student voice system, noting that the required time investment doubled or even tripled compared to the previous, more traditional approach. This observation prompted important questions among staff regarding the balance between efficiency and meaningfulness in the planning and execution of these initiatives. While the extended timeframe might raise concerns about resource allocation, the school leaders recognise the significance of anchoring these efforts in human rights perspectives and a shared understanding of the purpose of education. By emphasising the legal foundations to intrinsic value of prioritising the voices of students, the institution justifies the time spent on planning and facilitating these activities. This reflective approach not only highlights the commitment to inclusivity but also opens up space for contemplating the broader pedagogical implications, fostering a holistic examination of educational practices beyond the realm of student voice initiatives.

Conclusion

This chapter has explored the development of an inclusive student council in a special school for autism, highlighting the importance of amplifying and empowering diverse voices in educational settings. Through examining legal frameworks, communication styles, and traditional approaches, we have uncovered the challenges and opportunities in creating truly inclusive student voice initiatives.

The case study demonstrates how schools can move beyond traditional, often limiting, approaches in the organisation of student councils. By offering a variety of engagement activities, schools can ensure that all students, regardless of their communication style or social preferences, have meaningful opportunities to participate in decision-making processes.

Crucially, developing student voice activities and self-advocacy should be viewed as a continuous process of co-creation. While initial steps might focus on providing diverse opportunities for engagement, the ultimate goal should be to evolve inclusion alongside the growing awareness and skills of both students and staff.

To achieve genuine inclusion, schools must provide a range of accommodations and support, ensuring that all students have equal opportunities to participate. By integrating student voice into the culture of school life, educational institutions can create environments where all students, particularly those with autism, feel empowered to contribute to decisions affecting their education and well-being.

Reflective questions

1. What could be a long-term impact of the traditional as opposed to more inclusive student voice system for everyone involved and the wider community?
2. How do the presented ideas relate to your own setting and the way you approach student voice?
3. What other strategies or approaches could further diversify the opportunities for children and young people to enable and amplify their voice?
4. Are these strategies for diversifying student voice in contradiction with any of the current teaching approaches or development of life skills?

> **Takeaway activities**
>
> Choose one student voice question that is commonly asked in your setting, for example, the question of safety (physical, emotional, proactive, reactive, etc.). Taking into account every single child and young person within your setting, adapt the question into as many versions as needed to ensure understanding and suitability for their age, communication style, skills, and other unique characteristics. Consider the content of the question and the initial understanding of this somewhat-abstract concept, as well as the medium of communicating (from verbal and textual to concrete or kinaesthetic). How many different adaptations have you created?

References

Alderson, P. (2000). School students' views on school councils and daily life at school. *Children and Society*, 14, 121–134.

Assembly, U. G. (1948). Universal declaration of human rights. *UN General Assembly*, 302(2), 14–25.

Assembly, U. G. (1989). Convention on the Rights of the Child. *United Nations, Treaty Series*, 1577(3), 1–23.

Beattie, H. (2012). Amplifying student voice: The missing link in school transformation. *Management in Education*, 26(3), 158–160. https://doi.org/10.1177/0892020612445700

Benford, P., and Standen, P. (2009). The internet: A comfortable communication medium for people with Asperger syndrome (AS) and high functioning autism (HFA)? *Journal of Assistive Technologies*, 3(2), 44–53. https://doi.org/10.1108/17549450200900015

Biesta, G. (2011). *Learning democracy in school and Society: Education, lifelong learning, and the politics of citizenship*. Rotterdam: Sense Publishers.

Biesta, G., Lawy, R., and Kelly, N. (2009). Understanding young people's citizenship learning in everyday life: The role of contexts, relationships and dispositions. *Education, Citizenship and Society*, 4(1), 5–24.

Blank, M., and Sheila, J. (1986). Questions: A powerful but misused form of classroom exchange. *Topics in Language Disorders*, 6(2), 1–12.

Brown, K., Jolliffe, T., and Watt, K. (2022). *Beyond language: Understanding and supporting the diverse communication styles of autistic people*. London: Routledge.

Castro, S., and Palikara, O. (2016). Mind the gap: The new special educational needs and disability legislation in England. *Frontiers in Education*, 1. https://doi.org/10.3389/feduc.2016.00004.

Clark, C. (2017). Transformative approaches to student voice: Theoretical underpinnings, recalcitrant realities. *Social Inclusion*, 5(3), 23–33. Cogitatio Press. https://doi.org/10.17645/si.v5i3.970

de los Reyes, E., and Gozemba, P. A. (2002). *Pockets of hope: How students and teachers change the world*. Westport: Greenwood Publishing Group.

Department for Education (DfE) (2014). *Listening to and involving children and young people (statutory guidance)*. London: DFE. Available at: https://dera.ioe.ac.uk/id/eprint/19522/1/Listening_to_and_involving_chidren_and_young_people.pdf (Accessed: 29 December 2023).

Department for Education and Department of Health (2015). *Special educational needs and disability code of practice: 0 to 25 years*. Available at: https://www.gov.uk/government/publications/send-code-of-practice-0-to-25 (Accessed: 25 October 2023).

Fayette, R., and Bond, C. (2017). A systematic literature review of qualitative research methods for eliciting the views of young people with ASD about their educational experiences. *European Journal of Special Needs Education*, 33, 349–365. https://doi.org/10.1080/08856257.2017.1314111

Fielding, M. (2001). Students as radical agents of change. *Journal of Educational Change*, 2(2).

Fielding, M. (2004). Transformative approaches to student voice: Theoretical underpinnings, recalcitrant realities. *British Educational Research Journal*, 30(2), 295–311. Taylor & Francis. https://doi.org/10.1080/0141192042000195236

Fielding, M., and Bragg, S. (2003). *Students as researchers: Making a difference*. Pearson Publishing.

Finneran, R., Mayes, E., and Black, R. (2021). Pride and privilege: The affective dissonance of student voice. *Pedagogy, Culture & Society*. 1–16. https://doi.org/10.1080/14681366.2021.1876158

Flutter, J. (2007). Teacher development and pupil voice. *Curriculum Journal*, 18(4), 343–354.

Flutter, J., and Rudduck, J. (2006). *Consulting pupils: What's in it for schools?* London: Routledge.

Foucault, M. (1980). *Power/knowledge: Selected interviews and other writings, 1972–1977*. Translated by C. Gordon (Ed.), L. Marshall, J. Mepham and K. Soper. New York: Pantheon Books.

Gillespie-Lynch, K., Kapp, S. K., Shane-Simpson, C., Smith, D. S., and Hutman, T. (2014). Intersections between the autism spectrum and the internet: Perceived benefits and preferred functions of computer-mediated communication. *Intellectual and Developmental Disabilities*, 52(6), 456–469. https://doi.org/10.1352/1934-9556-52.6.456

Griffin, M. M., Taylor, J. L., Urbano, R. C., and Hodapp, R. M. (2014). Involvement in transition planning meetings among high school students with autism spectrum disorders. *Journal of Special Education*, 47, 256–264. https://doi.org/10.1177/0022466913475668

Gunter, H., and Thomson, P. (2007). Learning about student voice. *Support for Learning*, 22(4), 181–188. https://doi.org/10.1111/j.1467-9604.2007.00469.x

Hatfield, M., Ciccarelli, M., Falkmer, T., and Falkmer, M. (2017). Factors related to successful transition planning for adolescents on the autism spectrum. *Journal of Research in Special Educational Needs*, 2(2), 1–12. https://doi.org/10.1111/1471-3802.12388

Howard, P. L., and Sedgewick, F. (2021). 'Anything but the phone!': Communication mode preferences in the autism community. *Autism*, 25(8), 2265–2278.

Hull, L., Mandy, W., Lai, M.-C., Baron-Cohen, S., Allison, C., Smith, P., and Petrides, K. V. (2019). Development and validation of the Camouflaging Autistic Traits Questionnaire (CAT-Q). *Journal of Autism and Developmental Disorders*, 49(3), 819–833. https://doi.org/10.1007/s10803-018-3792-6

Hummerstone, H. (2018). *Facilitating communication between students on the autism spectrum and staff in secondary mainstream schools*. University of Southampton, Doctoral Thesis, 413 pp.

Kehoe, I. (2015). The cost of performance? Students' learning about acting as change agents in their schools. *Discourse: Studies in the Cultural Politics of Education*, 36(1), 106–119. Routledge. http://dx.doi.org/10.1080/01596306.2013.841356

Larson, R., Walker, K., and Pearce, N. (2005). A comparison of youth-driven and adult-driven youth programs: Balancing inputs from youth and adults. *Journal of Community Psychology*, 33(1).

Lasker, R. O. Z. D., Weiss, E. S., and Miller, R. (2001). Partnership synergy: A practical framework for studying and strengthening the collaborative advantage. *The Milbank Quarterly*, 79, 179–205.

Lewis, R., and Burman, E. (2008). Providing for student voice in classroom management: Teachers' views. *International Journal of Inclusive Education*, 12(2), 151–67.

Lodge, C. (2005). From hearing voices to engaging in dialogue: Problematising student participation in school improvement. *Journal of Educational Change*, 6(2), 125–146. https://doi.org/10.1007/s10833-005-1299-3

Lundy, L. (2013). Voice' is not enough: Conceptualising Article 12 of the United Nations Convention on the Rights of the Child. *British Educational Research Journal*, 33(6), 927–942.

MacBeath, J. (2006). Finding a voice, finding self. *Educational Review*, 58(2), 195–207.

Mannion, G. (2007). Going spatial, going relational: Why "listening to children" and children's participation needs reframing. *Discourse: Studies in the Cultural Politics of Education*, 28, 405–420. https://doi.org/10.1080/01596300701458970

May, H. (2004). Interpreting pupil participation into practice: Contributions of the SEN code of practice (2001). *Journal of Research in Special Educational Needs*, 4(2), 67–73. https://doi.org/10.1111/J.1471-3802.2004.00020.x

McLeod, J. (2011). *Qualitative research in counselling and psychotherapy* (2nd ed.). SAGE Publications.

Mitra, D. L. (2004). The significance of students: Can increasing "student voice" in schools lead to gains in youth development? *Teachers College Record*, 106(6), 651–688.

Mitra, D. L., and Gross, S. J. (2009). Increasing student voice in high school reform: Building relationships, improving outcomes. *Educational Management Administration and Leadership*, 4, 522–543.

National Autistic Society (2023). *What is autism?* Available at: https://www.autism.org.uk/advice-and-guidance/what-is-autism (Accessed: 02 November 2023).

Pellicano, E., Hill, V., and Croydon, A. (2014). *My life at school: Understanding the experiences of children and young people with special educational needs in residential special schools*. London: Office of the Children's Commissioner. Available at: http://www.childrenscommissioner.gov.uk/sites/default/files/publications/My_Life_at_School.pdf (Accessed: 02 November 2023).

Perry-Hazan, L. (2021). Conceptualising conflicts between student participation and other rights and interests. *Discourse: Studies in the Cultural Politics of Education*, 40(5), 1–16. Taylor & Francis. https://doi.org/10.1080/01596306.2019.1599324.

Quinn, S., and Owen, S. (2014). Freedom to grow: Children's perspectives of student voice. *Childhood Education*, 90(3), 192–201.

Rix, J., Hall, K., Nind, M., Sheehy, K., and Wearmouth, J. (2009). What pedagogical approaches can effectively include children with special educational needs in mainstream classrooms? A systematic literature review. *Support for Learning*, 24(2), 86–94. https://doi.org/10.1111/j.1467-9604.2009.01404.x

Rudduck, J., and Fielding, M. (2006). Student voice and the perils of popularity. *Educational Review*, 2, 219–231.

Rudduck, J., and Flutter, J. (2003). *How to improve your school: Giving pupils a voice*. Continuum Press.

Ryan, R. M., and Deci, E. L. (2000). Self-determination theory and the facilitation of intrinsic motivation, social development, and well-being. *American Psychologist*, 55(1), 68–78. https://doi.org/10.1037/0003-066x.55.1.68.

Sellman, E. (2009). Lessons learned: Student voice at a school for pupils experiencing social, emotional and behavioural difficulties. *Emotional and Behavioural Difficulties*, 14(1), 33–48. Taylor & Francis. https://doi.org/10.1080/13632750802655687

Shogren, K. A., and Plotner, A. J. (2012). Transition planning for students with intellectual disability, autism, or other disabilities: Data from the national longitudinal transition study-2. *Intellectual and Developmental Disabilities*, 50(1), 16–30. https://doi.org/10.1352/1934-9556-50.1.16

Sigafoos, J. (2006). Self-determination: Can we let the child determine the "best" treatment? *Paediatric Rehabilitation*, 9, 1–2.

Thomson, P. (2013). Coming to terms with 'voice'. In C. Wise, P. Bradshaw, & M. Cartwright (Eds.). *Leading professional practice in education* (pp. 78–89). SAGE Publications.

Topping, K. J. (2001). *Peer assisted learning: A practical guide for teachers*. Brookline Books.

Toshalis, E., and Nakkula, M. (2012). *Motivation, engagement, and student voice. Students at the Center Hub*. Available at: https://www.howyouthlearn.org/pdf/Motivation%20Engagement%20Student%20Voice_0.pdf (Accessed: 02 November 2023).

Wei, X., Wagner, M., Hudson, L., Yu, J. W., and Javitz, H. (2016). The effect of transition planning participation and goal-setting on college enrollment among youth with autism spectrum disorders. *Remedial and Special Education*, 37(1), 3–14. https://doi.org/10.1177/0741932515581495

Whitty, G., and Wisby, E. (2007). *Real decision making? School councils in action*. Institute of Education, University of London, UK: Department for Children, Schools and Families. Available at: http://eprints.ioe.ac.uk/2715/1/Whitty2007Real(Report).pdf (Accessed: 05 November 2023).

Wyness, M. (2009). Children representing children. *Childhood*, 16(4), 535–552. https://doi.org/10.1177/0907568209344274.

Zilli, C., Parsons, S., and Kovshof, H. (2020). Keys to engagement: A case study exploring the participation of autistic pupils in educational decision-making at school. *British Journal of Educational Psychology*, 90(3), 770–789.

Zimmerman, B. J. (2002). Becoming a self-regulated learner: An overview. *Theory into Practice*, 41(2), 64–70.

5 Sharing case studies of supporting SEND in schools drawing from three national contexts

Christine Sanders

> **Key words**
>
> Inclusive education, National contexts, Dyslexia, Autism, EAL, Behaviour

Introduction

It is made clear in the UN Convention on the Rights of the Child (1989) that every child has a right to education (Article 28), and this education 'must develop every child's personality, talents and abilities to the full' (Article 29), because every child, irrespective of their abilities, deserves an education that recognises their unique strengths and challenges. At the heart of developing this inclusive education lies an aspiration to create a classroom culture where diversity is embraced. A culture where differences are viewed as opportunities for growth and understanding and diversity is celebrated, understood and accepted by all. As has been argued by Liasidou (2012, pp. 13–14), *inclusive education* 'is fundamentally about issues of human rights, equity, social justice and the struggle for a non-discriminatory society. These principles (need to be) at the heart of inclusive education policy and practice'.

Reframing these values into everyday practice has challenges, but Knowles (2011, p. 9) offers a useful set of indicators that an inclusive school can implement:

- Children help each other.
- All adults support each other and work together.
- All adults and children treat each other with respect.
- Parents are welcomed, and there is evidence of a strong and mutually supportive partnership between the school and parents.
- The school has close links with the community, is involved in the work and activities of the local community, and the community has strong links with the school.

To explore how some of these suggestions are integrated into teachers' everyday practice, in this chapter I consider how teachers can work with pupils who are dyslexic, are autistic, or have English as an additional language (EAL); how school policies and practice, such as adapting resources, transition plans, or streaming, can create challenges for some pupils; and how reflective discussion between colleagues, children, and parents and carers can raise question and offer possible responses. I will be directly drawing upon my own experiences in a number of different national contexts. I have worked in primary school education for over two and a half colourful decades. It has been an exciting and incredibly rewarding journey, and I have had the privilege to work with hundreds of children across the globe from a variety of backgrounds in the United Kingdom, Switzerland, Mexico, and Australia.

Case Study 1: transition into the new school year

Freshly labelled books, brand-new sharp pencils, display boards with neat borders ready to display pupils' proud work; a tidy, neat, and organised classroom ready and eagerly awaiting the new class. Refreshed teachers after the summer break, excited pupils ready to see their friends and start the new school year, and relieved parents ready for the routine to begin again for another school year. The start of a new school year is a wonderful time. A fresh start for everyone. A common policy between and within schools in different national contexts is the use of a handover or transition meeting between teachers. Such a handover can refer 'to the activities that are implemented to facilitate children's transition' because 'children need continuity in their schooling to provide and promote long-term learning' (Alatalo, Meier, and Frank, 2016, p. 156). This could involve discussing pupils on the class list with the teacher, passing on lots of advice and numerous recommendations about pupils. Children who were working at or above the expected level in the previous class can be highlighted, and there is the opportunity to discuss in more detail pupils with special educational needs and disabilities (SEND).

This has been common practice for the schools I have worked in, and some of the following anonymised examples of shared comments may resonate with other teachers who have attended handover meetings that cover pupils with SEND:

> 'Jack's got ADHD, so he won't concentrate well.'

> 'Kane is autistic, so he won't join in lessons.'

> 'Robbie is working well below expected level in English, so get your teaching assistant to do some extra phonics during your English lessons, as he won't cope with working with the whole class.'

> 'Daniella doesn't have any English, so she can do some extra phonics.'

Reflective questions

1. What impact does this information have on (a) the new class teacher? (b) The pupils?
2. How does this information create or hinder an inclusive classroom?

Such statements demonstrate the everyday process of labelling and how this can influence the practice of teachers. This is particularly insidious in settings subject to a neoliberal ideology, since the almost-constant naming of children's performance, abilities, and difference against criteria and/or others can impact on their sense of self either positively or negatively (Wearmouth, 2021). It is important to adopt a more respectful and affirmative model in how we think about and talk about SEN and disability, because people recognise that certain challenges or impairments are associated with more stigma (ibid.) in society than others.

In the comments shared earlier, the pupils were negatively labelled before they had even set foot in my classroom. The information passed on in this form, while intended to prepare me as the next teacher to support the child, can limit the potential for inclusivity. I agree that children may have needs and differences requiring that classwork be adjusted to support them, but I firmly believe in getting to know my pupils, including them as much as possible, and letting them show what they can do. I believe this gives them an opportunity to shine rather than put them in a box with a closed lid before the school year has even started.

One of the most common areas for discussion in handover meetings is the sharing of adjustments that are being made to include dyslexic or autistic pupils. This has been a long-standing practice, still much needed, given that the British Dyslexia Association (2024) believes that around 10% of the UK population may be dyslexic, and there are around 160,000 autistic pupils in England (National Autistic Society (NAS), 2021). With so many affected, the next two case studies will focus on these specific educational needs.

Case Study 2: understanding disruptive behaviour

In my early days of teaching in North West England, I had Jordan in my Year 4 class (ages 8–9 years old). I was informed by his previous teachers that he was a polite, helpful, inquisitive, and curious child who always loved to chat with teachers and his friends at school. He achieved well in his Reception, Year 1, and Year 2 classes, and it was well known that he was a pleasure to have in the classroom. However, at the handover meeting, his previous teacher informed me that his grades had fallen throughout Year 3, mainly due to his disruptive behaviour in the class, and he was now labelled as 'working towards' or 'below' in most subjects. He excelled in PE and sport but often didn't make the cross-country or football teams due to his poor behaviour. I was told that he was disengaged in lessons and was not working to his full potential.

In the first few weeks of Year 4, Jordan would behave disruptively in the classroom. During lessons, he would make immature noises, call out, and distract others. He would 'lose' his book and pencil and try all sorts of creative avoidance tactics rather than be in his seat, working. The reaction of the other pupils in the class would encourage him to continue to be the 'class joker'. He would not complete his work and instead would try to talk and joke with his peers, go to the toilet, purposely break his pencil so it would need sharpening, and find any excuse not to complete his work or even attempt to start his work.

His behaviour deteriorated over the weeks and behaviour on the playground resulted in bullying and physical fights. He targeted other pupils in the classroom and on the playground and began to provoke, tease, and physically hurt them. His teachers tried a range of tactics to find out from him what was happening, but he didn't want to disclose anything. We wanted to develop a strong partnership with his mother to find a shared solution, but she said he was 'a nightmare at home' and he wouldn't talk to her either.

One day, Jordan's behaviour surprisingly changed during a history lesson. He was motivated, enthusiastic, and engaged in the lesson. He was asking and answering questions and contributing sensibly to class discussions. I was delighted and relieved and showered him with praise. I thought he'd made a positive change, however, when it came to completing the work. After the main input, he resorted back to being the class joker. He found numerous excuses to not complete the work set. I was so confused after he'd had such a positive lesson so far. What had changed? Unfortunately, the afternoon worsened, and his behaviour in the classroom and playground returned once again to being disruptive and challenging.

Reflective questions

1. What could be the cause of Jordan's initial change in behaviour?
2. Why would Jordan suddenly be engaged in a history lesson?

Wearmouth (2021, p. 23) argues that learners who are aware that they may have particular labels in class will 'continuously monitor the learning environment for cues regarding the degree to which they are accepted or rejected by other people'. She also points out that teachers need to explore the relationship between learning and behaviour to understand the difficulties children face and respond appropriately.

I had a long hard think about what had happened and discussed the situation with my colleagues to seek their support. With the special educational needs and disabilities co-ordinator (SENDCO) and with my newly qualified teacher (NQT) mentor, we dissected and analysed the history lesson piece by piece, and eventually we thought we found a possible answer.

For lesson inputs, I would often use PowerPoints on white backgrounds. This would then follow up with work to be completed on white worksheets or in pupils' books, where the pages are also white. The history PowerPoint that was used in this particular lesson was on a pale peach–coloured background. The text was dark and contrasting. The follow-up work after the lesson input was on white worksheets, and this was the point at which he had started to disengage. We wondered whether the colour of the paper could really have such a marked impact. For the following lessons, I edited the backgrounds on the PowerPoints and printed worksheets on a pale peach paper. I also checked that the font was Comic Sans, the font colour was clearly contrasted to the background, and the size of the font was enlarged.

It was such a relief to see that Jordan was more engaged in the following lessons and that he tried much harder to complete his work. He appeared slightly happier all day, and there were less incidents on the playground. I continued preparing my lessons this way with peach or other pale-coloured backgrounds on the PowerPoints, and Jordan often completed his work on coloured paper rather than in a workbook. A gradual improvement in Jordan's attitude was evident, and he was putting a lot more effort into his work. A simple adjustment to fonts, print size, colour, and layouts of PowerPoints and worksheets had massive positive consequences.

Wearmouth (2021) indicates a number of ways specific technologies and preparation of resources can support learning needs, and the British Dyslexia Association (BDA) offers a number of suggestions that can be useful to consider when supporting dyslexic pupils, or others, including:

- Readable fonts to use in the classroom include sans serif fonts, such as Arial and Comic Sans, as letters can appear less crowded. In addition, there are several fonts that have been designed for dyslexic readers, including Dyslexie, Opendyslexic, and Gill Dyslexic.
- Font size plays an important role, and that font size should be 12–14 point or equivalent (e.g. 1–1.2 em/16–19 px).
- Avoid underlining and italics, as this can make the text appear to run together and cause crowding, and instead use bold for emphasis.
- Avoid using all upper-case letters for continuous text, since lower-case letters are easier to read. Use single-colour backgrounds, and avoid background patterns or pictures and distracting surrounds.
- Use sufficient contrast levels between background and text, for example, a dark-coloured text on a light (not white) background.
- Avoid green and red/pink, as these colours are difficult for those who have colour vision deficiencies (colour blindness).
- Consider alternatives to white backgrounds for paper, computer, and visual aids, such as whiteboards, as white can appear too dazzling. Cream or a soft pastel colour is better, and some dyslexics will have their own colour preference.

In terms of supporting Jordan, I continued to meet with my NQT mentor and the SENDCO. We also discussed the findings with Jordan's mother to strengthen our partnership with her. It was arranged for Jordan to be tested for dyslexia, which he was eventually diagnosed with. He also had an eye test and proudly came to school one day with some round glasses: 'Just like Harry Potter's, Miss!' Jordan started writing on coloured paper rather than straight into his books. Displays and signs in my classroom were rarely on white backgrounds, and overlays were used for reading books and worksheets, which helped his confidence immensely.

After a few successful weeks, certificates in assemblies, and enjoying gaining a place on the football team, Jordan eventually admitted that he felt embarrassed that he could not do his work. He said he often could not read it and the words were blurred and hurt his eyes when he tried to read them. He said he was frustrated and 'felt stupid' in class and that was why he messed around. He also carried his anger and frustrations onto the playground, and this unfortunately resulted in aggressive behaviour towards other pupils. While this is just one account, it echoes the story of 'Katherine', her challenging behaviour, and the sense of shame, as shared by Wearmouth (2021, pp. 252–254).

This experience was a valuable learning curve for me, and since then I have made an effort to adjust lessons accordingly, so they are inclusive for pupils with dyslexia. Books and paper in schools were mainly white, which is not always appropriate for dyslexic pupils or those with visual impairment. Since that day, I always made sure PowerPoints and worksheets had pale backgrounds with contrasting fonts. Using these simple adjustments certainly improved relations, and Jordan was soon a different child. Happy, engaged, and keen to work hard. It was an eye-opener that a few changes for me as his teacher resulted in a huge change for Jordan.

Case Study 3: 'I had to eat my orange'

The World Health Organisation describes *autism* as a condition that is characterised by persistent differences in the ability to initiate and to sustain reciprocal social interaction and social communication, and by a range of repetitive, and inflexible, patterns of behaviour and interests (Wearmouth, 2021, p. 93). While such a description might seem restrictive and somewhat negative, similar patterns of behaviour became clear to me when I was working in an Australian school in Sydney with Christopher, who was a Year 6 (ages 10–11) autistic boy in my class.

Christopher was a happy and friendly boy, and lots of things were put in place for him at the school. He was streamed into the lowest set, but he was happy in a small group and showed understanding that he needed help with his work. He knew everything there is to know about Thomas the Tank Engine, and he also knew all the train timetables and tracks in Sydney. He was a very literal boy. When his grandma died, he did not show emotion, just the fact: 'Everyone dies and then their body stops working and we don't see them anymore.' He also knew a rule must not be broken. One of his rules was that he had to eat his orange after his lunch before he could go outside and play. 'The orange keeps me healthy,' he would tell people.

One day, an unplanned fire drill happened at lunchtime. Christopher refused to evacuate the school building – adamant that he had to eat his orange first. He was eventually carried out of the school building, kicking and screaming. He did not understand the seriousness of the situation. He could only understand that he had to eat his orange before he could go outside. That was the rule.

Reflective questions

1. What rules are put in place at school that children may find difficult to follow? Why might this be the case?

In a blog by Jaime A. Heidel (www.thearticulateaustistic.com, 14.6.22), it is stated that not following a rule can actually make autistic people feel physically uncomfortable and even sick. Many autistic students rely on rules and routines because they find any kind of change difficult; therefore, keeping their environment and routines predictable feels safer (NSA, 2024).

The incident with the fire drill led to a serious discussion between teachers and parents about how to deal with situations like this. We needed to find a way to communicate when a rule could be broken. A series of lessons and role-plays with Christopher were devised, teaching him that in very important situations, rules could be broken, especially if it was to keep people safe. We called these situations 'Red Rockets' – Christopher's choice – and if a trusted adult said that a time or situation was a 'Red Rocket', then Christopher understood that the rule could be broken to keep him or someone else safe. This took time and patience, but eventually, Christopher showed understanding. It was also a reminder for staff of how and when to use the term 'rule' throughout the day, knowing how literally Christopher, and perhaps other pupils, might respond to them. At the next fire drill, Christopher calmly said, 'This is a Red Rocket, so I must break the rule and go outside, so I don't get burned by the fire.'

Again, this is just one example of how reflection on an experience can lead to a greater understanding of one child, but also a better understanding of how different strategies or techniques could be beneficial more widely. In terms of support for autistic pupils, on the NAS website (2024), there is a range of guidance and advice for teachers, parents, and other significant adults.

While pupils with additional needs are a key group for teachers to support, children who have English as an additional language (EAL) can be mistakenly identified as having an additional need, so this is a group I turn to for case study 4.

Case Study 4: English as an additional language (EAL)

In comparison to my experiences of teaching in Australia, teaching at an international school in Switzerland was an idyllic setting for diversity. Pupils came from all over the world to a tiny village on a mountain in Switzerland. Rush hour was when the cows came down the mountain with their huge bells clanging, blocking the road. Snow was often so deep it was higher than the pupils, and washing your car or vacuuming on a Sunday was breaking the law. It was a great opportunity to work and live here.

My first class had eight pupils aged 5–7! Amazing, compared to the more usual 30 pupils per class in England or Australia. However, eight languages, eight backgrounds, eight cultures, a number of religions, and varying levels of schooling soon made the class interesting and thought-provoking to teach! The biggest challenge was the language barrier; pupils with little or no English were all expected to learn primary school subjects in English as the language of instruction at the school. Pupils can be defined as EAL if they have been using 'a first language other than English during early development and who may continue to use this language in the home or community setting throughout their schooling' (Dixon, Thomson, and Fricke, 2020, p. 310). However, in a classroom where English is not the standard language for pupils, the labelling of pupils as EAL seemed incongruent. At the same time, the classroom practice I developed to support their learning has similarities with known approaches. Visual aids, daily charades, and lots of smiles were daily practices in all classrooms. The curriculum was adapted to suit the needs of the school, and experiences were valued more than traditional lessons. Art lessons were a joy to teach, as the pupils could express themselves without having to use spoken languages. Music was always fun for the pupils, especially when it came to playing musical instruments, as they could all join in and play the rhythm (see Conteh (2023), García (2009), the National Subject Association for EAL (2024), and Sharples (2021) for a wide range of other examples).

One of the most powerful approaches for this class was to utilise and share the different languages and enable the children to adopt a peer learning style where the pupils supported and taught each other in their lessons (Topping, Buchs, Duran, and Van Keer, 2017). Counting in maths was often done in the languages of all pupils in the class, with pupils taking the lead for their own language and teaching the rest of the class how to count in a different language. Some pupils could be seen and heard practising this with their friends on the playground. Extra English lessons were offered to pupils who had the least amount of English, and these were often very hands-on and included lessons involving the local community, such as visiting the local farm to talk about the animals – names, colours, textures, food, sizes, features – all made interesting by the English teacher, who hardly ever kept the pupils in a classroom at a desk. Walking around the school grounds, visiting the local shops, and allowing the pupils to soak up their environment were extremely beneficial to these children. Such activities demonstrate that rather than each language having a shape and function that is distinct from another, 'languages work as one singular linguistic system', shaped by 'the social context of their interactions' (García et al., 2017, cited in Slaughter and Cross (2021, p. 41), enabling the children to build on their prior knowledge of language.

The adoption of a multilingual approach was extended by involving the families of pupils at the school. An annual International Day brought all the families together with stalls flying flags of their home countries and serving national dishes for all to enjoy. Families would wear traditional clothes and would teach songs and games from their home countries. Festivals and holidays for every country represented at the international school were also celebrated by all. Everybody – pupils, teachers, parents, and the wider community – was integrated within the learning the children experienced. Everybody was extremely happy, and it was such a learning journey for us all.

Unfortunately, sometimes systems and processes designed to support pupils' learning within a school can create barriers for including *all* pupils, which I now consider for case study 5.

Case Study 5: self-belief and public speaking

Whatever the national context, the community in which a school is situated can be central to the culture and ethos within the school. In Australia, this is heightened in a particular way; at any public event or gathering, the Aboriginal land on which the school building stands or where the gathering is happening must be acknowledged (Oxfam, 2015). For a while, I worked in a large private primary and secondary Jewish school in Bondi, Sydney. It hosted pupils from age 4 to 18. The primary school was three- to four-form entry. The school had recently removed the middle school and introduced Year 6 back into the primary school. I was responsible for teaching one of the four Year 6 classes. The classes were streamed for maths and English, and the pupils had a variety of specialist teachers for music, Jewish studies, Hebrew, science, and PE throughout their working week.

As the oldest pupils in the primary school, it was the role of Year 6 students (aged 10–11) in school assemblies to stand on the stage in front of all the pupils and staff and acknowledge the sacred land on which the school stood. Every pupil in the class had acknowledged the land, apart from Taylor. Much like Christopher from case study 3, Taylor wanted to follow the rules and said it was his turn to do the speech as everybody else in Year 6 had had a go. When asked if he would like to do it, he immediately replied yes. This was met with a lot of opposition from other staff members and his parents, who believed it would be too much for him and he would not be able to take the pressure. 'He's autistic, so he won't be able to do it' was the label that was evident. It was a large assembly hall, like a theatre with tiered seating and a large stage. A daunting task for most pupils! Taylor said he could do it. 'I'll be good at it,' he said. 'I will say the words in a loud and clear voice, and I will be very good at it.' He believed in himself. I made an informed judgement and decided to take a chance, while also considering Taylor's feelings, and asked him to take his turn on the stage. 'You're throwing him to the lions!' one staff member stated.

Taylor practised the words in his 'big, loud voice'. He knew to 'speak slowly so everyone could hear his important words'. He did not disappoint; he stood there proudly and clearly and confidently said, 'We begin today by acknowledging the Traditional Custodians of the land on which we gather today. We pay our respects to their Elders, past and present. We extend that respect to Aboriginal and Torres Strait Islander peoples here today." This was followed by an air fist bump and a whispered, "Yes!"

The amount of praise Taylor received from everybody – staff, pupils, and parents – after his public speech was so encouraging for him and his self-esteem. One statement that really said it all was when Taylor himself said, 'I did it, just the same as everybody else. I am like everybody else in my class.'

This experience taught me that knowing a pupil well and listening to their thoughts and feelings are crucial to their development, rather than keeping them in their labelled box. This is reiterated in the UN Convention on the Rights of the Child (1989), which states: 'Children who are capable of forming views have a right to receive and make known information, to express an opinion and to have that option taken into account in any matters affecting them' (Article 12).

This is an approach which has long been embraced by researchers and teachers working to respect individuality and empower pupils by developing their involvement in more inclusive educational practices, from Rudduck, who pioneered the term 'pupil voice' (Fielding, 2007), to more recent work by Mayes, Finneran, and Black (2019), Messiou (2019), Partovi and Wyness (2022), and Mursic's work covered in Chapter 4 and Woolhouse and Kay's approach discussed in Chapter 7 of this book.

However, a teacher's best intentions are not always realised, and the systems, processes, and organisation of education locally in schools and, more broadly, at a national level can thwart our plans.

Case Study 6: ability streaming

Working in a private school in Sydney, Australia, as a Year 6 (aged 10–11) teacher introduced me to the idea of streaming pupils, which in the USA is often termed *tracking*, which refers to how pupils are divided into groups, determined by their levels of educational ability or attainment, often determined by a one-off test (Francis et al., 2020). The idea of streaming is that pupils in these classes are working at their own ability level and therefore would not be left behind if they were struggling or become bored and unchallenged if they were waiting for others to catch up. The teachers of these streamed classes also would not need to differentiate or adapt their lessons as much as a teacher working with a mixed-ability group would.

In my Sydney school, four Year 6 form classes (around 90 children) were streamed into five ability classes for English and maths. The lowest stream was the smallest class, with around 12 pupils. Each class had the name of a colour, but the pupils were under no illusion that the colour names of these groups related to perceived ability. The pupils were streamed according to their performance in one whole year test, covering both maths and English. The test resulted immediately in labelling pupils as:

'Excelling expected level' – Red class
'Working above expected level' – Orange class
'Working at expected level' – Yellow class
'Working towards expected level' – Green class
'Working below expected level' – Blue class

Reflective question

1. What is the impact of streaming for different groups of pupils?

I was responsible for the Blue maths class and the Yellow English class. After I chatted with my colleagues who taught the other streamed classes, it became apparent that the streaming did have benefits, as some gifted and talented pupils in the Red and Orange classes were challenged and worked at a faster pace, especially in maths. It was felt that they did not get bored waiting for others, and the excitement of healthy competition was a motivator for pupils to keep pushing themselves. At the same time, pupils in lower streams could work at a slower, more comfortable pace that allowed for consolidation and practice of essential skills. However, research in the field has indicated that pupils in 'lower streams' make poorer progress than peers in the 'higher streams' (see Ireson, Hallam, and Hurley, 2005; Slavin, 1990; Steenbergen-Hu, Makel, and Olszewski-Kubilius, 2016; EEF, 2018). In classes that utilise some form of streaming, low-attaining learners fall behind by one or two months a year, on average, when compared with the progress of similar students in classes with mixed-ability groups, and this effect is particularly strong in mathematics, where setting is most common (Higgins et al., 2016).

In addition to concerns over academic progress, the pupils in the 'working below expected level' Blue maths class that I taught had extremely low self-esteem in the lessons and were not motivated to learn at all. The pupils knew that there were four streams above them which seemed impossible for them to reach, as they shared with me:

'We are the thick class.'

'I'm rubbish at maths.'

'I hate maths.'

'I'm too stupid to understand it.'

I found it difficult to accept the negative impact streaming had for the pupils in the lower streams. It was hard to see the pupils labelling themselves this way. The pupils lacked motivation and enthusiasm, no matter how exciting I tried to make the lessons. There was some similarity with Jordan from case study 1: These pupils also often joked around and were disengaged with the lesson content. As noted earlier in the chapter, these children experienced a sense of stigma because they had been negatively labelled by the school and, as a result, by themselves and their peers too, as also noted by Wearmouth (2021). One risk of labelling students as low-achieving can become a self-fulfilling prophecy; Francis et al. (2020, p. 636) studied 126 schools situated across England and found a correlation between placement in streamed sets and pupils' self-confidence, arguing that a gap in general self-confidence between students in the top and bottom sets widened between the start and end of their two-year study, particularly in the mathematics sets. This echoes the research findings of Ireson and Hallam (2009) from a decade earlier.

The impact appears to be different depending on which group a pupil is streamed into. In agreement with the claims made by Schofield (2010), Hallam and Parsons (2013, p. 393) found that 'overall, structured ability grouping (streaming and setting), of itself, has no positive impact on average attainment, although, depending on the level of curriculum differentiation, can widen the gap between low and high attainers'. So while streaming could be a successful strategy for the most capable students, it does little for students who find learning more challenging. Although, Hood (2020) suggests that while the impact on pupils streamed into lower-ability groups is generally negative, within-class attainment grouping (a practice used most frequently in primary schools) can be successful if groups regularly change, pupils can move between groups, and all have opportunities to receive high-quality instruction and to engage in rigorous tasks that are engaging and motivating.

Conclusion

In this chapter I have shared a range of real-life situations that have occurred in classrooms in various national contexts to consider the diverse experiences children have of learning and to think through how teachers can approach different issues in their everyday practices. In different ways, each case study has embodied some of the indicators listed at the start of this chapter that Knowles (2011, p. 9) highlights as representing inclusive practice. Most importantly, in my years of experience, I have found that it is developing respectful relationships between teachers, pupils, and parents that enables changes to happen and solutions to be found for the challenges children face.

Writing this chapter has also taught me that it can be OK to try out new things and to take considered risks when seeking to develop inclusivity – indeed, as has been noted by bell hooks (1994, p. 21):

> When education is the practice of freedom, students are not the only ones asked to share, to confess. Engaged pedagogy does not seek simply to empower students, any classroom that employs a holistic model of learning will also be a place where teachers grow and are empowered by the process.

I want to end on a positive note. I have experienced teaching pupils from a variety of races, religions, nationalities, and cultures. Each class that I have taught has been different and unique, and that is one of the many delights and rewards in this profession. No two classes have ever been the same, apart from one common factor: A happy and successful class is a class where pupils, irrespective of their background, nationality, culture, race, or religion, feel valued, safe, respected, and understood. In my experience, a happy class results in curious, keen, inquisitive pupils who embrace a love for learning.

Final reflective question

1. Look at the experiences and reflective questions shared in this chapter around how situations could be better understood and children could be better supported. What questions arise from experiences you have had working with children?

Takeaway activities

- Ask teachers you know to tell you a short story about one experience that made them reflect and change their practice.
- If you know a child that is struggling at school, ask them how they feel about the situation and what they would like to change.

References

Alatalo, T., Meier, J., and Frank, E. 2016. Transition between Swedish preschool and preschool class: A question about interweaving care and knowledge. *Early Childhood Education Journal*, 44, pp. 155–167.

British Dyslexia Association. 2024. Available at: https://www.bdadyslexia.org.uk/, accessed 24.1.24.

Conteh, J. 2023. *The EAL teaching book: Promoting success for multilingual learners*. 4th ed. Sage.

Dixon, C., Thomson, J., and Fricke, S. 2020. Language and reading development in children learning English as an additional language in primary school in England. *Journal of Research in Reading*, 43(3), pp. 309–328.

Dyslexia Institute to the Parliamentary Select Committee Education Endowment Foundation. 2018. *Education endowment foundation toolkit*. London: EEF. Available at: https://educationendowmentfoundation.org.uk/evidence-summaries/teaching-learning-toolkit/setting-or-streaming/

Fielding, M. 2007. Jean Rudduck (1937–2007) 'Carving a new order of experience': A preliminary appreciation of the work of Jean Rudduck in the field of student voice. *Educational Action Research*, 15(3), pp. 323–336.

Francis, B., Craig, N., Hodgen, J., Taylor, B., Tereshchenko, A., Connolly, P., and Archer, L. 2020. The impact of tracking by attainment on pupil self-confidence over time: Demonstrating the accumulative impact of self-fulfilling prophecy. *British Journal of Sociology of Education*, 41(5), pp. 626–642.

García, O. 2009. *Bilingual education in the 21st century: A global perspective*. Malden, MA: Wiley-Blackwell.

Hallam, S., and Parsons, S. 2013. The incidence and make up of ability grouped sets in the UK primary school. *Research Papers in Education*, 28(4), pp. 393–420.

Higgins, S., Katsipataki, M., Villanueva-Aguilera, A., Coleman, R., Henderson, P., Major, L., and Mason, D. 2016. *The Sutton Trust-education endowment foundation teaching and learning toolkit*. Available at: https://

durham-repository.worktribe.com/output/1606338/the-sutton-trust-education-endowment-foundation-teaching-and-learning-toolkit, accessed 24.1.24.

Hood, N. 2020. *Blog: "What does the research say about the impact of streaming, setting and attainment grouping on students?"* Available at: https://theeducationhub.org.nz/what-does-the-research-say-about-the-impact-of-streaming-setting-and-attainment-grouping-on-students/, accessed 5.3.24.

Hooks, B. 1994. *Teaching to transgress*. Routledge.

Ireson, J., and Hallam, S., 2009. Academic self-concepts in adolescence: Relations with achievement and ability grouping in schools. *Learning and Instruction*, 19(3), pp. 201–213.

Ireson, J., Hallam, S., and Hurley, C. 2005. What are the effects of ability grouping on GCSE attainment? *British Educational Research Journal*, 31(4), pp. 443–458.

Knowles, G. 2011. *Supporting inclusive practice.* London Routledge.

Liasidou, A. 2012. *Inclusive education, politics and policymaking*. Continuum.

Mayes, E., Finneran, R., and Black, R. 2019. The challenges of student voice in primary schools: Students 'having a voice' and 'speaking for' others. *Australian Journal of Education*, 63(2), pp. 157–172.

Messiou, K. 2019. The missing voices: Students as a catalyst for promoting inclusive education. *International Journal of Inclusive Education*, 23(7–8), pp. 768–781.

National Autistic Society (NAS). 2021. Available at: https://www.autism.org.uk/what-we-do/news/school-report-2021, accessed 30.1.24.

National Subject Association for EAL. 2024. Available at: https://naldic.org.uk/, accessed 24.1.24.

Oxfam. 2015. *Aboriginal and Torres Strait Islander cultural protocols*. Available at: https://www.oxfam.org.au/wp-content/uploads/2015/11/2015-74-ATSI-Cultural-Protocols-update_WEB.pdf, accessed 2.2.24.

Partovi, M., and Wyness, M. 2022. Breaking the silence: Working with pupil voice in Iranian primary schools. *Educational Review*, 74(2), pp. 226–242.

Schofield, J. W. 2010. International evidence on ability grouping with curriculum differentiation and the achievement gap in secondary schools. *Teachers College Record*, 112(5), pp. 1492–1528.

Sharples, R. 2021. *Teaching EAL: Evidence-based strategies for the classroom and school*. Multilingual Matters.

Slaughter, Y., and Cross, R. 2021. Challenging the monolingual mindset: Understanding plurilingual pedagogies in English as an Additional Language (EAL) classrooms. *Language Teaching Research*, 25(1), pp. 39–60.

Slavin, R. 1990. Achievement effects of ability grouping in secondary schools: A best evidence synthesis. *Review of Educational Research*, 60(3), pp. 471–499.

Steenbergen-Hu, S.,. Makel, M. C., and Olszewski-Kubilius, P. 2016. What one hundred years of research says about the effects of ability grouping and acceleration on K–12 students' academic achievement: Findings of two second-order meta-analyses. *Review of Educational Research*, 86(4), pp. 849–899.

Topping, K., Buchs, C., Duran, D., and Van Keer, H. 2017. *Effective peer learning: From principles to practical implementation*. Taylor & Francis.

United Nations Convention on the Rights of the Child. 1989. Available at: http://www.ohchr.org/EN/ProfessionalInterest/Pages/CRC.aspx

Wearmouth, J. 2021. *Special educational needs and disabilities in schools*. Bloomsbury.

6 Reimagining inclusive education

Power, status, and voice

Fiona Hallett and Graham Hallett

Key words

Voice, Inclusive education, Contextualised learning, Inclusive pedagogies

---

Introduction

The development of an inclusive approach to education policy in England since the 1981 Education Act has been significantly influenced by policies advocating shared approaches and joint working. In considering the needs of children and young people, all decisions are expected to result from processes that place the child at the heart of decision-making. To achieve this, it has long been expected that special educational needs professionals and parents should work in partnership (SEN Code of Practice, 2001) within a multi-agency approach and should consider the wishes of the child concerned. The movement towards enabling an active contribution from the child stems in part from the UN Convention on the Rights of the Child (UNCRC), which asserts the right of the child to be provided with information, to hold and express opinions, and to have these taken into account when decisions are made about them (Article 12, UNCRC, 1989).

It is clear, therefore, that all professionals involved in the education of a child experiencing difficulties in accessing an appropriate education suitable to their needs must listen to the parents of that child. This needs to be within a collaborative partnership that respects and acknowledges the unique insights that they possess, and that this willingness to listen and hear should also apply to the child. The exercise of this requirement has been subject to frequent review in England over recent years, leading to explicit criticism by parents of the difficulties many have experienced in being heard (Lamb Inquiry, 2010; House of Commons Education Select Committee Review, 2019, SEND Review, 2022), with more recent criticism suggesting that being heard can be disproportionally influenced by the specialist knowledge held by some professionals.

In this chapter, consideration is given to what is meant by *hearing* the voice of the child, to avoid the assumption that this means only a direct conversation between a child and a teacher, for example. It is intended to treat voice in a much broader way, to include the child's behaviour, their responses to what is being taught and how, their ability to form relationships and build friendships, and their expressed aspirations and ambitions, all of which might be seen as forms of communication. This will be accomplished through describing and exploring a pedagogical approach based on a contextualised learning activity introducing a student named Stephen that has been used successfully with higher education students following undergraduate and postgraduate programmes in both general and inclusive primary initial teacher education (ITE).

Pedagogical approach

The approach being described originated in the development of a module within an undergraduate inclusive education programme on behaviour. It was part of a suite of modules that focused on the four areas of need outlined in the 2001 SEN Code of Practice, the content of which included case study pupils who exhibited characteristics of the areas of need. The underlying premise was that these case studies would be used within an active learning approach based on problem- or contextualised-based learning.

Active learning was adopted for two reasons: The first was to recognise that educating emerging teachers to teach involves the active demonstration of the types of teaching that are supported by theory – in this case, the ideas of Dewey (1916) and Vygotsky (1978). The second was the expectation that content knowledge is best acquired through exploratory teaching methods that demonstrate aspects of pedagogical content knowledge, such as questioning, reflection, and collaboration.

Programmes of primary ITE have, inevitably, to cover a large area of curriculum content knowledge, to which must be added material related to inclusion, behaviour management, PSHE, and teaching theory. The organisation of such programmes, which is often on the basis of subject modules, can lead to fragmentation and to the need to overload modules with content delivery, rather than promoting teaching of a more active nature. In this module, it was decided to adopt an approach in which the tutor acted as a learning facilitator, teaching in a way where expectations were placed on the students to seek, explore, and engage in learning that expanded their content knowledge and related it to the practical elements already experienced in the course, which amounted to 16 weeks of school-based practice in two schools, one of which was a specialist setting for many of the students. This offered alignment with Dewey's position that learning is 'promoted through active experience and engagement' (Dewey, 1916) and that students 'can learn on their own and . . . [the teacher's] role is to remove obstacles and create conditions for active learning . . . not to instruct, provide answers . . . or tell people what they should learn' (Kolb, cited in Blasco, Kjaergaard, & Thomsen, 2021).

Additionally, the tutor was expected to provide a supportive teaching space, to create a safe environment for learning, again reflecting the expectation that modelling good classroom practice is an essential element of ITE. In this way, alignment was sought with theory, in this case the idea that the tutor should strive to continually keep their students within what Vygotsky (1978) describes as the zone of proximal development. Experience of teaching the module demonstrated a deep emotional engagement by the students with the case study child, in part because of the creation of this supportive teaching space, a result that undoubtedly strengthened the value of this element of the module. This led to the case study being used in other programmes, often as a free-standing session, and as a professional development session outside of ITE programmes.

Problem-based learning

Perhaps obviously, at the heart of problem-based learning (PBL) is the solution of a problem. PBL originated in medical education as a way of bringing together the extensive content knowledge acquired in the early years of training to be a doctor with the very necessary application of that knowledge in clinical settings to solve the 'problems of education' (Tan, 2003), as a way of addressing the gap between theory and practice. From these beginnings, the use of PBL has been adopted in a variety of contexts, including education (Kavanagh & Rainey, 2017), nursing (Seibert, 2021), and business management (Yazici, 2020). In education, the approach has been used in all stages of schooling, as well as in teacher initial and continuing training.

When a PBL exercise is introduced into the classroom, the problem is presented first, before any content knowledge is given, as it is the problem that is seen as the starting point for learning. The problem should be realistic and should be drawn from as close a real-world situation as possible, with the classroom being an obvious source of such situations. The problem should be challenging, leading to new ways of learning for the participants. In addition to challenging the current knowledge of the participants, the problem should also bring into consideration how attitudes affect responses.

Importantly, the approach is one that fosters a collaborative approach, requiring communication and cooperation between the participants as a response to what is a self-directed way of learning. In reaching a conclusion to the learning process engendered by the problem that has been set, it is necessary for a synthesis to be reached, requiring the integration of the views and judgements of the participants. It is likely that this will lead in disciplines such as medical education to a provisional diagnosis of a symptomatic condition. In this case, it was felt that an alternative was desirable, in an approach that became known as contextualised learning activity (CLA), rather than PBL. Rather than seeking a narrow synthesis/solution, the aim became to acknowledge the complexities that exist in the classroom, where educational aims can become intertwined with concerns about the diagnosis of learning difficulties, social work issues, economic disadvantage, and so on. This does not prevent a solution being reached by the group, but it does require a realisation that the proposed solution might not be one that would be reached in the real world, where policy differences might produce a situation other than that preferred by the group.

This synthesis should not be seen as the end of the process; any 'answer' that is reached should mark the beginning of an extended reflective learning process for those involved, to further develop content knowledge, to reflect on the process in relation to practice, and to consider in the light of these activities whether the solution previously reached remains tenable, or whether a reconsideration of the CLA would produce a different outcome.

The content selected for this CLA was the material contained in the SEND Code of Practice in use at the time of delivery, either the SEN Code of Practice (2001) or the SEND Code of Practice (2015).

The SEND Code of Practice

The most recent SEND Code of Practice (DfE/DoH, 2015) is subtitled 'Statutory guidance for organisations which work with and support children and young people who have special educational needs or disabilities', which gives a clear indication of the extent and scope of the material in a document that runs to 292 pages. Generally, the Code is a densely packed overview of all the content likely to be needed within the field, and therefore, not all of it will have a direct relevance to, for example, a classroom teacher at the beginning of their career. This tends to make engaging with the Code difficult, particularly within a content-led approach.

However, there has always been much in the SEND Code of Practice that is relevant to all teachers, and it is important that this material be accessed within initial teacher education. Chapter 2, Section 2 of the 2001 Code of Practice emphasises this, where it states that '[a]ll teachers are teachers of children with special educational needs', going on to say that this is therefore a whole-school responsibility, rather than one that rests with those holding special responsibility for SEN, such as the SENCo. In meeting that responsibility, it is clear that many of the requirements of the Code place demands on every teacher to listen to the voice of the child or young person, however that might be communicated.

Chapter 1 of the 2015 Code of Practice contains the principles that underpin SEND provision, which 'must have regard' to 'the views, wishes and feelings of the child or young person, and the child's parents' and 'the importance of the child or young person, and the child's parents, participating as fully as possible in decisions' (Section 1.1), designed to support 'the participation of children, parents and young people in decision-making', 'greater choice and control for young people and parents over support', and 'a focus on inclusive practice and removing barriers to learning' (Section 1.2).

Chapter 2 focuses on the need for important information to be available to children, parents, and young people to participate in decision-making and to allow them to communicate their wishes, a process that will depend on the involvement of all teachers to be successful. Chapter 3 emphasises the role of multi-agency working in providing effective support for children with SEND and makes it clear that parents and the child should be at the centre of this process, foregrounding the need to listen to, and act upon, the views/voice of the child.

In dealing with expectations on schools, the content of Chapter 6 of the Code should be familiar to all teachers. Included are sections dealing with improving outcomes for pupils with SEND, equality and inclusion, curriculum, and identifying needs, where the four areas of need are introduced and provision identified. An important element here is the idea of a graduated approach to meeting needs, which is based on the assumption that needs might change and that provision needs to be tailored to those needs as a result of careful classroom assessment processes, which might be seen to involve effective teacher–pupil communication. That any change in need might encompass both a diminished need for support as a result of effective support as well as one that increases is a point worth noting.

Chapter 9 is of equal importance to Chapter 6; this chapter includes information on statutory assessment processes, with a familiar emphasis on involving, and supporting, parents, children, and young people in decision-making, cross-agency working, and the sharing of information. Whilst it is probable that individual teachers will have limited input to the procedures involved in statutory assessment for education, health, and care plans (EHCP), this will not be so for the reassessment requirements of the EHCP process, where assessment, target-setting, intervention, and report-writing will all place burdens on those most in contact with the child involved, requiring thoughtful interactions to ensure that the voice and wishes of the child are heard and acted upon. For this reason, the CLA selected for this module was built around the last two years of a particular pupil's primary school experience, covering Years 5 and 6, when the pupil was 9 to 11 years old, and which culminated in the pupil's transfer to secondary education.

The contextualised learning activity

In addition to the obvious need to be fully conversant with the content selected for the CLA, in this case the provisions contained within the relevant SEND Code of Practice, school reports, etc., additional material was needed to support the picture that emerges as the teaching and learning develops. The impetus for the activity can be stated concisely, but this will represent only a small part of the story that will unfold as the teaching interaction continues, and it was felt that a script was needed to support this. This required the writing of a series of responses that anticipated the need to refer to any documents that might exist around such a case, drawing on similar documents from actual situations. It was necessary for this material to be fully internalised by the tutor to allow responses to be delivered spontaneously to increase the authenticity of the experience.

Delivering the CLA

In early iterations of the CLA, the participants comprised a group of approximately 25 second-year undergraduate primary ITE students in a timetabled seminar session lasting four hours, split into two parts. As confidence in the activity grew, it was used successfully with different group sizes and with different session lengths. The classroom was arranged in a semi-circle, with students facing the tutor. The group were asked to have only a notebook and writing implement with them. After some introductory words, the focus of the CLA was introduced.

The students were told that it was August and they were about to begin working as a newly qualified Year 5 teacher (Pupils aged 9–10 years old). The name of one of the pupils in their class was Stephen, who had only enrolled at Easter in the previous academic year, in Year 4, having transferred from a local special school. Group members were told that information about Stephen from a number of sources was available to them by questioning the tutor. The sources were outlined, which included educational and educational psychological reports, medical advice, social service assessments, and material from Stephen's parents and Stephen, copies of which were held by the tutor and shown to the students. Time was then allowed for the students to record their initial thoughts about Stephen and to consider appropriate questions.

To begin the information gathering part of the activity, students were told that they were to ask one question about Stephen, starting with a random student and then moving in turn around the group until everybody had contributed. It was emphasised that no individual follow-up questions would be allowed, all group members were to contribute, and notes could be taken. The questioning process then began and continued until every group member had asked a question. Generally, questions were answered by the tutor immediately, without referring to the written documents, unless a question was asked that sought specific information from a specific source. In responding, the tutor used their knowledge of the group to judge how to answer, offering support in some cases, and by challenging in others.

The next stage of the process was to allow a period of reflection on what had been learned, first individually, and then in small groups. This was then extended into a whole-group consideration of what was now known and, perhaps more importantly, what was not. A second round of questioning was then completed, starting with the student who had posed the final question in the first round, proceeding in the opposite way around the group; experience suggests that being first, with the need to think quickly, can be difficult, whilst being last can be frustrating if all the questions you have thought about are asked before the questioning reaches you. A further period of reflection, both individually and in groups, followed to pool the additional information that had been gained. It is worth noting that when working with smaller groups, a third or fourth round of questioning might be used, to ensure that sufficient information could be gathered to utilise the material that was available.

At this point, depending on the information gathered, the students begin to identify with Stephen as a member of their class, and so the next stage of the process was to link this material with their practice-based knowledge. In groups of three/four, the students were asked to suggest the strategies they would adopt in their classroom to meet the learning needs of all their class, and for Stephen in particular, given his relatively recent arrival in the school from a special school. Whilst an emphasis on learning needs was specified, it was made clear that this included all aspects of classroom practice, including behaviour management, something about which they, like many other newly qualified teachers, were likely to be apprehensive. Each group was then asked to share one of their suggested activities with the class, offering a justification for its selection; further contributions were then sought from each group, until all suggested activities had been shared and discussed.

In the final element of the first half of the CLA, the tutor debriefed the group. The source of the material on Stephen was identified, if that had not already emerged during the questioning, in the information gathering process connected to statutory assessment for a statement of SEN or for an EHCP, depending on when the CLA took place. This allowed connections to be made to the Code of Practice being used, extending the content knowledge being accessed. Any information about Stephen that had not been gathered during questioning was shared from the written sources, to further embed how information on a pupil with SEN is gathered. This allowed a whole-group discussion to occur about Stephen as a pupil and about how the strategies suggested by the group might be modified to utilise any new information. The session break that followed was of sufficient duration to allow the group further time for reflection on their experience so far of the CLA.

At the beginning of the second part of the seminar, the tutor noted the success of the Year 5 teaching for Stephen and moved the focus of the CLA to the beginning of Year 6. This is an important time for any pupil, with the process of applying for secondary education soon to begin. For a pupil subject to statutory assessment processes, it is of particular importance, as a transition review becomes necessary, preferably early in the school year, to allow consideration of appropriate arrangements for secondary education. The students were advised that all the material necessary for the review has been gathered from the sources recommended in the Code of Practice. They were now required to access this material, evaluate it, and make appropriate recommendations for Stephen's next steps, in the style of a statutory annual review.

With the students again seated in a semi-circle, a new round of questioning began, again starting at a random point in the arrangement of chairs. The process followed rules that were used previously, with one question required from each student, no follow-up questions, and time being given to record and reflect upon answers. Following reflection, a further round of questioning was conducted, although this was preceded by tutor input on the options open to Stephen, given the statutory assessment that exists and his presence in a feeder primary school for one secondary school, although living in the catchment area for another. Time was then allocated for the students to consider what they would recommend as the outcome of the transition review, and what resources would be needed to support this decision.

By this stage of the CLA, it was usual for the students to have developed a clear internal picture of Stephen, based on their experiences on school placement, to have become emotionally involved in his story, and to have become invested in his future, even though he had only come into being through their engagement with the questioning process. It was tempting to finish the CLA at this point, but this was never possible, because as soon as the tutor tried to bring the CLA to an end, the students would demand to know what happened to Stephen after transfer to secondary education. An ending had been built into the material written for the CLA which, when shared with the group, would lead to a further debate about what might have been done differently, further embedding reflective learning. Feedback for the session was universally positive, with comments complimenting both the material and the style of delivery.

Reflections

The contextualised learning activity outlined in this chapter paved the way for extensive reflective learning for the participants, both under the direction of the module tutor as the CLA unfolded and in subsequent activities and sessions. The interactive nature of the process also created an arena in which tutor reflection enabled immediate changes to the development of the activity. An example of this process which occurred on many occasions when the CLA was delivered was the need to interrogate the questions asked in the first round of questioning.

The concern here was that very little had been discovered about the educational achievements and learning needs of Stephen, as opposed to questions that sought to ascertain the 'diagnostic symptoms' that would support a label of need, for example, social, emotional, and mental health – that is, a within-child, deficit approach to the questioning. When this was discussed, the participants tended to be both surprised and chastened, as they recognised the disconnect; they had, arguably, missed the opportunity to gather the sort of information that would have helped in meeting the requirement to address Stephen's learning needs as term began. The second round of questioning tended to see a shift in focus, to better prepare the groups to meet those needs; in general, the ideas offered showed a very clear use of knowledge, skills, and learning activities, demonstrating a useful level of theory–practice development.

This shift in focus can be seen as perhaps the most important learning that occurred in the module in which the CLA was undertaken. Questions that focus on explaining a pupil's label would seem to be indicative of attitudes much more aligned with a medical model of SEND than a social/educational one. That students in ITE seem to have developed this attitude, presumably from their own experiences of education, schools, teachers, etc., indicates a need for this to be challenged at an early stage of becoming a teacher, if we are to develop a more inclusive education system where judgements about pupils are made based on professional assessments that involve voice, rather than in systems privileging diagnostic pathways, where the voices of those most closely connected with the pupil (and the pupil's) are lost. An understanding of how we define and respond to voice can be enhanced by the types of practitioner research that are fully grounded in theory.

Across this activity, the reflective process was strongly influential in ensuring that the students remained in the zone of proximal development (Vygotsky, 1978). Whilst ZPD was originally, and is usually, used in relation to children's learning, Eun (2019) reimagined the conceptualisation of ZPD in terms of recognising multiple voices and acknowledging conflicts and contradictions within the zone.

With regard to the former, Eun extends the focus on a presumed first (less-competent) voice and the second (more competent) voice to that of a third voice, 'defined as the larger context, such as the institutional and historical forces mentioned previously, that shape the social interactions between the first and second voices' (2019, p. 25). In relation to the CLA described here, the third voice is exemplified in the information held by the tutor.

In research conducted in 2008, Eun et al. also highlighted the importance of socio-political context, noting that

> [t]he third voice of testing spoke through the first voice of teaching which resulted in teachers teaching to the test and the students striving to obtain passing scores.
> (cited in Eun, 2019, p. 26)

Towards the end of the CLA described in this chapter, the student teachers recognised the conflict between their original questions, largely within-child and based upon a raft of labels at the forefront of practice, and their own perceptions of the need to focus on educational innovation, and responded to this with an apparent attitudinal change, however short-lived this might have been. Their emotional engagement with Stephen clearly enabled this shift, something that has also been the case when the CLA has been used with serving teachers.

Another systemic contradiction becomes obvious whenever this CLA is used with emerging, or serving, teachers – that of a perceived linearity in decision-making when conducting a statutory assessment for a child with SEND. For example, a local authority may resist statutory assessment and the granting of an EHCP due to budgetary constraints, whilst an educational psychologist or a school's medical practitioner might favour labelling or diagnosis through well-defined pathways, reflecting a medical model approach. Some schools, perhaps a majority, will see that the best placement for a child with SEN lies in specialist provision, whilst children's services departments might favour the retention of local ties for children at risk. Parents may be ambivalent, pro- or opposed to labels; indeed, it cannot be assumed that they will wish to communicate with those seeking an assessment of their child's needs, and the child or young person might be torn between loyalty to their parent/carer, their own ambitions, friendships made at school, or the ethos of a particular school and may not be able to unravel this ambivalence when trying to communicate their needs. In effect, the process may serve to silence the child, even where reviews occur, as the gap widens between ambitions, opportunities, and levels of acceptance.

Each stage of the CLA is designed to provoke participants to think about the difference between listening and hearing as aspects of asking questions and of group discussions. By detailing with what was, unfortunately, an unsuccessful attempt to reintegrate Stephen to a mainstream setting, in line with the graduated response, space was created for the exploration of a wide range of communication opportunities for all involved, focusing on best educational practice.

The acknowledgement of extended communication beyond that involving conversation opened up a range of interactions with Stephen based on his responses to classroom activities, social relationships, assessments, activities beyond the classroom, etc. Here, 'voice' could be seen as stemming from observations, achievements, self-efficacy, and from recognising that behaviour can be a powerful form of non-verbal communication. This requires an awareness of variables, such as changes to routines or triggers; areas of personal sensitivity, involving the child's family, for example; and thresholds, such as family upheavals leading to sleep disruption, rather than simply seeing challenging behaviour as being a 'within-child' attribute.

Crucially, the emotional evolvement of the students involved in the CLA in terms of picturing the child, becoming invested in his progress, and developing a strong desire for him to succeed resulted in a sense of loss when they realised that their hopes for Stephen may not have been fulfilled. This is another important lesson that all teachers must learn; in the end, what we invest in each and every child might not have the conclusion that we seek and wish for. In particular, student teachers began to question why the focus was on viewing the child, rather than schooling, as the problem, and from this they began to become passionate about how they, when qualified, could make a difference.

Conclusion

This activity is complex. First, the 'story' needs to be authentic, factually correct, and detailed. The tutor, and students, needs to analyse whether the child (and parent/carer) has sufficient experience, awareness, and knowledge of the educational system, as required by the SEND Code of Practice (DfE, 2015), to make informed choices in a process where the odds are often seen to be stacked against them. For instance, it could be that Stephen became the victim of a system that seeks to gather the voice of the child without, necessarily, truly hearing and engaging with that voice because of differing policy directions. Listening is not the same as hearing, which should be at the heart of the teacher–pupil relationship rather than something that we do as part of a statutory process.

Reflective questions

1. What question would you ask when told that someone would be joining your setting from another, very different setting?
2. Do you think that the types of question that might be asked are *predominantly* shaped by role, setting, political backdrop, or personal experience?
3. In this case, the voices of external experts were seen as more important than the voice of those working closely with Stephen and, more worryingly, the voice of the child. Why might that be?

Takeaway activities

- Adapt this series of activities for your own setting. Whose voice is lost? What needs to be considered? Who can make a difference? If you are not involved in a setting, review any of the undercover reports filmed by BBC Panorama – these include films about behaviour in a young offenders unit and psychiatric units.
- Think about the different ways that the voice of marginalised members of society can be silenced, and consider how such voices can be heard.
- Revise this activity from the point of view of a member of the caring profession who works closely with someone like Stephen whose voice is also unheard due to their role or position in the mechanisms of the state.

References

Dewey, J. 1916. *Democracy and education: An introduction to the philosophy of education*. New York: Macmillan.

DfE/DoH. 2015. *Special educational needs and disabilities code of practice: 0 to 25 years*. London: TSO.

DfE/DoHSC. 2022. *Consultation outcome SEND review: Right support, right place, right time*. Available at: https://www.gov.uk/government/consultations/send-review-right-support-right-place-right-time [Accessed 9th August 2023].

DfES. 2001. *SEN code of practice*. Nottingham: DfES.

Education Act. 1981. Available at: https://www.legislation.gov.uk/ukpga/1981/60/enacted [Accessed 17th August 2023].

Eun, B. 2019. The zone of proximal development as an overarching concept: A framework for synthesizing Vygotsky's theories. *Educational Philosophy and Theory* 51 (1): 18–30.

House of Commons Education Select Committee: Special educational needs and disabilities. 2019. Available at: https://publications.parliament.uk/pa/cm201919/cmselect/cmeduc/20/20.pdf [Accessed: 15th August 2023].

Kavanagh, S. S., & Rainey, E. 2017. Learning to support adolescent literacy: Teacher educator pedagogy and novice teacher take up in secondary English language arts teacher preparation. *American Educational Research Journal* 54 (5): 904–937.

Kolb, et al. 2014. Cited in Blasco, M., Kjaergaard, A., & Thomsen, T. U. 2021: 35. Situationally orchestrated pedagogy: Teacher reflections on positioning as expert, facilitator, and caregiver. *Management Learning*, 52 (1): 26–46.

Lamb Inquiry. 2010. *Special educational needs and parental confidence*. Available at: https://www.specialeducationalneeds.co.uk/uploads/1/1/4/6/11463509/full_report.pdf [Accessed 15th September 2023].

Seibert, S. A. 2021. Problem-based learning: A strategy to foster generation Z's critical thinking and perseverance. *Teaching and Learning in Nursing* 16: 85–88.

Tan, O. S. 2003. *Problem-based learning innovation: Using problems to power learning in the 21st century*. Singapore: Cengage learning.

United Nations Convention on the Rights of the Child. 1989. Available at: https://www.unicef.org.uk/wp-content/uploads/2016/08/unicef-convention-rights-child-uncrc.pdf [Accessed 15th August 2023].

Vygotsky, L. S. 1978. *Mind in society: The development of higher psychological processes*. Cambridge, MA: Harvard University Press.

Yazici, H. J. 2020. Project-based learning for teaching business analytics in the undergraduate curriculum. *Decision Sciences Journal of Innovative Education* 18 (4): 589–611.

7 Reimagining the role of children and young people's voices within the design of inclusive education

Clare Woolhouse and Virginia Kay

Key words

Voice, Children's rights, Multi-modal strategies, Inclusion

Introduction

In this chapter we outline the work undertaken within a school-based research project that directly involves children and young people in shaping it. The 'Visualising Opportunities: Inclusion for Children, Education, and Society' (VOICES_Ed) project was initially designed to reinterpret concepts, ideas, and practices relevant to educational and social inclusion.

In the initial phase of the study, children and young people from four schools in North West England were invited to take photographs during their everyday school activities that they felt represented inclusion or exclusion. Each photographer was asked to comment on why they had taken the photograph and what it meant to them. These annotated photographs then became the basis for school-based workshops within which other children and young people were able to engage with them, discuss issues of relevance to them, and create further materials to facilitate the exploring of issues that affected them, which have, in some cases, been collated into a resource toolkit for use in schools.

We will now briefly outline the underpinning thinking and approach to our study, describe the activities undertaken within the school workshops, and share examples before detailing how children's involvement in this type of research can contribute to redesigning lessons, curriculum, and/or policies within schools.

Reimagining how we understand educational inclusion

The ongoing VOICES study is timely in that we wanted to explore in depth how children and young people might be included within the design and delivery of education in a more inclusive way that was not superficial. This intention aligns to the requirements noted by Professor Robinson in Chapter 1 and to 'recognise the right of the child to education, and with a view to achieving this right progressively and on the basis of equal opportunity', as stated by the UN Convention on the Rights of the Child (Article 28.1, 1989). As teachers will know, there is also a need for children to be consulted on practices that affect them (Section 2B of Children and Families Act, 2014), and children shall be assured of their right to express views on matters which affect them. As Wickenden and Kembhavi-Tam (2014, p. 400) point out, 'children . . . have and can express their own views and these are often quite different from those of proxies such as parents or professionals who might have previously answered for them'.

Despite drastic changes in the experience of education between 2020 and 2022 due to the Covid-19 pandemic, the UK government has offered minimal guidance on how adults can listen and respond to the personal experiences of children which might affect their engagement with education. In order to start to address this gap in guidance, we seek to share practical examples that can be used to help practitioners, parents, and researchers understand how the experiences and priorities of children and young people can impact on their health and well-being and, therefore, their ability to engage within education.

The ongoing challenges presented by our post-pandemic society have created an urgent need to explore innovative and creative ways to engage children who are at risk of exclusion, marginalisation, or mental health difficulties and to foster new and enterprising, inclusive practice which makes the best use of the financial resources available, especially in light of the radical reforms planned in the latest SEN Green Paper (DfE/DoH, 2022). In addressing this need, a key tenet of the VOICES project has been to reject the idea that there is a clear, fixed, or incontestable understanding about what constitutes educational inclusion (Dunne et al., 2018). Rather, we seek to find out about the realities, feelings, and beliefs of children and young people in relation to their experiences of an education system, because throughout the world, 'policy initiatives such as the United Nations Convention on the Rights of the Child (1989) and Rights of Persons with Disabilities (2006) form a political backdrop for the development of educational practices based on principles of social justice' (Woolhouse et al., 2021, p. 423). Yet this does not mean that education will necessarily be experienced as inclusive or socially just by those within it. We therefore ask: What can we do to reimagine the ways in which children and young people's voices are listened to in developing inclusive practices within education?

Designing inclusive methods that involve multisensory pedagogies

It was important to the VOICES team that we choose a qualitative research method for data collection that we felt was as inclusive as possible; we wanted to minimise the barriers to participation and maximise the opportunities for children and young people to take part. It was felt that using participatory, creative, visual, and tactile pedagogical approaches would be the most suitable choice to enable a more collaborative and sensitive approach to research with children's stories. Such a holistic approach can also open up spaces for the sharing of emotional responses to situations and experiences, as Brown et al. (2020, p. 2) note:

> Through involvement in participatory visual research, children have an opportunity to document their experiences and critically reflect on the forces that influence those experiences. Thus, positioning children not simply as objects of research but as fully engaged collaborators in inquiry aligns with the value of framing children as competent social actors who both shape and are shaped by their environment.

To achieve this, a range of multisensory pedagogies for use with children and young people were designed, structured around the creation and sharing of photographs and other arts-based materials (for other examples, see Barley and Russell, 2019; Bertling, 2020; Lomax, 2020; McLaughlin and Coleman-Fountain, 2019; Shaw, 2021). We sought to create an innovative approach whereby children and young people were invited to produce and annotate anonymised photographs to instigate discussion as well as encourage artistic, creative responses. This approach builds on the work of MacDonald et al. (2019, p. 187), who contend that photo-related research with children 'should be participant driven and seek to apply photography as a means to document a community's strengths and concerns; generate knowledge and promote dialogue through discussion of photographs'.

The placing of children and young people, their views and experiences, in the centre of research is essential because they have often been under-represented in guiding research that informs the practice that is implemented with them (Faldet and Nes, 2021). We wanted the children involved to share experiences that their teachers, or researchers, may not be aware of, because, as Bernardi (2019, p. 60) notes, 'disrupting the normative canons for participation in research and explicitly recognising capability can encourage new possibilities in the presentation and emancipation of children' (see also Bradbury-Jones et al., 2018). In the VOICES project, we wanted children and young people to be able to critique the obvious, accepted, or taken-for-granted opinions and practices around educational inclusion and/or marginalisation. Using photographs can also enhance research because it can offer a space for thoughtful and reflective discussion from everyone involved.

There is a second key reason for using photographs and other arts-based approaches within our work, which is that they can enhance the potential for engaged, active learning. This use of multisensory pedagogies within education has its roots within the Montessori (2013) view of learning. Such pedagogies have been adapted to harness children's sense of wonder, use of art-based free play, and exploratory learning within a holistic approach by educational researchers, such as Alvarez et al. (2021, p. 3), who note that 'children can feel motivated to work collaboratively and productively in a group, make decisions and solve practical problems in their communities through creative and artistic expression'. While the VOICES project has mainly focused upon photographs taken by children and young people aged 5–17 in mainstream or specialist school settings, multisensory pedagogies have also been used effectively within research in early years and preschools (Mason et al., 2019; Widyana, et al., 2020), in higher education (Robinson, 2018; Sinclair, 2018), and in further or lifelong learning settings (Krajewski and Khoury, 2021; Papanastasiou et al., 2019). Having determined that we would use photo elicitation as a starting point for the study, it was also decided that we would employ a patchwork approach to later workshops which would utilise a range of different creative approaches, including drawing, origami sculpture, and the writing of very short scenarios, which are described in the rest of this chapter.

Data collection and sharing

The initial data collection involved working with eight schools. Following ethical approval and consent from staff, parents, and children, pupils in four schools in the north-west of England were invited to take photographs that they felt represented inclusion or marginalisation and to provide a short statement about what the photograph meant to them. Two of the schools catered for primary-aged children (5–11), and one of those included was a special educational needs and disabilities (SEND) setting. The other two schools were for secondary-aged pupils (11–18), one of which included specialist SEND provision. In all, 63 photographs were produced and anonymised using a software package that applied an 'art' filter onto the image so that individuals could not be identified, an example of which is shown in Figure 7.1. See Woolhouse (2019) for a more detailed description of the ethical choices made about collecting, anonymising, and sharing these materials.

Thirty of the images and accompanying comments were selected and used to develop school workshops undertaken with children and young people. The materials were also adapted as resources for undergraduate and postgraduate students on teacher education programmes and for continuing professional development workshops with school staff, SEND teachers undertaking the SENCO Award, and other professionals engaging in master's level study in inclusive education. The work has also been shared with four groups of higher education (HE) lecturers attending UK conferences and two groups attending European conferences to garner a wide range of interpretations as well as, more widely, with the general public through an installation

Figure 7.1 In the art classroom.

at the Tate art gallery in Liverpool. It was felt that by sharing the materials as widely as possible, thoughtful discussions would be provoked in response to the concerns raised within the project illustrated by children and young people. To allow our 'viewers' to reflexively consider the photographs, we asked prompt questions, such as:

1. Do the images represent inclusion or exclusion? Why?
2. Has anything been left out of the photograph? What would you add?
3. What questions do the images encourage you to ask?
4. Having talked about the image, have you changed your mind about inclusion?

The intention of working in this way with anonymised photographs and accompanying comments created by children and young people was to open up a safe space for a range of children, young people, and the adults with whom they work, to explore their own and contrasting perspectives about educational practice framed in a non-judgemental way (Woolhouse et al., 2019). Stockall (2013) suggests that sharing and engaging with multiple, diverse viewpoints can enable fruitful discussion and change understandings. As has been pointed out by Packard (2008, p. 63), 'visual methods [are] not simply a way to record or display data, but rather [are] a way to generate new knowledge, to tap into existing resources which would otherwise lie dormant, unexplored and unutilised'. In order to utilise the rich data emerging from discussions around the photographs, we also involved children aged 14–15 who attended the school workshops in writing short scenarios that conveyed their concerns to teachers. The anonymised photographs, scenarios, and individual keywords or questions were collated into a shareable physical toolkit that has been used in schools to explore issues and topics of concern.

The initial photographs and comments that had been gleaned during 2015–2017 were also shared with the general public in the exchange gallery at Tate Liverpool in June 2018, as detailed by Woolhouse et al. (2021). The week-long exhibition at the Tate Liverpool art gallery was designed to be interactive, and we recorded a wide range of materials that were contributed by visitors to the gallery. For example, under each of the photographs shared in the gallery, we provided a 'postbox' and blank cards so that visitors could offer thoughts and feedback on the images. Over the course of the week, over 200 cards were posted. In another part of the gallery, visitors were invited to create a self-portrait and add it to our 'community wall' if they wanted to live in a welcoming and inclusive society – 113 people did so. We had a corner of the exhibition where a poster described how children in Japan create origami cranes to wish for peace; origami paper and instructions were provided, and visitors were invited to create a crane and add it to the 'peace shelf'. By the end of the exhibition, this had become two peace shelves which included 84 paper origami cranes, 1 dog, 1 plane, 1 hat, 2 boats, 1 cat, 5 English-language and 1 German-language counting games, 2 flowers, and 15 random sculptures. In the rest of this chapter, we focus on discussing the materials collected within the VOICES project and detail the pedagogies employed to consider how we used photographs and other creative approaches to facilitate discussion.

Using photo elicitation to facilitate discussion

Throughout the VOICES project, we sought to use a wide variety of learning approaches to invite children and young people to share their experiences and guide us in developing a greater understanding of how they feel about their education. The central approach has been to use photo elicitation, where children produce and annotate photographs that can be the trigger for further discussions about inclusion or marginalisation in education; for example, one of the images we have used to prompt discussion is 'Nowhere to Sit' (see Figure 7.2):

Information card for 'Nowhere to Sit'

This photograph was taken by a male student aged 15.
He took this photograph as an example of exclusion, saying that there was 'nowhere to sit' for the boy standing up.
Prompt question: Do you think that the boy wants to sit down? Why?

Children and young people's voices in inclusive education 81

Figure 7.2 Photograph and information card: 'Nowhere to Sit'.

This particular image and the prompt question on the information card that accompanied it elicited a range of differing responses during workshops with secondary-aged young people, including the following:

- 'He may just be talking to the others/relaying a message for the teacher.'
- 'Sitting would make him a part of a group, and sitting is better than standing.'
- 'Looks like the boy is excluded. . . . Maybe he's only visiting to look what other groups are doing, while he has his own [group]. He could get a chair and sit where he stands if he [had] to.'
- 'The boy standing up looks in charge.'
- 'The boy standing up looks like he wants to join in and sit with the other boys. He is looking directly at them. However, the other boys seem to be looking away, purposely. It looks like they're ignoring him.'
- 'The boy standing looks engaged in what they're doing, suggesting that he wants to be involved in what they're doing.'
- 'This photo, I think, is about people not being friendly, because they have left them out'.
- 'No, I do not think so. He is quite happy standing up. It puts him in a position of dominance.'
- 'He looks like [name]. He's always standing up. Do you think he wants to sit down?'

The different range of responses received highlight how different young people can interpret the same image in different ways, possibly relating it to their own experiences or to those of their classmates, as demonstrated by the final comment, in which a friend was specifically named (anonymised by the researcher).

Through the aforementioned responses, it can be seen that the image alone is not of central value; the responses to the image hold much more power. As Chawla-Duggan et al. (2020, p. 40) argue, 'using photography and video recording solely to "collect data" overlooks the value of visual ambiguity'. The ambiguity of the images creates space for reflection; each viewer of each photograph is free to bring their own assumptions, emotions, and experience to their understanding of the images. When looking at a concept such as 'in(ex)clusion' (Dunne et al., 2018, p. 22), '*how things are* is often less important than *how people think* – or perceive – things are' (Flutter and Rudduck, 2004, p. 6), and the wide range of responses we have gathered demonstrates the potential of ambiguity to allow the power of different engagements and interpretations.

In the week of our installation in the Tate Liverpool gallery, there were over 3,300 visitors to our work and over 1,000 engagements on Twitter. Active engagement with our project, through offering thoughts and ideas about the photographs in our postboxes and the opportunity to create images for the self-portrait community wall or origami sculptures that then became part of the exhibition, was absorbing for many Tate visitors, who found the approach innovative and refreshing. One young visitor commented:

> It's great that there is so much to do. Galleries can be intimidating for young people or people not used to coming to galleries [and] [t]his is the best gallery I've been to; I didn't know we would get to do stuff.

Adapting for different school settings or subjects

Using visual and arts-based methods can maximise engagement opportunities for the widest range of children and young people, and although it does not completely negate power dynamics between the adults and children involved, it disrupts these more effectively than many other approaches (Holt, 2014). This approach can be used not only to investigate many aspects of the curriculum and different types of lessons but also to enhance learning within subject strands, with obvious links to using PSHE to explore issues such as bullying, homophobia, or racism, or other subjects, such as art or ICT, via creating, processing, and critiquing the images. There are also strong links to the English curriculum, with opportunities to write about perspectives, comments, stories, or scenarios or possible links to the drama curriculum, within which an embodied exploration of differing experiences can be undertaken. Reflection upon photographs can be employed in an enormous variety of ways in different school settings, and children and young people can easily take charge of this journey, as evidenced by one child in our project who took a photograph of a geography lesson she enjoyed. In Figure 7.3 we can see the outcome of a lesson on climate change and sustainability, which, in turn, could be used to prompt further discussion about such topics or to ask children about what they enjoy learning or what works when they are with other children, as indicated in the following prompt questions. Approaches such as those detailed in this chapter give a practical way to not only engage children and young people in giving feedback on what and how they are learning but to also provide a conduit through which young people can play a role in reflecting upon and redesigning the teaching and learning processes they have been involved in.

The views and experiences of children and young people can also inform the development of school policy both within their schools/settings and in the wider community. The possibilities are wide-ranging and limited only by the scope of the application. For example, other photographs from within the VOICES project have been used as a training tool for teaching assistants to prompt debate around what it means to be or feel included. Such discussion might also be invaluable to school leaders who wish to affect positive change in this regard. There is a strong link between student voice and effective school leadership (Jones and Bubb, 2021; Adderley

Figure 7.3 Photograph and information card: 'Painting Trees'.

Information card for 'Painting Trees'

This photograph was provided by a 10-year-old girl. She reported that she enjoyed this activity and said, 'Everyone painted pictures of the rainforest together, and we all had fun'.

Related questions to ask children

- What activities do you enjoy?
- How can you encourage other people to share the fun?

et al., 2015), and participatory research has been shown to help improve knowledge, policies, and practices for children and their well-being (Marinkovic Chavez et al., 2022).

In another instance, the photo elicitation approach is being used with schools in the Sefton region of North West England to explore children's experiences of transitioning between primary and secondary school. Children are taking photographs around their schools and then using these anonymised images to discuss excitement or concerns about moving between schools. The aim of this project is to share the images and comments from these sessions to develop a 'transition'-focused toolkit that can be shared with schools across the Sefton region. All this activity is important because researchers such as Ben-Arieh (2010) argue the need for those involved in creating child-related policies to acknowledge and better understand the interrelation between child well-being and policy, reminding us that effective and engaging methods of accessing pupil voice are an essential aspect of such development.

The examples we have provided in this chapter demonstrate how the work on the VOICES project so far has resulted in an innovative data resource that includes annotated images, keywords, and scenarios that have been used with a number of schools and local authorities in the UK during 2022–2024. Such resources are easy to adapt or add to in any setting, and as the exhibition at Tate Liverpool demonstrated, this can be about going beyond a school environment, into the wider community, offering innovative spaces within which children and young people are provided with a platform to speak of their experiences.

Conclusion

Throughout this project, we have sought to address the children and young people we work with as knowledgeable insiders who can teach us about their experiences of being included (or not) within education. We feel this approach has provided us with a greater understanding of differing experiences and thus can be the groundwork for creating stronger and more trusting relationships. We offer alternative ways to facilitate listening to children and young people's voices and so enhance reflections on inclusion and marginalisation within education and society. Describing our pedagogy via this chapter has offered a space for reflections on the ways that we can help transform how children and young people are involved in discussions about their rights, their experiences of social justice or of pressing social issues, such as climate change. The approach we took within our empirical research may also serve as a springboard for developing ways to better and more actively engage children and young people in the redesign of inclusive learning, policy, or environments that really attend to their needs and experiences.

Reflective questions

1. What do you like about the approach to photo elicitation and other arts-based methods described in this chapter?
2. What do you think might be some of the challenges with using it?
3. What other innovative or multi-modal pedagogies/methods could you develop to enable the voices of children and young people to be heard?
4. Think of a setting where you might work with children or young people. How could you use this approach to explore an issue of concern?

> **Takeaway activities**
>
> - Ask a group of children or young people to create self-portraits, and put them together in a wall display to show that they are members of a welcoming class or community.
> - Choose a topic – think about relevance and appropriateness for the age group you work with (i.e. climate change/exam stress/bullying/mental health/food poverty/making new friends). Ask the children or young people to take photos/draw pictures/or create collages to express how they feel about the topic. These can then be shared and prompt small group discussions, followed by more general large group feedback.

Acknowledgements

We would like to thank all those involved in the production of the photographs and other materials, the children and young people, their teachers and teaching assistants. We would also like to offer our special thanks to Lorraine Chester for facilitating such proactive engagement from teachers across the Sefton local authority.

References

Adderley, R.J., Hope, M.A., Hughes, G.C., Jones, L., Messiou, K. and Shaw, P.A., 2015. Exploring inclusive practices in primary schools: Focusing on children's voices. *European Journal of Special Needs Education*, 30(1), pp. 106–121.

Alvarez, I.M., Velasco, M.M. and Humanes, P.R., 2021. Linking curriculum content to students' cultural heritage in order to promote inclusion: An analysis of a learning-through-the arts project. *International Journal of Inclusive Education*, pp. 1–16.

Barley, R. and Russell, L., 2019. Participatory visual methods: Exploring young people's identities, hopes and feelings. *Ethnography and Education*, 14(2), pp. 223–241.

Ben-Arieh, A., 2010. Developing indicators for child well-being in a changing context. In McAuley, C. and Rose, W. (Eds) *Child well-being: Understanding children's lives* (pp. 129–142). Jessica Kingsley Publishers.

Bernardi, F., 2019. *Reclaiming childhood. Disrupting discourses of identity, autonomy and dis/ability, adopting Arts-based methods, Gramsci and Bourdieu. A cross-cultural study in Central Italy and North West England*. PhD Thesis, Edge Hill University.

Bertling, J., 2020. Expanding and sustaining arts-based educational research as practitioner enquiry. *Educational Action Research*, 28(4), pp. 626–645.

Bradbury-Jones, C., Isham, L. and Taylor, J., 2018. The complexities and contradictions in participatory research with vulnerable children and young people: A qualitative systematic review. *Social Science & Medicine*, 215, pp. 80–91.

Brown, A., Spencer, R., McIsaac, J.L. and Howard, V., 2020. Drawing out their stories: A scoping review of participatory visual research methods with newcomer children. *International Journal of Qualitative Methods*, 19, pp. 1–9.

Chawla-Duggan, R., Konantambigi, R., Mei Seung Lam, M. and Sollied, S., 2020. A visual methods approach for researching children's perspectives: Capturing the dialectic and visual reflexivity in a cross-national study of father-child interactions. *International Journal of Social Research Methodology*, 23(1), pp. 37–54.

Children and Families Act, 2014. Available from: https://www.legislation.gov.uk/ukpga/2014/6/contents/enacted [Accessed 14th October 2022]

DfE/DoH, 2022. *SEND review: Right support, right place, right time*. Available from: https://www.gov.uk/government/consultations/send-review-right-support-right-place-right-time [Accessed 14th October 2022]

Dunne, L., Hallett, F., Kay, V. and Woolhouse, C., 2018. Spaces of inclusion: Investigating place, positioning and perspective within educational settings through photo-elicitation. *International Journal of Inclusive Education*, 22 (1), pp. 21–37.

Faldet, A.C. and Nes, K., 2021. Valuing vulnerable children's voices in educational research. *International Journal of Inclusive Education*, pp. 1–16.

Flutter, J. and Rudduck, J., 2004. *Consulting pupils, what's in it for schools?* London: Routledge Falmer.

Holt, L., 2014. The 'voices' of children: De-centring empowering research relations. *Children's Geographies*, 2(1), pp. 13–27.

Jones, M.A. and Bubb, S., 2021. Student voice to improve schools: Perspectives from students, teachers and leaders in 'perfect' conditions. *Improving Schools*, 24(3), pp. 233–244.

Krajewski, S. and Khoury, M., 2021. Daring spaces: Creating multi-sensory learning environments. *Learning and Teaching*, 14(1), pp. 89–113.

Lomax, H., 2020. Multimodal visual methods for seeing with children. Chapter 4 in *Seeing the world through children's eyes* (pp. 55–71). Brill.

MacDonald, D., Dew, A. and Boydell, K.M., 2019. Representation and knowledge exchange: A scoping review of photovoice and disability. *Journal of Applied Arts & Health*, 10(2), pp. 185–201.

Marinkovic Chavez, K., Gibbs, L., Saracostti, M., Lafaurie, A., Campbell, R., Sweeney, D., Hernandez, M.T., Sotomayor, M., Escobar, F., Ordosgoita, R., Cadavid, D Garcia, D., Wright, M., Charalamppoulos, D., Miranda, E. and Alisic, E., 2022. Think big: A multinational collaboration to promote children's role as coresearchers in participatory research. *American Journal of Community Psychology*, 69(3–4), pp. 306–317.

Mason, G.M., Goldstein, M.H. and Schwade, J.A., 2019. The role of multisensory development in early language learning. *Journal of Experimental Child Psychology*, 183, pp. 48–64.

McLaughlin, J. and Coleman-Fountain, E., 2019. Visual methods and voice in disabled childhoods research: Troubling narrative authenticity. *Qualitative Research*, 19(4), pp. 363–381.

Montessori, M., 2013. *The Montessori method*. Transaction Publishers.

Packard, J., 2008. 'I'm Gonna Show You What It's Really Like Out Here': The power and limitation of participatory visual methods. *Visual Studies*, 23(1), pp. 63–77.

Papanastasiou, G., Drigas, A., Skianis, C., Lytras, M. and Papanastasiou, E., 2019. Virtual and augmented reality effects on K-12, higher and tertiary education students' twenty-first century skills. *Virtual Reality*, 23(4), pp. 425–436.

Robinson, H.M., 2018. Emergent digital literacy and mobile technology: Preparing technologically literate preservice teachers through a multisensory approach. In *Information and technology literacy: Concepts, methodologies, tools, and applications* (pp. 1167–1183). IGI Global.

Shaw, P.A., 2021. Photo-elicitation and photo-voice: Using visual methodological tools to engage with younger children's voices about inclusion in education. *International Journal of Research & Method in Education*, 44(4), pp. 337–351.

Sinclair, S., 2018. Creativity, criticality and engaging the senses in higher education: creating online opportunities for multisensory learning and assessment. In *Creativity and critique in online learning* (pp. 103–122). Cham: Palgrave Macmillan.

Stockall, N., 2013. Photo-elicitation and visual semiotics: A unique methodology for studying inclusion for children with disabilities. *International Journal of Inclusive Education*, 17(3), pp. 310–328.

United Nations Convention on the Rights of the Child, 1989. Available from: http://www.ohchr.org/EN/ProfessionalInterest/Pages/CRC.aspx

United Nations Convention on the Rights of Persons with Disabilities, 2006. Available from: https://www.un.org/development/desa/disabilities/convention-on-the-rights-of-persons-with-disabilities.html

Wickenden, M. and Kembhavi-Tam, G., 2014. Ask us too! Doing participatory research with disabled children in the global south. *Childhood*, 21(3), pp. 400–417.

Widyana, R., Astuti, K., Bahrussofa, M.F. and Githa, G.M., 2020. The effectiveness of jolly phonics and multisensory learning methods in improving preschoolers pre-reading skills. *International Journal of Innovation, Creativity and Change*, 11(8), pp. 113.

Woolhouse, C., 2019. Conducting photo methodologies: Framing ethical concerns relating to representation, voice and data analysis when exploring educational inclusion with children. *International Journal of Research and Method in Education*, 42(1), pp. 3–18.

Woolhouse, C., Hasting, C. and Hallett, F., 2021. Perspectives on inclusion: Close encounters of the creative kind. *International Journal of Art and Design Education*, 40(2), pp. 420–435. Available from: https://onlinelibrary.wiley.com/doi/10.1111/jade.12357

Woolhouse, C., Kay, V., Hastings, C., Hallett, F. and Dunne, L., 2019. *Developing creative communities to explore inclusion and exclusion with children*. BERA Research Intelligence.

Section II

Involving young people and adults in developing inclusive communities

8 'Nothing about us without us'

Developing inclusive and meaningful research collaborations with autistic young people and peers

Angela Wearn, Zoe Collier, Katie Jenkins, Lily Wearn, Niamh Carson, Catherine El Zerbi, Felicity Shenton, Liam Spencer, and Amy Pearson

---

Key words

Autism, Inclusion, Mental health, Pupil voice, Secondary education

---

Introduction

This chapter outlines the development of a peer-initiated research project focused on autistic young people's experience within mainstream secondary school and how staff training can be optimised to support the development of more inclusive educational environments. Our work together is specifically focused on amplifying the voice of autistic young people and preventing poor mental health within this group through improved collaboration across schools, young people, and training providers.

Traditionally, autistic and other neurodivergent young people have been excluded from informing and shaping research that affects them. To increase young people's voice in research, the National Institute for Health and Care Research (NIHR) Applied Research Collaboration (ARC) for the North East and North Cumbria brought together a diverse group of young people to identify important topics that could be addressed via research. The group identified the mental health and well-being of autistic adolescents as a priority, relevant to the everyday lives of themselves and their peers. Together with a group of researchers, some of whom are also autistic, they developed a project that would help address three simple questions: What is already happening within our region? What helps or does not help? And how can we make things better than they are now?

Our collaborative approach led us to connect with a variety of different partners who further supported the development of our study through a participatory workshop with a wider group of autistic young people and a steering group who acts as 'critical friends', helping us resolve questions or challenges we came across along the way.

The following chapter will outline the background to involving and including autistic young people in research, and the importance of focusing on the well-being of autistic secondary school pupils. We will share reflections and practical examples of how we worked together, the toolkits and frameworks that have underpinned our approach, and highlight how this learning might be applied to an educational context, to support the development of meaningful partnership working *with* rather than *for* pupils.

Background

Involving autistic young people in research

Autism refers to a lifelong neurodevelopmental disability that is characterised in relation to differences in social communication, repetitive behaviours/highly focused interests, and/or sensory challenges (this may be an over- or under-sensitivity to, for example, noise, light, touch, or textures) (American Psychiatric Association, 2022). There are high rates of co-occurrence with common mental health conditions, such as anxiety and eating disorders (Lever & Geurts, 2016; O'Halloran et al., 2022), and other forms of neurodivergence, such as ADHD or dyspraxia (May et al., 2018; Miller et al., 2021). Historically, knowledge and understanding around autism have been generated from research which lacked diversity or the involvement of the autistic community (Feinstein, 2011; Milton & Bracher, 2013; Onaiwu, 2020).

In large part, the poor involvement of the autistic community has been strongly linked to *epistemic injustice*, which broadly relates to injustice done to an individual in relation to their perceived knowledge (Baumtrog & Peach, 2019; Fricker, 2007). Epistemic injustice experienced by the autistic community within research (and, indeed, other contexts) has been vast (Chapman & Carel, 2022; Dinishak, 2021), with assumptions that non-autistic adults were better placed to describe and explain autistic experience than those who lived it (Botha & Cage, 2022; Milton, 2014). This is particularly pronounced in the context of young people and/or those with mental health concerns (Greenblatt et al., 2024) and often described in terms of two areas. The first, *testimonial injustice*, refers to young people's knowledge and experience being discredited due to their age, often placing greater confidence in adults' expertise and consequently marginalising young people's views, in some cases with particularly adverse outcomes (Baumtrog & Peach, 2019). The second form of epistemic injustice, *hermeneutic injustice*, refers to individuals (in this case, young people) being denied access to resources that help them understand their own experiences by those with more social power and/or being unable to contribute to a shared understanding (Fricker, 2007; Greenblatt et al., 2024).

Therefore, whilst autistic young people have often been involved in research as participants, they have traditionally had little say and/or steer in the direction and processes of autism-focused research itself, as one of our young co-investigators reflects:

> *Previously, young people (let alone neurodivergent persons) only connected with research through school textbooks, participating in surveys, or in some cases, providing their own human tissue. This lack of representation has ultimately led to the production of research and theories about autism which dehumanise and pathologise my community and how we exist in the world. To draw from my own personal experiences as a young autistic researcher, authentic and meaningful involvement in research entails academics prioritising the needs and interests of young people and viewing us as co-partners rather than as a vessel for their own agenda.*

The neurodiversity movement of recent years (Kapp, 2019) has aimed to rectify these injustices and, in many cases, incorrect assumptions, moving away from a deficit-based model of autism (i.e. focused on only the challenges that autistic people face) to a broader, neuro-affirmative approach which recognises diversity within the community, celebrates strengths, as well as identifies areas where support may be needed (Hartman et al., 2023). This, in turn, encourages the increased involvement of the autistic community in research that affects them (Fletcher-Watson et al., 2021; Milton, 2019).

Frameworks to support research involvement

The National Institute for Health and Care Research (NIHR), often termed the research arm of the Department for Health and Social Care, defines *public involvement* as working with or by members of the public, rather than 'to', 'about', or 'for' them (NIHR Centre for Engagement and Dissemination, 2021). This is different from *engagement* in research (where information is shared with communities) or *participation* in research (where people take part in a research study). Public involvement is now a requirement within research funded by NIHR and other major funding bodies in the United Kingdom. In addition to the moral argument, involving those who are most affected by a given issue can help ensure research is relevant, accessible, and acceptable to our communities, can support in identifying potential problems before they occur, and can minimise the likelihood of inadvertently causing harm (Brett et al., 2014; Dinishak & Akhtar, 2023; Fletcher-Watson et al., 2021).

The UK Standards for Public Involvement in research (NIHR, 2019) have therefore been developed as a set of values or principles that underpin good public involvement in research. They are often used as a framework for 'what good looks like' when involving others in research organisations and activity. They are also a tool to encourage reflection and continuous learning, facilitating understanding around what needs to be improved for better partnership working. These six standards are as follows:

- **Working together.** Work together in a way that values all contributions and that builds and sustains mutually respectful and productive relationships.
- **Inclusive opportunities.** Offer involvement opportunities that are accessible and that reach people and groups according to research needs.
- **Communications.** Use plain language for well-timed and relevant communications, as part of involvement plans and activities.
- **Support and learning.** Work together in a way that values all contributions and that builds and sustains mutually respectful and productive relationships.
- **Impact.** Seek improvement by identifying and sharing the difference that public involvement makes to research.
- **Governance.** Involve people in research management, regulation, leadership, and decision-making.

Despite the application of these standards and progression of public involvement in research over recent years, there are still groups who are less likely to be present within research spaces as partners, even in an advisory capacity, such as autistic children and young people. At its core, public involvement in research is underpinned by the mantra of 'Nothing about us without us', hinting towards the right for individuals, particularly individuals deemed vulnerable, to have input into decisions and activities that affect them. Indeed, the often-cited UN Convention on the Right of the Child (UNCRC, 1989) is as applicable to research as it is to education, stating that every child has the right to have their views taken into account in all matters affecting them. With this in mind, one of the most well-cited models of citizen participation from Sherry Arnstein (1969) was adapted by Robert Hart (1992) to demonstrate different ways children and young people may be involved in community activities; these models often applied to research involvement, but also of use within education and a range of other contexts.

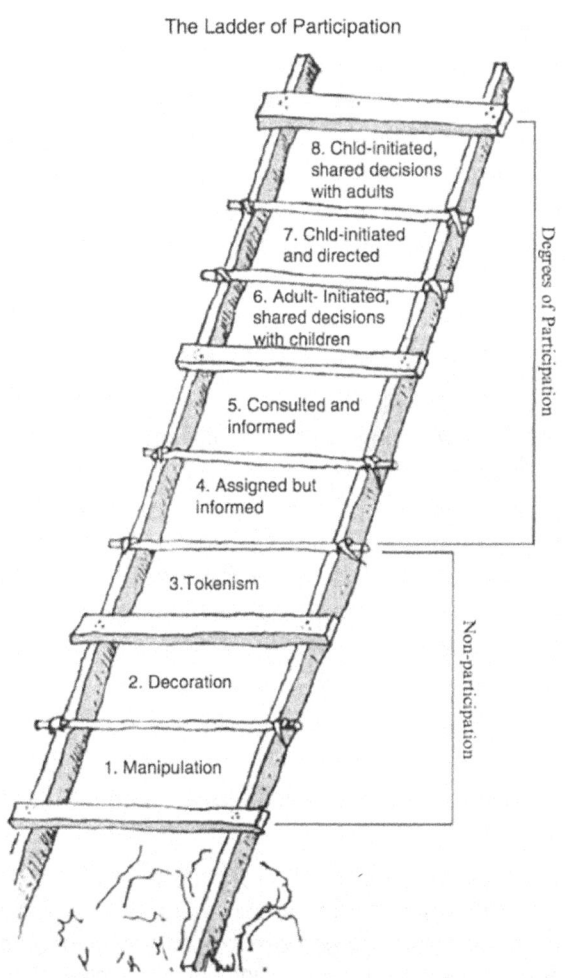

Figure 8.1 The Ladder of Participation – demonstrating ways in which children and young people may be involved in community activity.
Source: Hart (1992: 8).

Each rung on the ladder signifies a move towards more child-/young person–focused approaches and a more equal distribution of power; examples of each step are detailed in the following within the context of research/project involvement:

Manipulation. Young people being placed onto projects to influence others into agreeing with adults' agendas. The young people in this case having with no real understanding of their role and/or the issues that the project aims to address.

Decoration. Young people attending a project event as entertainment, or for having photographs taken, to make the event appear young person–friendly or focused. In this case, young people have had no real say or steer in the event itself.

Tokenism. Young people are invited onto a project team, often as representatives of young people or a minoritised group of young people, but have little to no opportunity to decide upon focus of the project or influence what is going to take place.

Assigned but informed. Young people have been fully informed of the focus of the work and have an understanding of the issues surrounding this but are given tasks with very little input or influence.

Consulted but informed. Young people have an opportunity to share their opinions in consultation exercises, which influence the direction taken by adults.

Adult-initiated shared decisions with children. A project has been initiated by adults; however, young people have genuine ability to inform and decide on some elements of this work.

Child-initiated and child-directed. Young people taking the initiative to develop a project and take the lead on carrying out the work. The author notes this may be particularly difficult in reality due to structural processes and the need for adult staff members to take responsibility for, for example, financial decisions.

Child-initiated shared decisions with adults. Young people initiate a project that they would like to take forward and link with adults to support them in this work. Together, both the young people and adults work together to develop and conduct the work.

This model has been critiqued for its linear nature, which suggests each step is better than the one before it; it is more accurate to emphasise the higher rungs of the ladder as different *degrees* of meaningful involvement, the appropriateness of which is dependent on the specific circumstance at hand (Hart, 2008; Jensen & Simovska, 2005; Mannion, 2003). Even in light of this criticism, Hart's (1992) model remains a good foundation for highlighting that the mere presence of young people within a group, team, or project is not enough to ensure genuine inclusion or involvement. Lundy (2007) describes four key components in working with young people that build upon Hart (1992) and align with the aforementioned UNCRC (1989):

- **Space.** Children must be given an opportunity to express a view.
- **Voice.** Children must be facilitated to express their views.
- **Audience.** The view must be listened to.
- **Influence.** The view must be acted upon, as appropriate.

These models can be applied as a principle-led foundation to inform practice and ensure the legal rights of autistic young people are embedded within the plans and process for involvement. However, as indicated within Hart's (1992) and Lundy's (2007) models, the involvement of autistic young people in both research and education must extend beyond tokenism to be truly meaningful and avoid negative unintended consequences (Brownlow et al., 2021; Milton, 2019).

Facilitating space and voice: priority-setting with young people

The Applied Research Collaboration within the North East and North Cumbria (ARC NENC) is an NIHR-funded partnership bringing together universities, health and social care providers, local authorities, voluntary and charity organisations, and members of the public across the region who work together to tackle health and social care inequality through research (NIHR ARC NENC, 2023). Following on from the launch of ARC NENC in 2019, a Young Person's Advisory Network (YPAN) was set up to ensure that young people had opportunity and space to meet, share ideas, express their views, and consider ways in which to become involved in health- and social care research. This network is coordinated by the ARC NENC's public involvement and community engagement (PICE) manager and brings together a diverse group of young people aged between 14 and 21, inclusive of those from ethnically minoritised communities, neurodivergent groups, and the LGBTQ+ community, amongst others.

Since the group was established, the YPAN has been involved in a number of activities, both project-specific and also informing and contributing to wider decision-making at a governance level (such as scoring funding call applications for their relevance and importance to young people). In late 2021, the YPAN came together to discuss what topics were most important to them and, as part of this, identify a key area of interest from which a research project could be based. The broad topic ultimately identified was the mental health and well-being of autistic secondary school pupils. The following reflections from four YPAN members highlight how they came to their decision:

> *Over the many meetings the YPAN enjoyed together, we established some of the key issues important to us. Through sharing stories of personal experiences, we learnt that we collectively felt that young autistic people are continuing to struggle in schools, with the support available being limited or insufficient. As we discussed further, we realised an important factor was a lack of research, and thus resources, in this area.*

> *The topic interested me, as I had recently left school so had seen first-hand how schools approach the topic of mental health, but was intrigued to learn more about autistic young people's experience in secondary schools and how this could be improved.*

> *We know from our experience that high school students often don't get asked about things that can really affect us – there have been lots of changes to how autistic young people were supported in my school, which we didn't find out about until afterwards, when it had already happened. No one asked what these changes would feel like for us.*

> *This piece of research is very dear to my heart and, on my part, was inspired by my own secondary school experiences as an undiagnosed autistic young person. Throughout school, I saw myself as an outsider among my peers, and despite how much I tried, I never felt like I truly 'fitted in' anywhere. Autism was taught through a series of social, communicational, and sensory 'deficits' and 'impairments', and autistic students who were clearly struggling and needed support from staff were instead made an example of. As a result of this environment, I had learned that in order to make it through school, I needed to just simply shut up and put my head down. For many years, I had struggled with my mental health and viewed myself as inadequate; it's only been a recent endeavour that I have started to challenge my own internalised ableism and re-conceptualise myself as a normal autistic person and rather than a defunct human.*

Focusing on audience and influence: co-producing a way forward

Building the team

Co-production is an approach to working together aiming for equal partnership and equal benefit (Redman et al., 2021). Whilst true equity in decision-making can be difficult when adults and young people work together, it is important to try to minimise power differences as much as possible and adhere to some key underlying principles and values that foster an environment that enables genuine co-production to take place.

The Co-Productive Collective (2021) outlines four key values at the heart of this approach:

- **Being human.** by valuing the diverse knowledge and experiences brought to the conversation and building relationships that are mutually beneficial based on honesty and trust.
- **Being inclusive.** Working to remove barriers to participation and recognising the strengths of all within the team, supporting development.
- **Being transparent.** Acknowledging the power balances and hierarchies exist and working to address these.

- **Being challenging.** Including a focus on continuous reflection, learning and improvement, and embracing new ideas and ways of working.

Demonstrating commitment to these principles was important to us from the outset, as well as our desire to demonstrate that co-production was more than just a word – it is authentic, genuine, and meaningful.

> *Genuinely involving young people in research means treating us equally, whether someone is 20 years old or 13 years old – their opinion is important and matters.*

> *This was an opportunity I had never seen before for people my age, and I think that's what makes it so special, valuing young people's voices and allowing us to be heard.*

Following the identification of our broad priority area, the PICE manager facilitated a meeting with two adult researchers (with a mix of personal and professional experience around the area) and six YPAN members in a mutually accessible location within the city centre. These meetings consisted of open discussion to (1) share general thoughts and experiences around the topic, (2) consider who may be suitable to include as part of a wider team, and (3) think about some broad but important questions that we ideally wanted our research project to address. Despite our diverse backgrounds, we found that we shared some similar experiences, frustrations, and supports during our own school experience, particularly amongst the autistic members of our group. In line with the principle of *being human*, sharing these thoughts and experiences as equals, where all views were acknowledged without judgement, supported relationship and trust building between group members. Individuals shared what they felt comfortable with and were under no pressure to share at all. This relaxed and informal approach supported the development of our shared understanding of the topic at hand and our cohesion as a team.

Through discussions we identified a strong common thread – that autistic well-being was often linked to experiences within high school, with school staff having (or having had) a significant impact on autistic pupils' feelings, thoughts, and experiences around school. We already knew from speaking to other family, friends, parents/carers, and from previous research in the area (e.g. Brownlow et al., 2021; Sproston et al., 2017; Williams et al., 2019), that our shared experiences were not unique to our small group alone, and how mainstream special educational needs and disabilities (SEND) provision was presented on paper was often not representative of young people's, families', and teachers' experience in 'real life' (The National Autistic Society, 2019). Given the huge barriers to accessing diagnostic assessment and associated support within the North East and North Cumbria (see North East Autism Society, 2023), we were particularly interested in further understanding and exploring this issue within the context of our region and wanted to answer these three broad questions:

- What is already happening within the North East and North Cumbria?
- What helps (or does not help)?
- How can we make things better than they are now?

From these three simple questions we began to build a picture of how we wanted to answer these questions, until we had an outline of what our project might look like, split into three stages, in keeping with the preceding questions. These were:

1. Mapping work and consultations to understand what autism-focused training teachers currently have access to within schools across the region.
2. Peer-led group conversations (called 'focus groups') to explore autistic young people's experiences, particularly in relation to staff–pupil interactions, and the relevance of this for mental health.
3. Stakeholder workshops to prioritise and co-develop recommendations that would be of value to training providers and schools.

To support more detailed development of these work packages, we developed our ideas around who should be involved. Ultimately, our core research team grew to include seven YPAN members, five adult researchers, and one mental health youth support worker from a local community organisation, with diverse backgrounds including autistic and non-autistic adults and young people, those with experience of poor mental health, carers, those with disabilities, those from ethnically marginalised communities, LGBTQ+ groups, and those living within areas of high socio-economic deprivation. We also created a separate steering group to support and help guide our project as 'critical friends'; this group included other young people as well as representatives from research, schools, public health, and the voluntary and community sector.

To maintain our central focus highlighting the views of autistic young people, we wanted to discuss our project with a wider group of autistic young people – to achieve this, we worked with a local children's charity, Children North East (https://children-ne.org.uk/), to organise and run a participatory workshop.

Participatory workshop

Fifteen autistic young people and eight adults (consisting of researchers and youth support workers) came together in a neutral location within the North East. Discussion points addressed the following areas:

- General thoughts about the research area and proposed study (e.g. relevance, other things we need to think about)
- How best to recruit autistic young people as participants
- Preferred ways to share experiences about school
- Safeguarding – how best to support people who might need additional support after taking part
- Important areas to ask about and discuss with participants
- How findings should be shared, and with whom
- What young people would like to see happen as a result of this research

The participatory workshop stood out as a really pivotal point for the development of our research proposal, seeking the input from our wider community of autistic young people. A real learning moment, I felt, was when we moved into the 'adult-free' section of our workshop. We had initially planned to offer an adult-free space for young people to freely discuss the topic themselves. The young people involved on the day did not feel this was necessary and appeared uncomfortable going forwards with it, so we abandoned that part of our workshop. This emphasised the need for us, as adults, to consistently listen and amend our approaches throughout, in line with those who we are working with, rather than rigidly sticking with approaches that reflect assumptions around what young people (as a collective) want. I have found this individualised approach particularly relevant when working alongside neurodivergent young people, who may prefer structure, and an older person they feel connected to, to support them in social situations.

Flexibility in approach has underpinned all our activities from the start and, in part, contributes to our core principles of *being inclusive* and *challenging* existing ways of working. While inclusivity is a difficult concept to define, given its broad and complex nature, we acknowledge that sometimes the simplest amendments, or coming to conversations with an attitude of acceptance, can have a big impact on making young people, and indeed all team members, feel valued, included, and able to participate in a way that works for them.

There has been lots of flexibility to work around everyone's commitments, by allowing us to work together or alone and doing in-person and online meetings – this made it really accessible for me. When developing the funding application, any and all questions were quickly answered, and all the young people and everyone else involved are always happy to help, as I had no experience working on funding applications. Over the many meetings, we have got to know each other and figured out what key issues are important to us, with everyone having different experiences. This made a great team, and we all hope to make a difference in secondary schools for young autistic people.

Sometimes it had been a hard week and I felt like I didn't have the energy to go to a meeting. It's good to know that we aren't judged for it and there are other chances and other ways to share our opinions.

During our participatory workshop, the wider group agreed that the impact of secondary school on autistic pupils' well-being and the role of school staff training were key issues relevant to autistic young people and repeatedly discussed within support groups. Individuals felt there were large differences in training and information both across and within schools. It was felt the main desired outcome for the project was 'more understanding of autism within schools'. However, other outcomes were also deemed important, boosting the confidence of autistic young people to advocate for themselves and to be involved in research and real change.

Whilst it is unlikely to fully reach these outcomes in one project alone, some more specific suggestions for our work were recorded in tabular format, with a column specifically outlining how we intended to take the feedback forwards into the development of our research proposal. This workshop summary was shared with participants, and any other comments welcomed – this was important, in case young people felt unable to share their point of view during the workshop and instead wanted to provide input via email or text. It was also important for us to share information in this way, so those who attended the workshop could see how their input was being taken forward to inform the detail of our research proposal application.

Moving forwards

We received a favourable opinion on our bid for research funding, and the project started in June 2022. Following that time, we have continued to work together to develop our project, iron out and navigate hurdles along the way. For example, as an attempt to *be transparent*, to acknowledge and reduce power differences within our core team, we invited young co-investigators to take part in training to increase knowledge and familiarity with concepts in and around academic research, such as informed consent and other ethical considerations, qualitative data collection, and analysis. Whilst admittedly not always possible, ensuring a greater number of young people than adults in meetings, and welcoming input from young team members first, can also help individuals feel more comfortable in expressing their views. We have also presented and discussed our work so far to researchers, practitioners, and the public, ensuring that the voice and experiences of autistic young people continue to be amplified across a diverse range of audiences as we progress our work together.

> *The work I've been doing in collaboration with the ARC YPAN has empowered me to challenge the notion that autistic people struggle within school settings not simply because they're autistic but rather because there is a lack of structural support for autistic young people. This experience has given me the opportunity to work alongside brilliant and inspiring researchers who have consistently regarded me as an equal. It's a sad reality that many autistic people will resonate with my secondary school experiences, and something must be done about it. With this project, I hope to put more up-to-date, neurodivergent-affirming autism training for educational professionals in place so that autistic young people can have more positive well-being and their struggles do not go overlooked, like mine did.*

> *In the time we've already spent working on this project, I've always felt a real positive connection between the team members. As a young person, this is my first experience working on a piece of research in this capacity, but I've always felt respected and valued by the adults involved in the project. I would hope this research can go on to help young autistic people receive the support they deserve in school, by producing appropriate resources that will be implemented in the North East and beyond.*

Learning for inclusive practice in education

The present chapter has outlined our rights- and principle-based approach to the inclusion of young people within research. Principle-led approaches are likely to be particularly valuable when working alongside groups who benefit from a high level of individualised and tailored support (Milton, 2019) and therefore have clear application to educational and other environments. We focus here on involvement beyond an advisory capacity, where young people have worked alongside adult professionals as partners and their views and experiences are included on an equal footing to others within the team. These power dynamics within co-production can be challenging to navigate (for example, our co-production approach is balanced against an institutional-level requirement for an adult lead to coordinate and take overall responsibility for the project); addressing and modifying existing power dynamics within an authoritative school environment may require an even greater amount of conscious effort and reflection. Nonetheless, educational establishments are well placed to support autistic and other young people in developing their own agency and advocating for themselves in wide-ranging contexts, such as via pupil leadership teams; within personal, social, health, economic (PHSE), and other lessons; in extra-curricular clubs; and/or whilst working with SEND support staff, amongst others.

> *Working on this project made me think about school and how they might be able to learn from how we have done things together – to really include people's thoughts and opinions on what is happening in school. Autistic and other neurodivergent people never get a say – we're told, 'it is what it is'. But changes can have such a big effect on us in comparison to other people – sometimes adults don't even realise that. Include us, ask us what we think, and listen to us like you would listen to other adults.*

Including the voice of pupils when planning a one-off event, or including a showcase of young people's work, or activities, for external visitors, can be a positive experience for all concerned, but there is clear value, and moral obligation, to go beyond this and truly incorporate the experience and perspectives of a diverse range of young people into all areas that impact them. This may relate to areas such as curriculum or policy development, SEND support/provision, recruitment of teaching staff, and so on. Given many pupils may have previous experience of feeling marginalised or not heard, particularly within a school setting (Lundy, 2007), true inclusion of young people's views will take time and may sometimes be uncomfortable, get challenging, and push the boundaries of traditional practice.

However, these conversations, albeit difficult, should be welcomed without consequence, as they are necessary for innovation and positive change to take place.

Moreover, a commitment to demonstrating and feeding back change that has come about as a result of young people's input and may result in improved relationships and trust within the school community (Brownlow et al., 2021). Given autistic young people are more likely to experience school-based distress (Connolly et al., 2023), victimisation and bullying (Rowley et al., 2012), and school exclusion (Paget et al., 2018; Sproston et al., 2017), trust and relationship building within this community are critical. Transparency of limitations in this regard is also key – when working in partnership, it is not always practicable to take forward every suggestion or amend wider rules and policies that exist at higher levels. Providing an explanation of why things cannot be taken forward, or taken forward only partially, in our experience, is often appreciated and understood by partners. It may also shine a light on areas for improvement on a wider scale, where professionals can use their power to push back as much as feasible on traditional approaches and structures that are ultimately having an adverse impact on young people.

As indicated in the preceding passages, the models and frameworks presented (i.e. Hart, 1992; Lundy, 2007; NIHR, 2019) can be drawn upon as a first step in the development of principles and values conducive to amplifying the voices of autistic young people in education. They can be used as tools in both planning and evaluation of meaningful involvement activity that extends beyond tokensim or 'ticking a box'. Deeper still, the principles of co-production outlined earlier (Co-Production Collective, 2021) have clear value for developing genuine partnerships between young people and adults and encourage a more equitable and inclusive approach to including autistic young peoples' perspectives within education policy and practice.

Conclusion

This chapter details the underlying principles and values of our work together, which, at its core, is focused on young person–initiated priorities, addressed through shared decision-making and collaboration across groups. Our approach has enabled us to highlight a key social issue affecting the lives of autistic young people, who previously have been excluded (1) from describing this issue in their own words, but also (2) from contributing to a shared understanding of what is still needed to resolve persistent mental health inequalities within the autistic community. We acknowledge that considering young people as equal partners may constitute a significant shift in perspective for some individuals and within some settings; however, the benefits for individuals, organisations, and the wider community are many. We hope that our approach and activity can serve as a point of good practice and reflection, encouraging genuine and meaningful steps forwards to include young people as partners in priority-setting, decision-making, and beyond.

Reflective questions

1. What are the important aspects to consider when aiming to work in partnership with SEND pupils?
2. How can we make sure young people feel safe and comfortable to share their thoughts and feelings around a given issue?
3. What can be put into place to ensure that collaboration with young people is diverse, is meaningful, and moves away from 'ticking a box'?
4. Which frameworks or guidance can help develop more equitable partnerships within your own setting?

Takeaway activities

- Bring together a group of young people to engage in an open priority-setting session, where they are encouraged to bring up any topics of importance relevant to the context you are working within. Consider feasible methods for collecting data/information about this topic (e.g. who should be asked and how), and plan how you might take these ideas forwards together.
- Work together with young people to develop a visual 'map' of those who should be involved in policy or practice changes within your setting. Using this map, identify accessible formats for engaging with and including all parties' views on a regular basis, including how they will receive clear feedback on the difference their input has made.

Acknowledgements

Special thanks go to our funders, NIHR ARC NENC, and all those involved in the development of our research project, particularly Kai Leighton, Elaf Alasi, Sally Sheridan, Wiki Sienkiewicz, and all the other young people who have given their time and shared their experiences to help shape this project. We would also like to offer our special thanks to our partners, Children North East and also Rhoda Morrow, Steven Takunda, and Andy Purvis, who have provided some much-needed advice, guidance, and support from the early stages of our work.

References

American Psychiatric Association. (2022). *Diagnostic and statistical manual of mental disorders* (5th ed., text rev.). https://doi.org/https://doi.org/10.1176/appi.books.9780890425787

Arnstein, S. R. (1969). A ladder of citizen participation. *Journal of the American Planning Association*, *35*(4), 216–224. https://doi.org/10.1080/01944366908977225

Baumtrog, M. D., & Peach, H. (2019). They can't be believed: Children, intersectionality, and epistemic injustice. *Journal of Global Ethics*, *15*(3), 213–232. https://doi.org/10.1080/17449626.2019.1695280

Botha, M., & Cage, E. (2022). "Autism research is in crisis": A mixed method study of researcher's constructions of autistic people and autism research. *Frontiers in Psychology*, *13*, 1050897. https://doi.org/10.3389/fpsyg.2022.1050897

Brett, J. O., Staniszewska, S., Mockford, C., Herron-Marx, S., Hughes, J., Tysall, C., & Suleman, R. (2014). A systematic review of the impact of patient and public involvement on service users, researchers and communities. *The Patient-Patient-Centered Outcomes Research, 7*, 387–395. https://doi.org/10.1007/s40271-014-0065-0

Brownlow, C., Lawson, W., Pillay, Y., Mahony, J., & Abawi, D. (2021). "Just Ask Me": The importance of respectful relationships within schools. *Frontiers in Psychology, 12*, 2281. https://doi.org/10.3389/FPSYG.2021.678264/BIBTEX

Chapman, R., & Carel, H. (2022). Neurodiversity, epistemic injustice, and the good human life. *Journal of Social Philosophy, 53*(4), 614–631. https://doi.org/10.1111/josp.12456

Co-Production Collective. (2021). *What does co-production mean to us?* https://www.coproductioncollective.co.uk/what-is-co-production/our-approach

Connolly, S. E., Constable, H. L., & Mullally, S. L. (2023). School distress and the school attendance crisis: A story dominated by neurodivergence and unmet need. *Frontiers in Psychiatry, 14*, 1–24. https://doi.org/10.3389/fpsyt.2023.1237052

Dinishak, J. (2021). Autistic autobiography and hermeneutical injustice. *Metaphilosophy, 52*(5), 556–569. https://doi.org/10.1111/meta.12514

Dinishak, J., & Akhtar, N. (2023). Integrating autistic perspectives into autism science: A role for autistic autobiographies. *Autism, 27*(3), 578–587. https://doi.org/10.1177/13623613221123731

Feinstein, A. (2011). *A history of autism: Conversations with the pioneers*. John Wiley & Sons.

Fletcher-Watson, S., Brook, K., Hallett, S., Murray, F., & Crompton, C. J. (2021). Inclusive practices for neurodevelopmental research. *Current Developmental Disorders Reports, 8*(2), 88–97. https://doi.org/10.1007/s40474-021-00227-z

Fricker, M. (2007). *Epistemic injustice: Power and the ethics of knowing*. Oxford University Press.

Greenblatt, A., Lee, E., Ashcroft, R., & Muskat, B. (2024). Epistemic justice and injustice among youth with mental health concerns. *Children and Society, 38*(4), 1–20. https://doi.org/10.1111/chso.12781

Hart, R. A. (1992). *Children's participation: From tokenism to citizenship* (Vol. 4). UNICEF. https://www.unicef-irc.org/publications/100-childrens-participation-from-tokenism-to-citizenship.html

Hart, R. A. (2008). Stepping back from 'the ladder': Reflections on a model of participatory work with children. In *Participation and learning: Perspectives on education and the environment, health and sustainability* (pp. 19–31). Springer Netherlands.

Hartman, D., O'Donnell-Killen, T., Doyle, J., Kavanagh, M., Day, A., & Azevedo, J. (2023). *The adult autism assessment handbook: A neurodiversity affirmative approach*. Jessica Kingsley Publishers.

Jensen, B. B., & Simovska, V. (2005). Involving students in learning and health promotion processes – clarifying why? what? and how? *Promotion & Education, 12*(3–4), 150–156. https://doi.org/10.1177/10253823050120030114

Kapp, S. K. (2019). *Autistic community and the neurodiversity movement: Stories from the frontline*. Springer Nature.

Lever, A. G., & Geurts, H. M. (2016). Psychiatric co-occurring symptoms and disorders in young, middle-aged, and older adults with autism spectrum disorder. *Journal of Autism and Developmental Disorders, 46*(6), 1916–1930. https://doi.org/10.1007/s10803-016-2722-8

Lundy, L. (2007). "Voice" is not enough: Conceptualising Article 12 of the United Nations Convention on the Rights of the Child. *British Educational Research Journal, 33*(6), 927–942. https://doi.org/10.1080/01411920701657033

Mannion, G. (2003). Children's participation in school grounds developments: Creating a place for education that promotes children's social inclusion. *International Journal of Inclusive Education, 7*(2), 175–192. https://doi.org/10.1080/13603110304784

May, T., Brignell, A., Hawi, Z., Brereton, A., Tonge, B., Bellgrove, M. A., & Rinehart, N. J. (2018). Trends in the overlap of autism spectrum disorder and attention deficit hyperactivity disorder: Prevalence, clinical management, language and genetics. *Current Developmental Disorders Reports, 5*(1), 49–57. https://doi.org/10.1007/s40474-018-0131-8

Miller, H. L., Sherrod, G. M., Mauk, J. E., Fears, N. E., Hynan, L. S., & Tamplain, P. M. (2021). Shared features or co-occurrence? Evaluating symptoms of developmental coordination disorder in children and adolescents with autism spectrum disorder. *Journal of Autism and Developmental Disorders, 51*(10), 3443–3455. https://doi.org/10.1007/s10803-020-04766-z

Milton, D. E. (2014). Autistic expertise: A critical reflection on the production of knowledge in autism studies. *Autism, 18*(7), 794–802.

Milton, D. E. M. (2019). *Beyond tokenism: Autistic people in autism research*. The Psychologist.

Milton, D. E. M., & Bracher, M. (2013). Autistics speak but are they heard? *Medical Sociology Online, 7*(2), 61–69.

NIHR. (2019). *UK standards for public involvement*. https://drive.google.com/file/d/1U-IJNJCfFepaAOruEhzz1TdLvAcHTt2Q/view

NIHR ARC NENC. (2023). *About the NIHR Applied Research Collaboration (ARC) North East and North Cumbria (NENC) – plain language summary*. https://arc-nenc.nihr.ac.uk/resources/about-the-nihr-arc-north-east-and-north-cumbria-plain-language-summary/

NIHR Centre for Engagement and Dissemination. (2021). *Briefing notes for researchers – public involvement in NHS, health and social care research*. https://www.nihr.ac.uk/documents/briefing-notes-for-researchers-public-involvement-in-nhs-health-and-social-care-research/27371

North East Autism Society. (2023). *How do waiting lists look in your area?* https://www.ne-as.org.uk/how-do-waiting-lists-look-in-your-area

O'Halloran, L., Coey, P., & Wilson, C. (2022). Suicidality in autistic youth: A systematic review and meta-analysis. *Clinical Psychology Review*, *93*, 102144. https://doi.org/10.1016/J.CPR.2022.102144

Onaiwu, M. G. (2020). "They Don't Know, Don't Show, or Don't Care": Autism's White privilege problem. *Autism Adulthood*, *2*(4), 270–272. https://doi.org/10.1089/AUT.2020.0077

Paget, A., Parker, C., Heron, J., Logan, S., Henley, W., Emond, A., & Ford, T. (2018). Which children and young people are excluded from school? Findings from a large British birth cohort study, the Avon Longitudinal Study of Parents and Children (ALSPAC). *Child: Care, Health and Development*, *44*(2), 285–296. https://doi.org/10.1111/cch.12525

Redman, S., Greenhalgh, T., Adedokun, L., Staniszewska, S., & Denegri, S. (2021). Co-production of knowledge: The future. *The BMJ*, *372*. https://doi.org/10.1136/bmj.n434

Rowley, E., Chandler, S., Baird, G., Simonoff, E., Pickles, A., Loucas, T., & Charman, T. (2012). The experience of friendship, victimization and bullying in children with an autism spectrum disorder: Associations with child characteristics and school placement. *Research in Autism Spectrum Disorders*, *6*(3), 1126–1134. https://doi.org/10.1016/j.rasd.2012.03.004

Sproston, K., Sedgewick, F., & Crane, L. (2017). Autistic girls and school exclusion: Perspectives of students and their parents. *Autism & Developmental Language Impairments*, *2*, 239694151770617. https://doi.org/10.1177/2396941517706172

The National Autistic Society. (2019). *The autism act, 10 years on*. All Party Parliamentary Group on Autism (APPGA).

UN. (1989). *Convention on the rights of the child*. https://www2.ohchr.org/english/law/pdf/crc.pdf

Williams, E. I., Gleeson, K., & Jones, B. E. (2019). How pupils on the autism spectrum make sense of themselves in the context of their experiences in a mainstream school setting: A qualitative metasynthesis. *Autism*, *23*(1), 8–28. https://doi.org/10.1177/1362361317723836

9 The inclusive design of a digital education programme – contribution and experiences of people with accessibility needs

Esther Murphy, Daniela Bratković, and Alisa Vivoda

> **Key words**
>
> Digital education, Accessibility, Inclusive design, Co-creation strategies

Introduction

Nowadays, full inclusion in society may also be equated with presence and participation in the digital world. Despite the sharp increase in the use of digital technologies and the expansion of the opportunities they offer, people with intellectual disabilities (ID) are still more likely to be excluded from the digital world than people without disabilities (Chadwick et al., 2022), which is confirmed by statements from people with ID themselves (Johansson, Gulliksen and Gustavsson, 2021). Research shows that digital exclusion leads to social exclusion and can consequently have a negative impact on well-being and quality of life in general (Chadwick, 2022; Murphy, 2021; Lake et al., 2021). People with intellectual disabilities highlight that using digital technology enables them to stay in contact with other people and to participate in various entertainment activities (Fabris, Bratković and Žic Ralić, 2023). Digital literacy also improves a person's employability (Lyons et al., 2019). Low digital skills, a lack of accessible devices and programmes, poor internet connections (Chadwick et al., 2022), poor financial opportunities, and a lack of adequate education are just some of the reasons for the digital exclusion of people with ID (Heitplatz, 2020). Rapid technological development requires fast learning and upgrading of digital skills (Asmar, Van Audenhove, and Marien, 2020), which is a major challenge for people with accessibility needs, especially those with ID.

When it comes to promoting digital literacy, a challenge is that existing educational opportunities for the general population are not accessible to people with ID. Due to their limited formal education, service providers are required to organise informal computer workshops, but in addition to training people with a disability, digital skills education for supporters is also needed (Heitplatz, 2020). Article 24 of the UN Convention on the Rights of Persons with Disabilities clearly states that all persons with disabilities have the right to education without discrimination and on an equal basis with others, including general higher education, vocational training, adult education, and lifelong learning (UN, 2006). Over the past three decades, great progress has been made in the field of inclusive education (Florian, 2019), but the focus has tended to be on children, while the education of adults with disabilities has generally been neglected. Significant digital skills inequity at national levels exists, ranging from inspiring examples of transition and post-secondary education programmes for adults in some countries (Björnsdóttir, 2017; Love, Baker and Devine, 2019) to the non-existence of such programmes in others.

A major challenge in achieving digital inclusion is accessing appropriate and accessible education that meets the needs and interests of people with intellectual and other developmental disabilities. Heitplatz (2020) suggests that the reason for this is that people with ID are often ignored or not asked for their opinions and wishes, as society often perceives them as vulnerable and incompetent. This is not only the case in the creation of digital literacy education but also in the development and evaluation of other support programmes and interventions (Sheehan and Hassiotis, 2017). However, the situation in this area is improving, and the need for the active participation of people with disabilities is increasingly recognised. A great example of people with intellectual disabilities taking an active role in co-creating online activities is described by Spassiani et al. (2022). During the Covid-19 pandemic, when users could not meet in person at the organisation, they had the opportunity to contribute their ideas and help in organising online events, such as quizzes, workshops, dance classes, etc., and designing online content for others.

Recently, especially after the Covid-19 pandemic, there have been many studies on the topic of digital technology and people with ID (Caton et al., 2022; Chadwick et al., 2022; McCausland et al., 2021). However, this topic should not only remain at the level of academic society and research, but concrete policies and initiatives also need to be developed that will actively work towards the realisation of digital inclusion at local, national, and international levels (Reisdorf and Rhinesmith, 2020). This requires the collaboration of different stakeholders, public administrations, service providers, users, their families, and all other people who support them.

Access to digital or online information and services on an equal basis to others and ensuring accessibility of information and communication technology (ICT) at minimal cost are prescribed in Article 9 and Article 21 of the UN Convention on the Rights of Persons with Disabilities (2006). Many other international and national legal documents that regulate the right to inclusion of people with disabilities, including digital inclusion, have also been adopted, but unfortunately, even many years after their adoption, implementation issues persist.

The context just described served as the basis for designing the innovative EU project Digi-ID, which aims to contribute to the digital literacy of people with ID and their right to self-determined access and use of digital technologies. Digi-ID PLUS is an EIT Health–funded interdisciplinary, user-centred innovation project led by Dr Esther Murphy from Trinity College Dublin in Ireland that joins with partners from Sweden, France, and Croatia, including the Faculty of Education and Rehabilitation Sciences, University of Zagreb, Croatia. Guided by the principles of inclusive participation and the human rights approach, the project encourages digital inclusion of people with accessibility needs, simultaneously providing them with lifelong learning and promoting inclusive employment opportunities. The project has received full ethical approval from research ethics committees in both countries, and in Ireland, an additional ethical process with collaborating disability services.

Methodology

Establishing Citizen Advisory Panel (CAP)

In this section, we present the inclusive programme design adopted via establishing our Citizen Advisory Panel. While the participation of people with ID in research is limited (Cook and Inglis, 2012), the positive impact of involvement is recognised (Conroy et al., 2021). The objective of the CAP model was to address not only the limited research participation opportunities due to the identified barrier of complexity of informed consent for this community (Doody, 2018) but also the critical issue of high unemployment, by creating inclusive employment roles within the programme.

We outline the establishment of the Citizen Advisory Panel (CAP) in Ireland, their role in our co-creation and co-design process, and the process of replicating the model and education content in other countries, such as Croatia, who have developed their own CAP and e-learning content, overseen by Digi-ID colleagues from the University of Zagreb in Croatia.

In Ireland, for our preliminary engagement in establishing the CAP, we consulted with a national umbrella advocacy organisation and collaborating services to support the inclusive recruitment process. In consultation with collaborating disability services, we conducted accessible information sessions with the individuals and supporter(s) to discuss and clarify their job roles and responsibilities, code of conduct, and payment matters. An accessible information guide about the nature and scope of the role was developed, shared, and discussed with all individuals and supporters.

Accessible email communications were developed to engage with the CAP to schedule meetings, share project work for review, and create an interactive space and rapport amongst members to share views and update the group on community and advocacy activities and news. Each member was asked whether they would like to include a support person, if they wished to, in our project communication emails and meeting attendance. All members were encouraged to participate actively in each meeting, with turn-taking guidelines in place to ensure each member had opportunity to voice views, experiences, and ideas. One-to-one meetings were also scheduled with individual members to carry out a specific piece of project work and, if necessary, to provide tailored support or any task clarification needs (Murphy et al., 2022).

Some CAP members have represented the project at national, EU, and international conferences, where they voiced their views on digital inclusion and have explained their role in the co-design and co-creation processes of our education programme.

The study has received full ethical approval from Trinity College Dublin's Faculty of Health Sciences Ethics Committee and from all the collaborating disability services ethics committees, and following the translation of the project's accessible materials, the same process has been replicated in all EU partner countries in respective languages and similar engagement with their collaborating services. One of the partnering countries that have been replicating the model is Croatia.

Citizen co-design and co-creation

Online learning is not a new concept, with several excellent offerings available, such as Udemy and Coursera, amongst others. However, these platforms currently do not have the ability to meet the goals of DigiAcademy. In the following section we will present some of the key differentiators of our solution.

The platform and its content have been specifically co-created and co-designed to meet the learning outcomes. No video-based e-learning platform on the market currently offers an accessible, personalised learning experience for people with low levels of digital skills. The platform allows the user to tailor their learning path to their needs, with the help of a supporter (social worker, caregiver), and utilises artificial intelligence (AI) to identify the best learning strategies for each user based on their profile and learning behaviour. The course content is presented by people with ID, who both act as ideal tutors as well as motivational peer role models.

Co-creating our accessible education programme

The first co-creation phase was content development and platform design. This phase involved focus groups and consultations for platform development, along with the co-creation of education content and technology development. Focus groups with people with ID were conducted to explore digital access, use, and inclusion experiences to gather data for content co-creation of the educational programme. Groups of approximately six to eight individuals were facilitated online and in person once social restrictions lifted. Focus group topic guides were designed and reviewed with our CAP. They included open-ended questions about, for example, (1) health, well-being, and social inclusion needs; (2) how technology is currently used to support; and (3) what helps/hinders the use of technology. Focus group participants also engaged in discussions about digital skills education topics, how they like to engage with education (e.g. content format, assessment), and reviewed design work with us. Questions were tried out with CAP in advance of the focus groups as a means of testing accessibility, making some accessible language adjustments to ensure eliciting the most authentic responses from research participants.

Recent design sessions have focused on our platform's registration process. Sessions have covered, for example, the use of QR codes, passwords, usernames, and biometrics.

A sample session question included: 'Tell us about how you find logging in with a username and password.' Or 'This is a picture of a QR code. Tell us, have you seen or used QR code before?' Our open-ended question approach is coupled with a showcase of examples and visuals relating to each topic. This approach is designed also as a learning process to raise awareness and increase digital literacy of everyday digital tasks.

Co-design

The second phase was the citizen review and testing. This phase has engaged a group of people with ID, who were not engaged with the requirement-gathering focus groups, to be programme testers. This group has engaged in prototype testing and evaluation to refine and quality-assure programme content and platform design elements. User testing was focused on asking about the user's experience accessing and using the accessible digital skills education programme. A one-to-one user testing interview will follow best practice guidelines on solution design accessibility (Chadwick et al., 2022; Murphy et al., 2019) and in accordance with Web Content Accessibility

Guidelines (WCAG) 2.1. We ran 15 rounds of user testing, both online and in person, to include the user testing feedback in shaping various iterations of the prototype, making modifications and adjustments to ensure the final prototype incorporates all user testing feedback. User testing sessions have entailed observation of the tester using the programme by the researchers (i.e., exploring the site, experience of user interface, navigating through the education programme) and eliciting feedback from the user using a semi-structured format guided by the interview schedule.

The current format is a two-hour focus group once a month, with stretched breaks incorporated. The testing has been delivered online, and we show a run-through of the accessible assessment prototype to users. We have also successfully shared the prototype link with users, who then can independently try it out and give feedback during our online discussion, or later via email or WhatsApp voice note, and to share photos. Questions that are asked are specific when it comes to the design elements. 'Is this clear?' 'Which one do you like most? Design A, B, C?' We present visuals relating to any new topics or features, which doubles as a literacy learning process to upskill on technical language and activities.

Meaning, value, and impact

Meaningful work and payment

DigiAcademy is committed to developing meaningful employment opportunities and equitable pay for individuals with ID and autism. Within the Irish context, the 2017 Census reported that there is a pay discrepancy between people living with a disability and their non-disabled peers; those with a disability earn 21.3% less, while for people with an ID, only 15% of working age were employed (Irish Central Statistics Office, 2017; National Disability Authority of Ireland, 2019).

Communication and connection

We have identified positive impact for individuals who have accessible information about digital skills which enables them to use digital resources which consequently equips them to communicate their views and experiences more effectively. This development fosters deeper connections with those around them and enhances their ability to connect with new digital environments, participation in new tasks, and potential for new learning. Technology bridges gaps in social interactions and provides the tools and skills for people to engage more fully with family, peers, and the world around them.

Confidence

As an individual acquires digital skills, they are exposed to a new sense of autonomy and the potential to improve their quality of life themselves. The learners and teachers experience a sense of accomplishment and self-assurance, which ultimately instils ambition and growth of mindset. The digital educators expanded their own knowledge and confidence during their work with the team, enabling them to showcase their own digital experiences to support their peers' digital engagement. They said:

> 'I loved the experience and really felt empowered and respected as the teacher.'

> 'I had great fun. . . . Before, I couldn't use email. Now I can't believe I am the teacher for others to learn.'

> 'I really enjoyed working together to produce the tutorials. I love knowing my videos can help others get started and be more independent.'

Insights from individuals' supporters also revealed growth in confidence turning into a ripple effect amongst peers. As noted by a speech and language therapist echoing the sentiment expressed by all supporters in our CAP: 'He has grown in confidence, and his communication has developed alongside his digital abilities. He speaks to his peers about the experience and helps them with getting started using their technology, showing them accessibility features.'

Support

Finally, the role of support is essential, especially that of family members, support workers, health professionals, teachers, and peers, as they can help ensure that the journey into the digital space is both positive and empowering. Our participants have shown that the presence of a person who provides caring and knowledgeable guidance and encouragement is crucial to the process of learning and growth. This support enhances the learning process while simultaneously providing a safety net for the individual.

Irish impact stories

Mei Lin

Mei Lin was one of the first teachers and CAP members on the DigiAcademy programme, which she does in addition to working in a recruitment company part-time. Mei Lin is a strong communicator who began her journey with a passion for technology and being in front of the camera. She enjoys using social media and wanted to support others who were nervous and wanted to learn how to use it safely. A young woman with Down syndrome who attended one of our workshops where we showcased Mei Lin's teaching remarked:

> 'Mei Lin is really amazing. She seems like an actress and having great fun! She is inspiring. I love drama, and I would like to have a job like Mei Lin.'

This young woman later also trained with us to work as a DigiAcademy teacher, teaching about how to use Microsoft Teams.

Cormac

Cormac is a DigiAcademy teacher whose course focuses on the accessibility functions of iPads and smartphones. Since starting with DigiAcademy, while attending a disability day service, Cormac has now progressed to further education and remains part of the Citizen Advisory Panel team. He is keen to bring other people on the same learning journey as himself. He contacted his new college course director to ask for some time in his week to take part in his Citizen Advisory Panel meetings.

Darren

At the outset, Darren found it difficult to actively engage in our first two meetings; he was also relying heavily on his speech and language therapist to express his views and communicate with the group. One of the main issues he expressed at the start was the social exclusion of living in a rural location and the positive impact that technology had had upon this experience:

> 'Living in a rural location makes it hard to have a social life. The only time I can talk to anyone is on WhatsApp or Messenger.'

During the CAP meetings, intentionally designed as a fun, creative environment to enable social interaction and exchange of learning, Darren became more and more confident, active, and participatory, communicating mostly independently from his therapist. He spoke with great self-awareness and recognition of the progress he had been making and was now encouraging other peers to participate more fully too:

> 'In the first meeting, I was nervous to get out to this group. What helped me was, just give it a go and get used to talk to the group, and confidence will come up and see how you will enjoy it!'

After five CAP meetings, he was also inspired by his peers in the group to share digital skills knowledge with our community; therefore, the team supported him in recording a short video, where he explained to our community how to use the screen reader on the phone and where he offered his support to all the people who would like to know more:

> 'I have learnt a lot from my peers in the group, and it was great to help them on how to use the screen reader.'

When asked about his overall experience being a CAP team member, he expressed positive emotions, emphasising the confidence he had developed owing to the CAP meetings:

> 'I was happy that I was put up to it, here with the meeting with all ye, and see how the whole programme is going. Thanks to give me the confidence to do this.'

James

When James first joined our team, he could not use email. He did not have an account. He relied on his support worker to share his email to ensure James received our online meeting invite. James, a quiet young man with an ID, had previously relied extensively on his supporter, but after three months on our team, he stopped a meeting to ask who had received the meeting invite, and through this he learnt that he needed email. This sparked James to begin the process, and through engagement with a one-to-one session to support him, he developed a deep interest in learning all the ways that email could support his independence. This led naturally to James's training with us as our Gmail and WhatsApp teacher. Since James became a DigiAcademy teacher, his own service also now uses DigiAcademy on a weekly basis, and the benefits of this have been noted for both learners and staff by the centre manager:

> 'We have seen over 30 people who didn't have or use regularly set up email, thanks to James's video tutorials and his encouragement.'

Another young man with intellectual disability also felt inspired by our digital educator James and reported:

> 'It is so inspiring how James has learnt how to use Gmail, and now he is teaching other people doing the same. I love technology, and I learnt a lot of digital skills. I would love to become a digital educator as well.'

James's key worker emphasised how James is now feeling part of the team and learning new digital skills and the ripple effect of inspiring his peers in his own ID service, stating that he 'has been inspired as well' and he is 'sharing this project and [his] experiences with [his] peers'.

James has also presented his work at his service national conference to over 300 attendees and participated alongside the DigiAcademy founder in a national news interview about digital inclusion (see Figure 9.1).

Croatian experience

Position of people with disabilities in Croatia

Although Croatia was one of the first countries to sign and ratify the UN Convention on the Rights of Persons with Disabilities in 2007, there are still many rights that need to be better implemented. A research project conducted in 2023 shows that national policies and regulations

Figure 9.1 James presenting his work.

are mainly in line with the Convention, but that mechanisms for more effective implementation of social policies and the realisation of rights guaranteed by law still need to be put in place (Sikirić et al., 2023). People with disabilities in Croatia are users of the social welfare system and face serious barriers to employment, independent living, and becoming active members of the community (Bratković, Lisak Šegota, and Alimović, 2023), especially when it comes to people with ID (Bratković, Mihanović, and Lisak, 2018).

Regarding the use of digital technologies, Žajdela Hrustek, Šimić, and Čižmar (2022) found that most people with disabilities in Croatia use mobile phones and the internet, but there are still many of them who only participate in a limited number of digital activities and need additional education. In another study conducted with people with ID, Masnjak Šušković et al. (2023) confirmed that there is much space to improve their digital skills and support them to become more independent in their use of technology.

Joining Digi-ID PLUS

Due to the need for accessible education in the field of digital skills which meets the needs and interests of Croatian citizens with ID, a Croatian team from the Faculty of Education and Rehabilitation Sciences, University of Zagreb, joined the Digi-ID PLUS project in 2022. Although the main goal of the project is to contribute to digital inclusion, we also see it as a great opportunity to encourage people with accessibility needs to take an active role in the creation of educational programmes, receive payment for their work, and improve other aspects of social inclusion.

The model developed in Ireland was transferred to Croatia, with adaptations needed due to the different socio-economic and cultural circumstances. In the summer of 2022, we began the search for members of the Croatian Citizen Advisory Panel through our national partner organisations, that is, service providers for people with ID. It was important that participants had experience in using digital technologies, but also that they were interested in the topic. Six people became members of our Citizen Advisory Panel, each as a representative of one partner organisation.

As a first joint activity, we organised an in-person meeting, with the aim of getting to know each other, presenting the project in detail to our panellists and answering all their potential questions. Information booklets in an easy-to-read format were prepared, with associated pictures as visual support. It was very important to make sure that potential participants were informed about all the activities and their role before giving voluntary consent to participate in the project.

Following the Irish model, we now have meetings approximately once a month, sometimes online, sometimes in person, in a group or individually, with each of the panellists. Our meetings usually consist of discussing current project activities, testing DigiAcademy, watching and commenting on video courses, and agreeing on further tasks. During the meeting, there is always enough time for informal conversations, sharing news, and just getting to know each other. We find this part especially important to get closer to each other and strengthen team cohesion; indeed, it has been shown that building social bonds and good relationships is a key element of working with people with ID (Scott and Havercamp, 2018).

When testing DigiAcademy, panellists are asked many simple and concrete, open-ended questions, which we find is the best way to explore their thoughts and suggestions for improving the platform and giving them freedom to apply different ideas. However, since some of them find it difficult to produce their own suggestions, we find it useful to prepare some options for them to choose from if they wish. For example, we can start by asking an open question: 'Which page colour do you like?' But if the person cannot answer, we need to find another way to explore their opinion. For people with higher support needs, we can offer some options so they can make a choice. For example: 'Do you prefer a page which is more orange, purple, or green in colour?' The most important thing when involving people with ID in the development of such a programme is to find an appropriate level and type of support, and this applies to both adults and children. Active support and supported decision-making are two concepts which need to be implemented to ensure that every person with ID can choose, vote, and thus make their suggestion (Devi, 2013).

In addition to evaluation of the educational platform and video courses, we try to evaluate our own work as often as possible. We encourage our CAP members to tell us how satisfied they are with their role in the project, to express ideas for new activities, and to tell us how we can improve our work. Such discussions help us determine the further course of the project and to divide the tasks so that they correspond to the interests and preferences of the panellists.

We think it is important that panellists talk about their work themselves so they are included in dissemination activities too, such as national and international conferences and other public events.

From the perspective of the Croatian CAP

In this paragraph, we would like to present the panellists' personal views on being part of the project team throughout the process so far. The most common reason given for joining the project is the desire to learn more about digital technologies. One panellist felt very honoured to be invited to join the project team:

> 'I was speechless that I as a user would be a representative, the only user from my centre, that it would be me.'

At our first meeting, almost all panellists were excited, nervous, and some of them were even a little scared because of the new people and not knowing what to expect. Now that they all know each other and have taken part in a lot of activities together, they are all happy to be part of the team. Here are some of their statements:

> 'I met new people, colleagues – this is now like meeting friends.'

> 'It's great! Because I can learn all about internet, Facebook, Zoom . . .'

> 'It is very interesting, and I'm satisfied. I can learn new things.'

When it comes to their favourite activity so far, they have different preferences:

> 'I liked the time when we were learning on PCs, in the faculty, when we wrote our names on DigiAcademy and registered with e-mail.'

> 'Well, I liked the best when we were on PCs. I don't have any reason, just it was great, very interesting.'

'I like the most when we were on television and when I was recording video courses. That was somehow the best.'

'I liked the recording so much, when I was talking about WhatsApp, what it is for and how it is used.'

Being a DigiAcademy teacher, the role of teaching others is an aspect they are very proud of and one of their favourite parts of the job.

We use different working methods: group meetings, individual online conversations, working in pairs, etc. One panellist prefers to work individually/in pairs rather than in a group:

'When you were with me in the Association, well, that was good, you and I, when we worked alone, you remember? It's good when you work together. When there are more of us, it's a little more difficult for me, it's a little harder to understand. It's better when you work in pairs.'

There were activities which some panellists did not like very much. A panellist said:

'You know what, I like the least when we have meetings on our phone. It's better in person. I think we should have more meetings in person next year.'

Although online meetings can have many disadvantages, such as connection issues and interrupting others, we have found that there are also advantages for some panellists, as they are more open and conversational online than in a face-to-face meeting. Some previous research agrees that people with ID are more open and feel safer to talk in the online environment (Spassiani et al., 2022). It is important to include panellists in tasks which they are comfortable with. For example, one panellist stated:

'It's nice when we meet in the faculty, but when I go to the conference, when I have to perform, I'm shy. To me it's a little bit . . . you know . . .'

So when we were preparing a joint speech for the international conference, the panellist was not forced to speak in front of others, but instead he helped prepare the presentation and, in this way, made a contribution.

Being part of the team is a new aspect in the lives of these six people:

'It is unusual to me. I've never been going to meetings before. But I like it.'

They feel proud and respected by other team members. Moreover, they feel important because they are teachers of others and emphasise the significance of peer support:

'If I know how to use some apps that others don't, I can teach them. . . . It's nice to help others.' (P3)

'[S]o we can teach others and explain them. As we are doing now, it's actually very important. Like we are professors, we are in the team.' (P4)

'I feel important when I go to conferences.' (P6)

Over time, we have noticed that the panellists are more communicative, talk spontaneously, and ask questions. They also give more feedback, share opinions and ideas. Some of their wishes and suggestions for improving the project are:

'Maybe that we include more people . . . and that we hang out more in person, communicate, and talk more about smartphones and this stuff.'

'I'd like to film a short video . . . about us and what we do in the project.'

A particularly important aspect of the project is being paid for their work, as the following quote proves:

'Look, it was the first salary I have ever received. . . . But the project will also end. . . . All good things come to an end.'

This statement underlines a problem that worries all CAP members – what happens when the project ends? Unfortunately, it is a frequent problem in Croatia that while there are great projects, there is a lack of sustainable systematic solutions. Therefore, we should encourage service providers to give people with ID the opportunity to actively participate in the creation of educational and other support programmes and their evaluation. The inclusive approach used in this project should not just be an example of a good practice but a common practice. Involving people with disabilities, as target users and experts by experience, in the co-creation of educational and other support programmes intended for them is beneficial in several ways. Apart from the fact that they know best and can tell us how to make programmes accessible, useful, and adapted to their needs and interests (Sanders and Stappers, 2008), inclusive participation also has a positive impact on the persons themselves by improving self-confidence, sense of usefulness, self-determination, self-advocacy skills, and overall well-being, which is confirmed in this project.

Tomislav's story

When Tomislav joined the project in September 2022, he was able to use the smartphone for various purposes: communicating with others, searching for information on the internet, using social media, etc. He had no experience of using a laptop or PC. Recalling the days when he joined our team, Tomislav says he was pleased and honoured to be invited as the only person and representative of his centre. His main reason for joining the project was to learn something new about digital technology. At our first meetings, Tomislav seemed shy and was not very talkative. He answered only briefly and sometimes even seemed as if he was not very interested. He confirms that he was a little nervous and excited at the first meetings and had stage fright. Shortly after joining the project, he expressed a desire to learn how to use Zoom, which he had never used before. With the support of his assistant, Tomislav installed Zoom on his smartphone and joined our online project meeting. Now he is one of the DigiAcademy teachers creating video courses on how to use Zoom for the Croatian population. His great work in the project was recognised in his local community, so a local TV station invited him for an interview to present his work and the project activities he is involved in. The interview was broadcast on a television programme about inspiring people with disabilities who break down prejudices.

Over time, Tomislav has become more communicative and committed. At the meetings, he answers questions more often, shares his thoughts about DigiAcademy, and makes suggestions for improving the project. He spontaneously talks to other members of the Citizen Advisory Panel about various topics, even those not connected to the project. He looks forward to our project meetings and suggests that we should work together more often. He himself recognises that he was ashamed at first, whereas now he is more open and talkative. Now Tomislav can join a Zoom meeting independently and is still learning about the different Zoom options. He is happy that he has met new people and made friends through the project. He is proud to be part of the team and is looking forward to teaching his peers about Zoom with the support of DigiAcademy and his own video courses.

To conclude the paragraph, we reproduce a quote from Tomislav:

> 'I will continue to work on the project and do my best . . . [a]nd I won't give up on this project, that's 101%.'

This paragraph is based on the observations of the project team members and Tomislav's own insights. We would like to thank Tomislav Pauli for sharing his story with us.

Conclusion

In conclusion, Digi-ID PLUS stands as a pioneering initiative in the realm of digital inclusion for individuals with ID across Europe, Croatia included. Collaborative endeavours have culminated in the development of DigiAcademy, a digital education platform co-created with insights from over 500 individuals with ID and their advocates. Crucial to the project's success are the Citizen

Advisory Panels (CAPs), composed of individuals with ID who provide invaluable perspectives throughout the co-creation process. The replication of CAPs across EU partner countries underscores the project's commitment to fostering inclusivity and diversity. Despite strides made in inclusive education, particularly for children, adults with disabilities face significant digital literacy barriers, limited access to accessible technologies, and societal marginalisation. The Covid-19 pandemic has further accentuated the urgency of addressing digital inclusion, prompting increased research scrutiny and calls for tangible policies and initiatives.

Efforts to promote digital inclusion must involve collaborative engagement among diverse stakeholders, including public administrations, service providers, individuals with disabilities, their families, and advocates. Compliance with international legal frameworks, such as the UN Convention on the Rights of Persons with Disabilities, advocating for equitable access to digital resources is paramount. Nonetheless, persistent implementation challenges necessitate ongoing efforts to surmount obstacles and ensure meaningful digital inclusion for individuals with ID.

Furthermore, the methodology employed in establishing CAPs within the Digi-ID PLUS project embodies a drive to foster meaningful participation and representation of individuals with ID throughout the research process. This inclusive model not only addresses barriers to research participation but also creates opportunities for inclusive employment roles, thereby contributing to broader societal inclusion efforts. The work and research conducted within the Digi-ID PLUS project have yielded insightful findings. DigiAcademy has not only improved employment opportunities but also bolstered the confidence levels and communication skills of individuals with ID. Moreover, it has underscored the essential role of support in facilitating learning and growth. In this context, support encompasses various stakeholders, including family members, support workers, health professionals, teachers, and peers. The presence of caring and knowledgeable guidance and encouragement is crucial to the process of learning and development.

The integration of the Digi-ID PLUS project in Croatia represents a significant stride in addressing the digital inclusion needs of individuals with ID. Collaborating with the University of Zagreb, the project aims to empower individuals with ID through education and active participation in programme creation. Adaptations to the Irish model were made to suit Croatian contexts, facilitating the recruitment of members for the Croatian Citizen Advisory Panel (CAP) and ensuring an inclusive environment. The project emphasises individualised support, decision-making, and ongoing evaluation, with panellists' perspectives highlighting the transformative impact on their lives. Our impact stories exemplify the project's commitment to empowerment and inclusivity.

To ensure sustainability and continued use of DigiAcademy, in Ireland the programme is now being set up as a profit-for-purpose company to continue employment opportunities for people with ID and is partnering with disability and education providers and employers to pilot the programme with more widely running, accessible in-person and online orientation and onboarding.

Should you wish to learn more about the project and explore opportunities to participate in new partnerships to pilot our English-language version via our accessible e-learning platform DigiAcademy, you can reach the team via email: esther@digi-academy.org

If you would like to watch short snippets of our teachers in action and listen to their views of working in our team: https://tinyurl.com/3jds7ax2.

Acknowledgements

We would like to thank all our collaborating services in Ireland and Croatia and extend our sincere gratitude to all involved in supporting our programme. Most especially, we wish to express heartfelt thanks to all members of our Citizen Advisory Panel for their invaluable work with us and commitment to advocating for digital access and inclusion for our community of people with ID. They are, in Ireland, Amy Fulcher, Brian Hogan, Christina Burke, Cormac Hanley, Darren Heduan, Denise Breslin, Fionn Crombie Aongus, Ifiok Umo, James Delaney, Joe McNamara, Lia Gogarty, Linda Byrne Duffy, Mei Lin Yap, and Sarah Boyne. And in Croatia, they are Nika Balija, Nikola Cikojević, Maja Keršanc, Tomislav Pauli, Enes Redžic, and Jan Tomislav Vrbić. Well done to you all for your dedicated work and highly valuable contribution to the project – your work has inspired this chapter, and we hope to encourage many more to learn new skills to lead the digital lives of their choice too.

Reflective questions

1. From your experience and perspective, what challenges do people with accessibility needs face in using digital technology for social inclusion?
2. What is your experience with the co-creation process in digital or other educational settings with young or adult people, students, or people who use disability services?
3. Why is it important that people themselves are involved as experiential experts in such inclusive education practice and research?

Takeaway activities

- Ask the young people or adults with accessibility needs to share their knowledge, interests, and experiences with using digital technology in peer-support and wider inclusive environment.
- Think about digital skills that would be useful to the people you are working with, and investigate what they would like to learn about. Encourage individuals who know how to use digital technology to teach others in the group; enable time and settings for peer teaching activities.
- Try to create an inclusive co-design process with innovative accessible digital tools or materials described in the chapter that will improve digital skills and active participation. Think about other tools, methods, and strategies that can be used in digital education and inclusion.

References

Asmar, A., Van Audenhove, L. and Marien, I. (2020) Social support for digital inclusion: Towards a typology of social support patterns, *Social Inclusion*, 8(2), pp. 138–150. https://doi.org/10.17645/si.v8i2.2627

Björnsdóttir, K. (2017) Belonging to higher education: Inclusive education for students with intellectual disabilities, *European Journal of Special Needs Education*, 32(1), pp. 125–136.

Bratković, D., Lisak Šegota, N. and Alimović, S. (2023) Izazovi neovisnog življenja iz perspektiva osoba s invaliditetom, roditelja i stručnjaka [Challenges of independent living from the perspective of people with disabilities, their parents and professionals], in: D. Miholić and M. Mirić (eds.) *Mapiranje sastavnica neovisnog življenja, Prikaz rezultata istraživanja iz projekta Platforma 50+ [Mapping the components of independent living, Presentation of research results from the project Platform 50+]*. Zagreb: Edukacijsko-rehabilitacijski fakultet Sveučilišta u Zagrebu., pp. 33–102.

Bratković, D., Mihanović, V. and Lisak, N. (2018) The possibilities of independent living and community inclusion of persons with intellectual disabilities, in: G. Ajdinski and O. Rashikj-Canevska (eds.) *5th International Conference "Transformation towards sustainable and resilient society for persons with disabilities"*. Skoplje: Institut for special education and rehabilitation, Faculty of Philosophy, University Ss. Cyril and Methodius, pp. 465–480.

Caton, J. B., Gillooly, A., Hatton, C., Flynn, S., Oloidi, E., Jahoda, A., Maguire, R., Marriott, A., Mulhall, P., Taggart, L., Todd, S., Abbott, D., Beyer, S., Gore, N., Heslop, P., Scior, K. and Hastings, R.P. (2022) Digital participation of people with profound and multiple learning disabilities during the Covid-19 pandemic in the UK, *British Journal of Learning Disabilities*, 51(2), pp. 163–174.

Chadwick, D., Ågren, K.A., Caton, S., Chiner, E., Danker, J., Gómez-Puerta, M., Heitplatz, V., Johansson, S., Normand, C.L., Murphy, E., Plichta, P., Strnadová, I. and Wallén, E.F. (2022) Digital inclusion and participation of people with intellectual disabilities during COVID-19: A rapid review and international bricolage, *Journal of Policy and Practice in Intellectual Disabilities*, 19(3), pp. 242–256.

Chadwick, D.D. (2022) 'You want to know that you're safe': Experiences of risk, restriction and resilience online among people with an intellectual disability, *Cyberpsychology: Journal of Psychosocial Research on Cyberspace*, 16(3). Available at: https://doi.org/10.5817/cp2022-3-8.

Conroy, N.E., McDonald, K.E. and Olick, R.S. (2021) A survey study of the attitudes and experiences of adults with intellectual disability regarding participation in research, *Journal of Intellectual Disability Research*, 65(10), pp. 941–948.

Cook, T. and Inglis, P. (2012) Participatory research with men with learning disability: Informed consent, *Tizard Learning Disability Review*, 17(2), pp. 92–101.

Devi, N. (2013) Supported decision-making and personal autonomy for persons with intellectual disabilities: Article 12 of the UN convention on the rights of persons with disabilities, *The Journal of Law, Medicine & Ethics: A Journal of the American Society of Law, Medicine & Ethics,* 41(4), pp. 792–806.

Doody, O. (2018) Ethical challenges in intellectual disability research, *Mathews Journal of Nursing and Health Care,* 1(1), pp. 1–11.

Fabris, A., Bratković, D. and Žic Ralić, A. (2023) Self-assessment of friendships and social inclusion of adults with intellectual disabilities, *Specijalna edukacija i rehabilitacija,* 22(3), pp. 183–200.

Florian, L. (2019) On the necessary co-existence of special and inclusive education, *International Journal of Inclusive Education,* 23(7–8), pp. 691–704.

Heitplatz, V.N. (2020) Fostering digital participation for people with intellectual disabilities and their caregivers: Towards a guideline for designing education programs, *Social Inclusion,* 8(2), pp. 201–212.

Irish Central Statistics Office (2017) Census of Population 2016. Available at: https://www.cso.ie/en/media/csoie/newsevents/documents/census2016summaryresultspart1/census2016summarypart1.pdf

Johansson, S., Gulliksen, J. and Gustavsson, C. (2021) Disability digital divide: The use of the internet, smartphones, computers and tablets among people with disabilities in Sweden, *Universal Access in the Information Society,* 20, pp. 105–120.

Lake, J.K., Jachyra, P., Volpe, T., Lunsky, Y., Magnacca, C., Marcinkiewicz, A. and Hamdani, Y. (2021) The wellbeing and mental health care Experiences of adults with intellectual and developmental disabilities during COVID-19, *Journal of Mental Health Research in Intellectual Disabilities,* 14(3), pp. 1–16.

Love, M.L., Baker, J.N. and Devine, S. (2019) Universal design for learning: Supporting college inclusion for students with intellectual disabilities, *Career Development and Transition for Exceptional Individuals,* 42(2), pp. 122–127.

Lyons, A., Zucchetti, A., Kass-Hanna, J. and Cobo, C. (2019) Bridging the gap between digital skills and employability for vulnerable populations, the future of work and education for the digital age, *Think 20 Japan.*

Masnjak Šušković, L., Bratković, D., Bohaček, A.-M and Fabris, A. (2023) The use of digital technology for social inclusion among people with ID, in: *The 11th Scientific Conference with international participation "It's about people 2023: Social and technological development in service of security and dignity".* Maribor: Alma Mater Europaea, pp. 88–99.

McCausland, D., Luus, R., McCallion, P., Murphy, E. and McCarron, M. (2021) The impact of COVID-19 on the social inclusion of older adults with an intellectual disability during the first wave of the pandemic in Ireland, *Journal of Intellectual Disability Research,* October, 65(10), pp. 879–889.

Murphy, E. (2021) Patients as co-designers and co-innovators: Between theory and practice, in: *Digital transformation of health care, EPF Congress, summary report.* Available at: https://www.eu-patient.eu/globalassets/library/epf-congress-report-2021_final_web.pdf

Murphy, E., McCausland, D., Carroll, R., McCallion, P. and McCarron, M. (2019) Exploring the relationship between technology usage and social inclusion for older adults with intellectual disability in Ireland, *Journal of Intellectual Disability Research,* 63(7), p. 645.

Murphy, E., Shiels, O., Yap, M.L., Angus, C., Delaney, J., Hogan, B., Burke, C., Heduan, D., Breslin, D. and Fiori, S. (2022) "I Feel Proud That with This App We Can Help Other People with Intellectual Disabilities": The role of an expert by experience digital inclusion citizen advisory panel, *Disabilities,* 2(4), pp. 715–735.

National Disability Authority of Ireland (NDA) (2019) Factsheet 2: Employment and disability, in: *National Disability Authority.* Dublin, Ireland: National Disability Authority, May. Available at: https://nda.ie/file-upload/nda-factsheet-2-employment-briefing-information.pdf (accessed on 16 November 2023).

Reisdorf, B. and Rhinesmith, C. (2020) Digital inclusion as a core component of social inclusion, *Social Inclusion,* 8(2), pp. 132–137.

Sanders, E.B.-N. and Stappers, P.J. (2008) Co-creation and the new landscapes of design, *CoDesign,* 4(1), pp. 5–18. Available at: https://doi.org/10.1080/15710880701875068.

Scott, H.M. and Havercamp, S.M. (2018) Promoting wellness in people with intellectual and developmental disabilities through relationships, *Current Developmental Disorders Reports,* 5(3), pp. 150–156. Available at: https://doi.org/10.1007/s40474-018-0144-3.

Sheehan, R. and Hassiotis, A. (2017) Digital mental health and intellectual disabilities: State of the evidence and future directions, *Evidence Based Mental Health,* 20(4), pp. 107–111.

Sikirić, D., Novak, T., Kiš Glavaš, L., Runjić, T., Milković, M., Mašić Fabac, V. and Miholić, D. (2023) Usklađivanje nacionalnog zakonodavstva s Konvencijom o pravima osoba s invaliditetom, Prikaz rezultata istraživanja iz projekta Platforma 50+ [Alignment of national legislation with the Convention on the Rights of Persons with Disabilities, Presentation of research results from the project Platform 50+], in: D. Miholić and M. Mirić (eds.) *Mapiranje sastavnica neovisnog življenja, Prikaz rezultata istraživanja iz projekta Platforma 50+ [Mapping the components of independent living, Presentation of research results from the project Platform 50+].* Zagreb: Edukacijsko-rehabilitacijski fakultet Sveučilišta u Zagrebu, pp. 7–53.

Spassiani, N.A., Becaj, M., Miller, C., Hiddleston, A., Hume, A. and Tait, S. (2022) 'Now that I am connected this isn't social isolation, this is engaging with people': Staying connected during the COVID-19 pandemic, *British Journal of Learning Disabilities*, 51(1), pp. 99–110.

United Nations Convention on the Rights of Persons with Disabilities (2006) Available at: https://www.un.org/development/desa/disabilities/convention-on-the-rights-of-persons-with-disabilities.html

Žajdela Hrustek, N., Šimić, D. and Čižmar, Ž. (2022) An instrument for measuring needs of vulnerable groups in terms of digital inclusion, in: N. Vrček, L. Guàrdia and P. Grd (eds.) *Proceedings of the Central European Conference on information and intelligent systems*. Varaždin: Fakultet organizacije i informatike Sveučilišta u Zagrebu, pp. 107–115.

10 Rooted in Nature

Improving the involvement of young people as research advisors

Elaf Alasi, Kacie Hodgson, Charley McFarlane-Troy, and Catherine El Zerbi

---

Key words

Co-produced research methods, Young advisors

Rooted in Nature study

Our research project was named after the Rooted in Nature programme designed and delivered by our study partner, Middlesbrough & Stockton Mind. This social prescribing programme was developed to help people enjoy nature-based activities as part of looking after and improving their health in Middlesbrough. Clients were people who might not usually consider nature-based activities and those who have health and other challenges in their lives that can be a barrier to accessing nature. Previous studies have shown some health and well-being benefits from engaging in nature-based activities (Seeland et al., 2009; Jennings & Bamkole, 2019). Research has also indicated social benefits from engaging in nature for young people living in economically under-resourced urban cities (Birch et al., 2020; McEachan et al., 2018). It was important to do this project, as Northern England is disproportionately affected by health inequalities relative to the rest of the country (Bambra et al., 2014), a situation that was exacerbated by the impact of the Covid-19 pandemic (Munford et al., 2021). The place in which the programme was run – Middlesbrough – at the time of the study was ranked as having some of the most income-deprived neighbourhoods in England (Indices of Deprivation, 2019). Around 37% of under 16s lived in low-income families, which was worse than the average for the North East region (22.6%) and England (17%) (Public Health England, 2021).

We, an interdisciplinary team of academic researchers and the lead at Middlesbrough & Stockton Mind, co-wrote a funding proposal to look at the potential health benefits of Middlesbrough & Stockton Mind's nature-based delivery programme. In December 2021, our 'Rooted in Nature' pilot study was 1 of 12 projects selected as part of the government's UK Research and Innovation's cross-research council-funded 'Mobilising Community Assets to Tackle Health Inequalities' research programme. The study started in January 2022, and our aim was to use arts-based methods to understand what young people most valued about participating in local nature-based activities as part of Middlesbrough & Stockton Mind's Rooted in Nature programme, and how such activities might improve young people's health and well-being.

Advisory sessions with young people began early in the pre-application stage. In preparing our funding proposal, Middlesbrough & Stockton Mind staff held three preliminary focus groups with young people involved in their nature-based programme to gain their views on the priorities for the research and feedback on potential methods for working with young people (Fancourt, 2017). Young advisors described different motivations for involvement in nature-based activities, including benefits for the community as well as their own health. Regarding research methods, they were positive towards photography, with some mentioning utilising cameras they already possessed, while others talked about using their smartphones. In response, the design of Rooted in Nature utilised arts-based methods in the form of photo elicitation (Beilin, 2005; Croghan et al., 2008; Packard, 2008; Thomson, 2008) to understand what young people value most about nature-based spaces and activities.

DOI: 10.4324/9781003459651-13

Why involve young advisors in research?

Children and young people's right to be involved in research and the research process

UK public law acknowledges that children under the age of 18 years possess knowledge, judgement, and foresight, therefore recognising and protecting their right to be listened to and be adequately informed on matters that concern them. The fundamental rights of children to survival, growth, participation, and the fulfilment of their potential are enshrined in the UN General Assembly's Convention on the Rights of the Child (1989) and in England are protected by law through the Human Rights Act 1998, the Children Act 2004, the Equality Act 2010, and the Children and Families Act 2014 (British Academy, 2019). Despite certain legal protections, the active involvement of children and young people in the decision-making and design of health- and social care policy and research is often fragmented. A large body of academic literature on childhood (e.g. Cavet & Sloper, 2004; Franklin & Sloper, 2005; Tisdall & Elsley, 2011) and national standards for professionals (General Medical Council, 2020; National Institute for Health and Care Excellence, 2021) clearly highlights the need for researchers, policymakers, and healthcare practitioners to adopt rights-based and inclusive approaches to communicating with and involving children and young people in decisions that directly affect their lives. To our knowledge, however, this literature has not yet been aligned with the involvement of children and young people in our field, which is applied health research.

Potential benefits for young research advisors

At the start of the study, we asked our Rooted in Nature youth partners to share an invite amongst their networks to find young advisors to join us. We stated that potential benefits for young advisors can include seeking to 'empower' them to become advocates for the health of themselves and their peers. Our hope as researchers was to provide young advisors with knowledge and skills to voice their concerns, make decisions, and advocate for policies and practices that promote fairer and better health outcomes. As young research advisors, children and young people can gain an awareness of the different health conditions affecting children and young people in our region, while also gaining research knowledge, skills, and experience, such as developing critical thinking skills, research literacy, and an understanding of the scientific process, which we hope can benefit them academically and professionally. Additionally, advising on a research project exploring the potential benefits of nature may increase knowledge and awareness of environmental issues that may not only benefit our young advisors' health (and university researchers' too) but also have broader ecological and societal gains in terms of promoting conservationism and sustainability (Reid et al., 2008). Support and guidance from university researchers may also help young advisors develop the knowledge, skills, and confidence needed so that they can advocate for the changes they want to see, though benefits from being a young advisor will vary depending on children and young people's interests. Our young advisor Elaf mentioned that a key benefit offered by our Rooted in Nature study was the flexibility around getting involved in aspects that best suited a young person's interests, which was made clear from our initial invite.

Elaf added that a further benefit was learning about scientific writing, particularly thematic analysis and processes such as the coding of transcripts to develop themes, and delving deeply into the array of meanings that different words and phrases may hold. Elaf added that our project demonstrated how photography can be used to show more than words, to help the interview process with young people. Another benefit included learning about new concepts relating to health and nature, which allowed an awareness and deeper understanding of health, social, environmental, and educational challenges faced by young people in North East England. Building working relationships with university researchers can also enhance skills, such as communication, critical thinking, problem-solving, designing youth-friendly research materials, and training in qualitative analysis, all of which are transferable skills which potential universities and employers look for so could be useful in the future. Collaborative approaches to working with young people, such as providing training opportunities to enable knowledge and skills to carry out various stages of the research process in which they are most interested and, importantly, in ways that are fun, are already established and highly valued in the academic fields of education (Carrington et al., 2010), geography (Cahill, 2007), and increasingly, in health research with adults (Holmes et al., 2019). Our young advisors mentioned how contributing to Rooted in Nature also helped with enhancing personal statements for university admission and CV development, such as writing skills and leading published outputs, such as this chapter, as well as a peer-reviewed article as a named co-author, contributions that enhance a sense of voice and confidence. Catherine (principal investigator) also connected Elaf and Kacie with colleagues who offered more varied research opportunities. For example, Elaf is a named co-applicant on an NIHR funding application to establish a children and young people's research partnership across our region, and both Elaf and Kacie are young advisors on a research project looking to optimise the provision of staff training to support positive mental health in autistic young people in schools.

As applied health researchers and young advisors, we strongly believe that children and young people need to be actively involved in research about their lives so they can bring their lived experiences, voices, and concerns to help shape research priorities as early as possible, to ensure the findings are valid, relevant, meaningful, and actionable. To not include children and young people as advisors undermines their *right* to be involved in matters that concern them. It is also clear, from our experiences of working alongside our young advisors, that they are keen to participate in knowledge production about their lives, and to take on the responsibility of such involvement. Through our experiences in Rooted in Nature as university researchers, we could see how working with children and young people enhanced the quality of research so that appropriate questions were asked, and that findings were interpreted in a way that echoed the values and perspectives of children and young people, though acknowledge that in practice this can be hard to achieve (McLeod, 2007), especially given the time, training, and resources required to make it happen. Elaf also points out that young people may be more likely to get involved in health research when they know that other young people are part of the research team. This corresponds with previous research showing that when young people see that their peers are actively involved and invested in the research process, it may encourage to take part in research young participants who might otherwise have not, including those who have been under-represented in the past (Rose & Shevlin, 2004; Carrington et al., 2010). This is especially helpful, as study recruitment of children and young people participants by adult researchers can be a challenging step in the research process.

Benefits to research and society

Making time and space by allocating funding and providing research training to support young advisors has broader societal benefits too. As Elaf indicates, the positive involvement of young advisors could lead to a lifelong interest in research and advocacy for youth issues. How we make space to enable young advisors to share their insights and experiences is different for each project, requires more staff time than projects without young advisors and a more flexible approach, as specific resources are required for each young advisor. As we have learnt through Rooted in Nature, there are at least five basic issues which need to be considered during the pre-application stage, namely, identifying from the outset young people's interests, preferences, and training needs in terms of understanding the research process, to ensure that they can contribute in meaningful ways; planning communication around young people's preferences and commitments, including modes and frequency of meetings; developing young people's awareness of local research advisory opportunities; identifying how young advisors would like to be paid for their work on research projects; and addressing how future development opportunities for continuity, progression, and sustainability can be facilitated by researchers.

Improvements for researchers on how to involve young advisors

Enhancing young people's understanding of the research process

Researchers should provide young advisors with co-designed and accessible printed information to ensure that a young advisor understands their role and responsibilities from the beginning of a project, or preferably before a project even starts, and so they have this information to hand which they can refer to throughout. Before meetings take place, we encourage all researchers to ensure they have checked for any reasonable adjustments required for young advisors, such as vision, physical accessibility, and dietary requirements, in order to accommodate any needs, as legally required by the UK's Equality Act 2010. Making the research process truly 'inclusive' is not a straightforward process, as there are practical, ethical, political, and financial challenges which must be carefully considered in advance when planning a study, particularly around equity, power, empowerment, and voice (Nind, 2014; Bradbury-Jones et al., 2018). In Rooted in Nature, our approach to co-production with public advisors was guided by INVOLVE (2012) principles which strive to work in ways that are respectful, supportive, transparent, accountable, responsive, and that provide fairness of opportunity. Notwithstanding, there were many technical issues arising throughout the research process which had not been foreseen by the research team. We learnt that these issues were rife and affected most co-produced research studies, such as the impact of recruitment delays on co-production training timelines, as well as peaks and troughs in communication with the research team, and delays in issuing payments for advisory work due to institutional financial processes. Most importantly, we underestimated the time and resources required to provide high-quality research training to our young advisors so that they could be equitably involved. We have reflected on our experiences and have outlined our learning at the end of this chapter, which we hope is useful to others who are also working towards democratising the process of knowledge production through involving children and young people.

When planning funding applications, budgets should be properly allocated to cover staff time for providing research mentorship (e.g. one hour per month for each young advisor) and developing project-specific research training for young advisors. While we did create and deliver training on the research process for Rooted in Nature, this was not co-designed with our young advisors, due to time and budgetary constraints. While we made progress in beginning to develop training, more funding is now required to create a bespoke research training programme with young advisors for the next stage of study development. In the field of applied health research, more work is required to co-design research training with children and young people in ways that are engaging, interactive, creative, and fun. To do this, we believe that researchers will benefit from working with children and youth practitioners, as well as adopting interdisciplinary approaches that bring together learning from education, the arts, humanities, community development, health, and medicine, to produce research training and data collection methods for working with young people in relation to exploring who they are, the choices they make, and the lives they lead. Indeed, as Elaf points out, exploring nature with young people served as a tool for education and learning (e.g. identifying species of plants and trees), which the use of photo elicitation optimised. Going forward, and based on our experience, bringing together different disciplines for methodological innovation offers ways to enhance the agency of children and young people in health research to improve the quality of both learning and data and therefore produce more relevant knowledge.

Communication

Mode of meetings

Meetings using jargon-free language via various platforms, such as email, Zoom, WhatsApp, and text message, will help young advisors understand their role over time. Researchers should also check with all young advisors at the start of study whether they require access to any necessary technologies so they can keep in touch, depending on their needs, to ensure that a young person is not at a disadvantage due to financial and communication barriers. For example, they may need a SIM card, mobile phone, internet, or laptop access to be able to keep in touch with the researchers and to contribute effectively, which is necessary to keep young advisors up to date on the stages of the research process, especially during busier times. These potential costs should be included in funding applications. The research team could also include creative methods in meetings, such as graffiti walls, flip charts, and Post-its, or Google Jamboard if online, to capture non-verbal thoughts and feedback, and to encourage imaginative and creative thinking (Alminde & Warming, 2020). Further, if data collection has stopped, it means that there is no further analysis to be conducted, which young advisors need to know about to factor into their plans. Elaf suggests communication methods and regular updates could include thus:

- Fortnightly email updates on overall study progress, and for researchers to update on any forthcoming project opportunities and respond to any questions
- Monthly Zoom group meetings with young advisors
- Monthly phone calls or messages to check in with young advisors to see how their role is going

Again, frequency and mode of communication should be factored into funding applications and project timelines. Elaf suggests that once a project ends, and to maintain momentum, it would be useful to create a social media platform to share information of forthcoming research advisory opportunities for young people. This platform could also form a network for young people to share information and could be a place where young people can ask questions to current young advisors and researchers.

Elaf added that face-to-face meetings are better for longer meetings (over three hours), which can lead to productive discussions and interactive learning, as well as a better understanding and connection to the project. In-person meetings also allow young advisors to socialise with a network of young people with similar interests. Holding meetings online can be more convenient for young advisors as they would not need to travel and can participate from homes or a preferred location – this is best for meetings that are up to three hours, as it may take the young person up to an hour or more to get to a meeting destination – meaning, two hours will be spent commuting for a meeting not lasting long. Online meetings can be more accessible to young advisors with mobility challenges or disabilities, as they can use assistive technologies. Additionally, young advisors may appreciate the savings on transport cost associated with online meetings; however, research teams should ensure that any travel expenses are booked and paid for in advance, so the costs associated with an advisory role are never a financial burden for young people. For young advisors who cannot attend in-person meetings, the researchers should facilitate a hybrid option whereby they can attend the meeting online via video call. During the meeting, they can be on-screen while others are in-person, so they do not miss out on important information. It is also important to provide opportunities for young advisors to contribute to creative outputs from a study, such as writing a blog or making a film about what the research found, to enable ways to communicate study findings in a visual way and potentially reach relevant audiences through social media and beyond academia (Stanley et al., 2019).

Frequency of research meetings

Elaf highlights the importance of keeping young advisors 'in the loop' with regular updates on the research process and study progress, such as delays or whether there are any new opportunities for research involvement. The frequency of meetings should depend on the design of the study and how complex the project is. For example, if a project is a pilot study in the early stages of development, then it may not need as frequent in person meetings as it would if it were at a more advanced stage. Frequency should also depend on which stage of the research process the project is at, as advisory work is usually more intensive during the planning, analysis, and writing-up stages, which may need more frequent contact time. As noted previously, fortnightly emails on study progress are a good way to keep in touch, as it means despite the young advisor being busy during the day, they can check emails for project updates. Even if project meetings are infrequent, maintaining a consistent schedule can help young advisors stay informed and involved. Young advisors often have priorities, such as school or college, exams, and family commitments, so it is important for researchers to be flexible with dates and times, which may include offering meetings, especially research training days, during school holidays, on weekends, and in early evenings during the week after school. Be mindful that a young advisor may have homework or extracurricular activities, and therefore there might be some days when they cannot attend. School hours should be avoided, so young advisors can attend without conflicting and jeopardising their education. During school holidays or summer breaks, young advisors may have more flexibility in their schedules, so it can be a better time for more intensive meetings or training workshops. Once a meeting schedule is established, researchers should try to stick with that date and time, as this helps young advisors plan their commitments and activities around the study meetings. If there is a large group meeting (rather than one-to-one or paired), a survey or poll may be needed to decide the best time and day for everyone – if working alongside a large team of young advisors, it might be useful to hold the same meeting over two different sessions to accommodate more young people.

Increasing awareness of advisory opportunities for young people

Elaf found out about our Rooted in Nature young advisory role through an online flyer distributed on Facebook and Twitter by our community partners. Prior to this, Elaf was unaware that such opportunities existed and said he would have gotten involved in research sooner had it been known. Kacie found out about our Rooted in Nature young advisory role through an email from a youth worker, and like Elaf, they previously did not know that these opportunities existed. To address this gap, Elaf and Kacie suggest some communication strategies to reach out to children and young people, particularly through schools and youth groups, to let them know of research advisory opportunities, as follows:

- Distributing flyers with details for potential young advisors via school social media and noticeboards in corridors
- Delivering workshops on young advisory opportunities in schools, led by current young advisors and university researchers
- Using group chats on platforms such as WhatsApp
- Sharing information through child- and youth-focused voluntary, charity, and social enterprise partners
- Offering incentives to existing young advisors and young ambassadors to spread the word through their networks
- Hosting workshops and events including food and entertainment in community settings, such as youth clubs, facilitated by existing young advisors and university researchers
- Asking schools to share information in assemblies and form classes

These strategies could be a way for children and young people to find out what a young research advisor is, what the benefits and challenges are, and to ask professional researchers any questions. Raising awareness would need to be facilitated in a way that is fun and engaging for children and young people, using child- and youth-friendly language and colours. To do this, researchers could work alongside local voluntary, charity, and social enterprise partners to ensure the content of workshops is accessible and inclusive.

Paying young advisors for their work

Consideration needs to be given to the fairest ways to remunerate young advisors for their work on research projects, based on what works best for them. We had factored in five hourly meetings with young advisors for Rooted in Nature; however, in practice, young advisors spent much more time helping us. Renumeration for young advisors was based on NIHR's public contributor policy, which is a rate of £25 per hour, with a young advisor paid the same amount as an adult advisor would be. In most cases, this payment was made via shopping vouchers rather than cash, though a choice was offered. The decision to utilise vouchers was to issue payment immediately and to minimise the amount of paperwork and waiting time (around four weeks) for a cash payment to be processed through the university. To minimise costs for attending training and workshops, we booked trains and ordered taxis, which were paid for in advance via the university, to remove any financial barriers to involvement. Elaf suggests that hourly wages would be more appropriate where young people are frequently involved in the delivery of the research, such as weekly data collection for peer action research over several months. Elaf also proposes that rather than offering money, if a young advisor enjoys the research project, maybe the researchers could offer a scholarship to do a course at university, so that they can continue to work in that field in the future.

Future planning: what now?

We hope the lessons we have learnt from our Rooted in Nature pilot are useful to researchers who are planning on co-producing research with young advisors. It is important that young advisors are included in the design of research projects from the pre-application stage and are given an opportunity to be named co-investigators, should they wish. Communication and research training need to be regular as well as accessible, interactive, and engaging so young advisors can see how a research study develops over time to properly understand the research process. What is needed to do this are dedicated funding for time and resources, multi-sector partnerships, and interdisciplinary approaches to create participative mechanisms for children and young people to learn, communicate, and contribute their views and ideas on research priorities, approaches, and methods. In enabling these conditions, we believe the inclusivity, accessibility, diversity, and ultimately, scientific quality, relevance, and impact of applied health research will be improved.

Conclusion

In summary, we will incorporate the following points in future research projects with children and young people:

- Build an online network for young advisors to share experiences, ask questions, and find out information on forthcoming research advisory opportunities.
- Invite local young people to join projects during the pre-application planning stage where possible so they are involved from the very start, so that they understand and can contribute to the vision and aims of the research.
- Provide paper and digital copies outlining the potential role of a young advisor and how a young person can adopt it based on their interests, so that they are engaged and understand opportunities and responsibilities from the beginning of a study.
- Check for any reasonable adjustments for young advisors, such as vision, physical accessibility, and dietary requirements, to accommodate any needs.
- Provide accessible material specifying what the role of a young advisor is, outlining how it works and the activities involved, so it is clear to potential young advisors from the outset.
- Invite young advisors to join funding proposals as named co-applicants once they have an understanding of the research project and an overview of the research process and have defined their study advisory role in line with their interests.
- Provide young advisors with any necessary technologies so they can keep in touch, depending on their needs.
- Pay travel expenses for young advisors in advance, to remove any financial barriers to research involvement.
- Provide flexibility regarding meeting times, venues, and format.
- Provide co-designed research training that is accessible, interactive, and fun.
- Be honest about project progress, and circulate fortnightly email updates, even when the project is quiet, to ensure young advisors are informed on which research activities they can contribute to, so that they can plan their time.
- Hold monthly online meetings to catch up on the project and for any questions.
- Offer young advisors flexibility between vouchers or cash, and be up front about the waiting times for cash payments to be processed through the university.
- Potentially offer non-monetary remuneration, such as paying tuition for college or university courses linked to a young advisor's career interests.
- Ensure that potential participants are aware that a research project is co-produced with young advisors, as this may allay any concerns about adults misrepresenting and misinterpreting their experiences.
- Provide opportunities for young advisors to contribute toward creative outputs from a study, such as the production and dissemination of films and blogs.
- Ensure there are adequate developmental opportunities for young advisors to progress to the role of co-investigator, should they wish.

Reflective questions

1. What do you think might be some of the challenges of researching with young people?
2. What methods could you develop to enable young people to be involved in evaluating practice?

Takeaway activities

- Ask a group of young people to create a visual representation of their local community using photographs, video, or drawings.
- Use the visual representation as a prompt to discuss with young people what they like about living in their community, and what the challenges they face are.

Acknowledgements

Rooted in Nature was supported by the United Kingdom Research and Innovation (UKRI) Arts and Humanities Research Council's 'Mobilising Cultural and Natural Assets to Combat Health Inequalities' (Grant Award AH/W008033/1). CE is funded by the National Institute for Health and Care Research (NIHR) Applied Research Collaboration (ARC) for the North East and North Cumbria (Grant Award NIHR200173). NIHR ARC for the North East contributed towards funding the time for our young advisors to contribute to the writing of this chapter.

References

Alminde, S., & Warming, H. (2020) Future workshops as a means to democratic, inclusive and empowering research with children, young people and others. *Qualitative Research*, 20(4), 432–448. https://doi.org/10.1177/1468794119863165

Bambra, C., Barr, B., & Milne, E. (2014) North and south: Addressing the English health divide. *Journal of Public Health*, 36(2), 183–186.

Beilin, R. (2005) Photo-elicitation and the agricultural landscape: 'Seeing' and 'telling' about farming, community and place. *Visual Studies*, 20(1), 56–68. https://doi.org/10.1080/14725860500064904

Birch, J., Rishbeth, C., & Payne, S. R. (2020) Nature doesn't judge you–how urban nature supports young people's mental health and wellbeing in a diverse UK city. *Health & Place*, 62, 102296. https://doi.org/10.1016/j.healthplace.2020.102296

Bradbury-Jones, C., Isham, L., & Taylor, J. T. (2018) The complexities and contradictions in participatory research with vulnerable children and young people: A qualitative systematic review. *Social Science and Medicine*, 215, 80–91. https://doi.org/10.1016/j.socscimed.2018.08.038

British Academy. (2019) *Childhood policy milestones.* Available: https://www.thebritishacademy.ac.uk/publications/childhood-policy-milestones-chronologies/. Accessed 21st May 2023.

Cahill, C. (2007) Doing research with young people: Participatory research and the rituals of collective work. *Children's Geographies*, 5(3), 297–312. https://doi.org/10.1080/14733280701445895

Carrington, S., Bland, D., & Brady, K. (2010) Training young people as researchers to investigate engagement and disengagement in the middle years. *International Journal of Inclusive Education*, 14(5), 449–462. https://doi.org/10.1080/13603110802504945

Cavet, J., & Sloper, P. (2004) The participation of children and young people in decisions about UK service development. *Child: Care, Health and Development*, 30(6), 613–621. https://doi.org/10.1111/j.1365-2214.2004.00470.x

Croghan, R., Griffin, C., Hunter, J., & Phoenix, A. (2008) Young people's constructions of self: Notes on the use and analysis of the photo-elicitation methods. *International Journal of Social Research Methodology*, 11(4), 345–356. https://doi.org/10.1080/13645570701605707

Fancourt, D. (2017) *Arts in health: Designing and researching interventions.* Oxford University Press.

Franklin, A., & Sloper, P. (2005) Listening and responding? Children's participation in health care within England, *International Journal of Children's Rights*, 13, 1/2, 11–29. https://doi.org/10.1163/1571818054545277

General Medical Council. (2007) *Professional standards: 0–18 years: Guidance for all doctors.* Available: https://www.gmc-uk.org/-/media/documents/gmc-guidance-for-doctors---0-18-years---english-20200211_pdf-48903188.pdf. Accessed 12th January 2024.

Holmes, L., Cresswell, K., Williams, S., Parsons, S., Keane, A., Wilson, C., . . . & Starling, B. (2019) Innovating public engagement and patient involvement through strategic collaboration and practice. *Research Involvement and Engagement*, 5, 1–12. https://doi.org/10.1186/s40900-019-0160-4

Indices of Deprivation. (2019) *The English Indices of Deprivation 2019. Index of multiple deprivation decile 1 in Middlesbrough.* Ministry of Housing, Communities and Local Governments. Available: https://lginform.local.gov.uk/reports/lgastandard?mod-area=E06000002&mod-group=AllUnitaryLaInCountry_England&mod-metric=1506&mod-type=namedComparisonGroup. Accessed 10th November 2024.

INVOLVE. (2012) *Briefing notes for researchers: Involving the public in NHS, public health and social care research.* Eastleigh: INVOLVE. Available: https://breakthrought1d.org.uk/wp-content/uploads/2023/08/INVOLVE-Briefing-Notes-for-Researchers.pdf Accessed 10th November 2024.

Jennings, V., & Bamkole, O. (2019) The relationship between social cohesion and urban green space: An avenue for health promotion. *International Journal of Environmental Research and Public Health*, 16(3), 452. https://doi.org/10.3390/ijerph16030452

McEachan, R. R., Yang, T. C., Roberts, H., Pickett, K. E., Arseneau-Powell, D., Gidlow, C. J., Wright, J., & Nieuwenhuijsen, M. (2018) Availability, use of, and satisfaction with green space, and children's mental wellbeing at age 4 years in a multicultural, deprived, urban area: Results from the Born in Bradford cohort study. *The Lancet Planetary Health*, 2(6), e244–e254. https://doi.org/10.1016/S2542-5196(18)30119-0

McLeod, A. (2007) Whose agenda? Issues of power and relationship when listening to looked-after young people. *Child & Family Social Work*, 12(3), 278–286. https://doi.org/10.1111/j.1365-2206.2007.00493.x

Munford, L., Khavandi, S., Bambra, C., Barr, B., Davies, H., Diran, T., Kontopantelis, E., Norman, P., Pickett, K., Sutton, M., Taylor-Robinson, D., & Wickham, S. (2021) *A year of COVID-19 in the North: Regional inequalities in health and economic outcomes*. Northern Health Science Alliance, Newcastle.

National Institute for Health and Care Excellence. (2021) *Babies, children and young people's experience of healthcare* (Clinical guideline [NG204]). London: NICE. Available: https://www.nice.org.uk/guidance/ng204. Accessed 26th February 2024.

Nind, M. (2014) *What is inclusive research?* Bloomsbury Publishing.

Packard, J. (2008) 'I'm Gonna Show You What It's Really Like Out Here': The power and limitation of participatory visual methods. *Visual Studies,* 23(1), 63–77. https://doi.org/10.1080/14725860801908544

Public Health England. (2021) *Child health profile for Middlesbrough: March 2021*. Department of Health & Social Care. Available: https://fingertips.phe.org.uk/profile/child-health-profiles/data#page/1/ati/402/are/E06000002 Accessed 10th November 2024.

Reid, A., Jensen, B. B., Nikel, J., & Simovska, V. (2008) *Participation and learning: Developing perspectives on education and the environment, health and sustainability*. Springer Netherlands.

Rose, R., & Shevlin, M. (2004) Encouraging voices: Listening to young people who have been marginalised. *Support for Learning*, 19(4), 155–161. https://doi.org/10.1111/j.0268-2141.2004.00341.x

Seeland, K., Dübendorfer, S., & Hansmann, R. (2009) Making friends in Zurich's urban forests and parks: The role of public green space for social inclusion of youths from different cultures. *Forest Policy and Economics*, 11(1), 10–17. https://doi.org/10.1016/j.forpol.2008.07.005

Stanley, Z., Lauretani, P., Conforti, D., Cowen, J., DuBois, D., & Renwick, R. (2019) Working to make research inclusive: Perspectives on being members of the Voices of Youths Project. *Disability & Society*, 34(9–10), 1660–1667. https://doi.org/10.1080/09687599.2019.1619232

Thomson, P. (2008) *Doing visual research with children and young people*. London: Routledge.

Tisdall, K., & Elsley, S. (2011) *Children and young people's participation in policy-making: Making it meaningful, effective and sustainable*. Available: https://era.ed.ac.uk/bitstream/handle/1842/20973/Participation-briefing-1.pdf?sequence=1

United Nations. (1989) *Convention on the rights of the child*. Available: https://www.unicef.org.uk/wp-content/uploads/2019/10/UNCRC_summary-1_1.pdf Accessed 10th November 2024.

11 Creating neuro-mixed learning environments in higher education

Allison Moore and Paul Davies

> **Key words**
>
> Neurodivergence, Neuro-mixed, Inclusion, Universal design for learning

Introduction

Since its emergence in autistic communities in the 1990s, the concept of neurodivergence has been applied to a wide range of other neurological differences, including, but not limited to, ADHD (attention deficit hyperactivity disorder), dyslexia, dyspraxia, dyscalculia, Tourette's, and mental ill health. What these disparate ways of being in and experiencing the world have in common is that they diverge from neuro-majority cognitive processing styles (Bertilsdotter-Rosqvist, Stenning & Chown, 2020). It is estimated that one in seven people in the UK is neurodivergent (Farrant & Owen, 2023), although American research suggests that, globally, as much as 10–20% of the population could be neurodivergent (Mahto, Hogan & Sniderman, 2022). It is not unreasonable to assume, therefore, that significant numbers of students in higher education (HE) are neurodivergent, although identifying the exact prevalence is far from easy. Current data collection relies on self-disclosure (Clouder et al., 2020); some forms of neurodivergence, such as ADHD, dyslexia, and dyspraxia, are subsumed under the umbrella category of specific learning differences (SpLD) (Sedgwick-Müller et al., 2022), and many students do not have a formal diagnosis. However, the first Unite Students Applicant Index report, 2022–2023, found that 7% of 2,038 university applicants to undergraduate degrees reported being autistic (an increase of 3% on the previous year), and 8% had ADHD/ADD.

There is an acknowledgement at an institutional level that neurodivergent students may require support. Those students who have an identified label of neurodivergence are protected by equality legislation and are usually entitled to access an 'inclusion team' producing individualised support plans. Nevertheless, quality, co-produced training on neurodiversity is rarely mandatory in UK universities, and there is frequently a lack of awareness amongst academic staff about what neurodivergence is and, therefore, what adjustments to teaching, learning, and assessment may be required (Little, Pearson & Gimblett, 2023). Further, given that significant numbers of neurodivergent adults are undiagnosed (O'Nions et al., 2023), it is likely that teaching staff have far greater numbers of neurodivergent students in their classrooms (and among departmental colleagues) than official data indicate or they may realise.

In this chapter, we will define 'neurodivergence', and some of its related terminology, which is often misunderstood and incorrectly used. Due to neurodivergent students frequently feeling they are not adequately supported, there is a high drop-out rate compared to their peers (Cage, De Andres & Mahoney, 2020; Cage & Howes, 2020). Research also highlights that, although most staff in UK universities have received diversity and equality training, it is limited in terms of how reasonable adjustments should be implemented, leaving staff lacking in confidence (Little, Pearson & Gimblett, 2023). We will examine the importance of understanding the impact educators can have in a neuro-mixed class.

Reflecting on our experiences of designing and delivering the MA in critical autism studies (CAS) at a university in North West England, we will share our approach to teaching and the attitudes we adopted to demonstrate how successful teaching neuro-mixed classes can be. We will focus on two areas in which small changes can bring about significant improvements to the experiences of all students. First, we outline principles of universal design for learning (UDL), which underpinned the development and delivery of the MA in critical autism studies and can result in a positive and rewarding experience for *ALL* students across all age ranges. We will offer examples of changes which can be made to teaching spaces of all kinds and suggest new practices for teachers and lecturers to implement. Second, we will consider the sensory environment and its impact on learning for neurodivergent (ND) students. Sensory sensitivities were included in the diagnostic criteria for autism for the first time in 2016, and research indicates that hyper- or hyposensitivities are features of other neurodivergences (Bijlenga et al., 2017; Kamath et al., 2020; Prato et al., 2024). We provide an overview of the eight sensory systems that can negatively impact ND students and offer simple solutions or changes which can be made to ameliorate their negative consequences. Whilst the focus of this chapter is on the university experience, it is applicable to all buildings, including home teaching, where neurodivergent children and adults are expected to learn. We hope that if you work in any teaching setting, then this advice can be applied to your own specific circumstances. When reading this, if you do not work in the HE sector, we suggest substituting 'teacher' for 'lecturer', as we believe many of the suggestions we make can be adapted to fit any environment.

What is *neurodivergence*?

Although the terms 'neurodiversity' and 'neurodivergence' have entered into everyday language, confusion continues over terminology and how to use it. 'Neurodiversity' refers to the cognitive differences between every single human individual, a biological fact of 'the infinite variation in neurocognitive functioning in our species' (Walker, 2014). It originated as a concept within the autistic community in the 1990s to signify that, like nature and biodiversity, *all* human beings are different in many respects and should be respected for it.

The term 'neurodivergent' is applied to a person who has a different cognitive make-up from 'neurotypical'. This important taxonomical distinction is intended to prevent discussions about 'normal' and 'abnormal'. The term *neurodivergence* was coined by Kassiane Asasumasu (2015), who stated that '[n]eurodivergent refers to neurologically divergent from typical. That's ALL' (sherlocksflataffest.tumblr.com. 2015). Neurodivergent people do not exist in silos, experiencing numerous 'intersections' and identities, including gender, race, sexuality, as well as disability. Many neurodivergent people will also have a range of co-existing medical conditions – co-morbidities – which can include physical (usually visible) disabilities or cognitive disabilities or mental ill health (usually hidden) (Casanova et al., 2020). Neurodivergence is not a mental health condition itself, albeit some neurodivergent people *may* have co-morbid mental ill-health, for example, anxiety, depression, etc., but this is usually because of inhabiting a world not designed for neurodivergent people (Lai et al., 2019).

The term 'neuro-mixed' can be understood as a corollary of the concept of neurodiversity, where diversity is a natural feature of social groups. What is attractive about using *neuro-mixed* is that it acknowledges neurological variation without reifying the neurodivergent/neurotypical binary, and in so doing, it transgresses dominant discourses that position neurodivergence as extraordinary to the 'cognitive and socially ordinary' neurotypicality (Bertilsdotter Rosqvist, Hjorth & Nygren, 2023: 407). University classrooms (much like any other classroom or nursery spaces) are spaces in which neuro-mixed learning and cross-neurotype communication take place (Bertilsdotter Rosqvist, Hultman, et al., 2023), but these spaces need to be cultivated so everyone can thrive.

Neurodiversity and neurodivergences are often incorrectly conflated with the neurodiversity movement, which is a social justice lobby aimed at advancing the civil rights of and promoting acceptance for ALL neurodivergent people. It supports the right of people to view their neurodivergence as an identity, to celebrate and take pride in it. It does not deny that, for some people, it can be very disabling. A common misrepresentation of the neurodiversity movement is that it only reflects the needs of autistic people erroneously referred to as 'high-functioning'. This disregards the fact that from the outset, the ND movement's 'values include the most significantly disabled, but also that those individuals themselves were among . . . [the] earliest pioneers' (Ballou, 2018). Further, the use of *functioning* labels runs the risk of minimising or rendering invisible the support needs of people classed as 'high-functioning', a term applied to autistic people without a learning disability (Keates, Martin & Waldock, 2024). It is often wrongly assumed that 'high-functioning' individuals of all ages, like those whose academic abilities have secured them a place at university, are able to 'function' without any support. Irvine and MacLeod's (2022: 51) literature review found that a significant barrier for autistic students was 'staff who considered university attendance to indicate there was no need for support'. The research highlights that there is a pressing need for additional support. Writing in 2009, Symonds notes that many initiatives aimed at accommodating neurodivergent students' needs are 'apologist in their attempts to redress the balance for students' (244). Unfortunately, the research literature suggests that this still continues to be the situation for many students, hence our call for these adjustments to be implemented as early as possible in children's educational journey to maximise their potential for learning.

What do we know about the university experiences of neurodivergent students?

In a recent narrative synthesis exploring the experiences of neurodivergent students in HE, Clouder et al. (2020: 771) identified that, in general, participants reported

> poor treatment, lack of support, inflexibility from lecturers . . . [a]nd perceptions of discrimination and judgemental attitudes when they disclose their learning difficulties.

When broken down to specific forms of neurodivergence, things become less clear. In part, this is because there is limited research in some areas and/or some neurodivergences tend to be conflated with the broader label of specific learning difference (SpLD). In UK universities, ADHD is seen as an SpLD, and there continues to be limited research into the needs and experiences of ADHD students (Sedgwick-Müller et al., 2022). There is more research here from America and a better understanding of how ADHD might impact university life, such as increased chances of non-completion of studies and lower academic outcomes compared to their non-ADHD peers (Sedgwick, 2018). It is also important to remember that many neurodivergent pupils and students will have co-occurring conditions that fall under the ND umbrella, hence the growing use of the term AuDHD. Under the UK Equality Act (2010), universities have a statutory duty to ensure that disabled students are not disadvantaged compared to students who are not disabled. Research suggests university (and school) staff continue to lack an understanding that they are legally obliged to make reasonable adjustments for disabled students (Little, Pearson & Gimblett, 2023), and it is often only at the point of assessment that adjustments are made.

Alternative assessments, which accommodate cognitive differences, are intended as a tool of equality but can serve to remind the student of their difference, that they are 'other' or 'less than' the neurotypical learner. What ND students learn is that 'what meets with approval in the institutional meritocracy is the student's ability to fit in and be less "other"' (Symonds, 2009: 245), to be less neurodivergent. In order to be effective, adjustments or accommodations to learning, teaching, and assessment need to be built into curriculum design and pedagogic practice, not just bolted on to assessments. In her research with American autistic students, Sarrett (2018: 685) found that even when accommodations were made, less than one-third of participants did not feel they addressed their 'sensory, social, academic or psychiatric needs'.

Many ND people arrive at university with a history of negative experiences of education that, for some, have led to ongoing educational trauma, which he defined as 'the inadvertent and unintentional perpetration and perpetuation of harms in schools' (Gray, 2019: 1). Over 70% of autistic people are educated in mainstream school (Mesa & Hamilton, 2022), but many of them report that school is a difficult place for them (Goodall, 2018; Wood, 2020), hence our assertion of the importance of universal design for all educational settings and age phases. A recent longitudinal study that followed autistic pupils transitioning from primary to secondary school found that, post-transition, 'many experienced bullying and poor mental health' (ibid., p. 1). Horgan, Kenny, and Flynn's (2023: 533) systematic review of research into the experiences of autistic young people in mainstream secondary school identified that negative experiences had a profound impact, engendering 'feelings such as anxiety, loneliness, dread, anger and frustration'. These experiences will deeply influence ND students' experience of and attitude to university. Before they are able to engage in academic life, they must try to overcome the mental barriers caused by their past educational trauma. Much of the existing research and practice in relation to education and neurodivergence erroneously locate the 'problems' that neurodivergent students encounter within the individual, due to their neurodivergence (#AttentionUK, n.d.).

Staff training and awareness of neurodivergence have a significant impact on neurodivergent students' experiences. In UK universities, mandatory training on equality and diversity is often delivered within the framework of the Equality Act 2010. This does not address neurodivergence specifically and is limited in terms of how one might accommodate diversity in students' needs in practice. In Little, Pearson, and Gimblett's research into staff's attitudes towards reasonable adjustments and understanding of implementation at one UK university, one participant said:

> The training I have received so far deals with the legislative framework and when and what adjustments should be put in place. What it has failed to do is tell me how to put in place those adjustments where they are difficult or where to seek assistance in doing so.
> (Little, Pearson & Gimblett, 2023: 139)

Designing the MA in critical autism studies

The MA in critical autism studies (CAS) began in 2020. From the outset, there was an explicit commitment to encouraging experts by experience to join the programme, including neurodivergent people and their parents/carers. For this to be realised, inclusion was built into the fabric of curriculum design and approaches to teaching, learning, and assessment. It had to acknowledge and actively aim to redress the barriers that many neurodivergent students face, as well as take steps to mitigate, where possible, earlier negative educational experiences. This was aided by the subject itself. CAS is thought to consist of three components. First, it critically considers the power relations that shape autism, who has the power to define what autism is, where its diagnostic boundaries are, and when those boundaries should change. The second element is enabling narratives that challenge medical, deficit-laden discourses of autism. The third is a commitment to creating new, interdisciplinary methodological and theoretical frameworks for analysing autism.

To have epistemic integrity, CAS must be inclusive of autistic voices (Woods et al., 2018), and it should be critical of any approach, irrespective of discipline, that marginalises or dismisses the voices most affected by its claims to knowledge (Davidson & Orsini, 2013). Therefore, CAS, in definition and practice, emphasises inclusivity. However, in order to put these definitions into practice, we needed to recruit neurodivergent students. Standard minimum entry criteria for a master's programme is a lower second-class degree, but Department for Education (DfE), Office for Students (OfS), and UCAS data highlight that students with disclosed disabilities are less likely to complete their undergraduate degree or attain a first- or upper-second-class undergraduate degree (Bolton & Hubble, 2021). Higher Education Statistics Agency (HESA) data shows that 36% of autistic students who enrolled for an undergraduate degree in 2019 had not completed three years later, a higher dropout rate than for any other disability (North East Autism Society, n.d.). Given that fewer autistic (and potentially other neurodivergent) people have completed an undergraduate degree and would, therefore, be disadvantaged by this entry requirement, we decided to accept applications from 'experts by experience' even if they did not have a first degree. Instead, their application was assessed on the basis of their personal statement and an interview. Similarly, applicants to master's programmes are usually required to provide an academic or employment reference. Given many neurodivergent people's negative experiences of education, they may be unable to provide an academic reference to support their application. The Buckland Review of Autism Employment report states that only three in ten autistic people of working age are in employment which makes it difficult to get an employer reference (DWP, 2024: 5). In these cases, applicants were able to provide a character and suitability reference from someone who had known them for some time. These small adjustments removed significant barriers to accessing the course and have contributed to a large proportion of applicants from neurodivergent people each year.

Universal design for learning

Under UK law, neurodivergent students are entitled to various reasonable adjustments so they are not disadvantaged. However, there are problems with this approach to inclusion. First, accessing these 'entitlements' requires students to (1) have a diagnosis and (2) disclose their diagnosis. As noted, many students start university without a formal diagnosis or are unaware of their neurodivergence (O'Nions et al., 2023); others, due to their experiences of systemic discrimination and stigma, have understandably chosen not to share their diagnosis. Second, because academic staff receive limited training on the practicalities of making reasonable adjustments, they can lack confidence in implementing them (Little, Pearson & Gimblett, 2023). This is compounded by the fact that maintaining student confidentiality usually means that staff are unaware of *why* they are making the adjustments (ibid.). In their research, Little, Pearson, and Gimblett (2023: 143) observed that some staff were suspicious that reasonable adjustments could be used to gain an unfair advantage compared to their peers (see also Cameron & Billington, 2017). Thirdly, what is considered 'reasonable' can be subjective and is variable, leading Milton, Martin, and Melham (2017: 81) to note, 'The notion of reasonable adjustment raises the question: "what constitutes reasonable and who decides?"'

To mitigate problematic current approaches, we advocate the use of universal design for learning (UDL), 'an antidote to the bolt-on provisions for students "with issues"' (Hamilton & Petty, 2023: 6). UDL is an educational framework that aims to remove barriers to learning and maximise achievement for all students (Edyburn, 2010). It is based on the three principles of multiple means of engagement, representation, and action/expression. Providing multiple means of engagement is based on the awareness that there is a variety of ways in which students can be motivated to learn. Some need learning to be highly structured, with expectations clearly communicated at the outset, whereas others are stimulated by learning new things in spontaneous ways (https://udlguidelines.cast.org/engagement, accessed 4 May 24).

Once students' interests have been harnessed, it is important to maintain that using formative feedback, varying difficulty levels of activities, and fostering the development of a community of learners. In order to engender and sustain interest, the learning environment must be safe enough for students to express themselves, to take risks and make mistakes (ibid.).

A multiple means of representation refers to presenting information in a range of ways to meet different learning styles and needs, but it also goes beyond that. If a subject area has very precise or technical terminology, it is important to clarify this so that learners are able to speak and interpret the language of their subject. Scaffolding students' understanding is important here too. Processing information quickly can be overwhelming for some, and they may find it difficult to ascertain what is critical information and what is peripheral. So utilise prompts and cues to identify the most important information that a student needs to take away from a lesson. This can be done during the learning session or after. One technique used on the MA in critical autism studies was to produce a short five-minute audio recording to highlight the essential ideas and concepts we wanted students to understand; they were called 'In a Nutshell'.

Multiple means of expression 'allows for learners to demonstrate their knowledge in various ways' (Milton, Martin & Melham, 2017: 83). Most discussions in classrooms are based on spoken language, and there is still an overreliance on the written word when it comes to assessments. There may be non-speaking people in the class, and they may use alternative forms of communication, which means it can take them longer to be able to make their point than someone using spoken language. Many people, irrespective of neurodivergence, can become situationally non-speaking due to anxiety, distress, or being overwhelmed by environment (Autism Understood, 2024). Whilst some methods suit some subjects better than others, clearly, it is incumbent on us to build in different ways people's 'voices' can be heard and valued, however they are articulated. Expressing oneself, especially when it comes to assessments, also takes practice and organisational skills, another area where tutors can scaffold learners.

Thinking about the environment: addressing the sensory needs of neurodivergent students

One of the easiest adjustments to make to neuro-mixed classes concerns the environment. It is estimated that up to 90% of autistic people have either hyper- or hyporeactivity sensitivities to sensory inputs (Balasco, Provenzano, & Bozzi, 2019). The latest *Diagnostic and Statistical Manual* (*DSM5*) for the first time includes environmental challenges as part of the diagnostic criteria for autism as '[h]yper- or hyporeactivity to sensory input or unusual interest in sensory aspects of the environment' (CDC, 2024), with many people experiencing both hyper- and hyposensitivities to their environment. Although diagnostic features of autism research indicate that they are also present in other neurodivergences, including ADHD (Bijlenga et al., 2017; Kamath et al., 2020) and Tourette's syndrome (Prato et al., 2024). Hypersensitivity can be understood as a heightened reaction to a sensory input. For example, a light might be experienced as so bright that it can feel painful. Hyposensitivity, on the other hand, is where the person experiences a reduced reaction to sensory input compared to neurotypical people. This might include an inability to feel pain, heat, or hunger, which could lead to serious health concerns if not addressed.

Thinking about the teaching environment is the first step in creating positive neuro-mixed learning spaces for all ages and in all environments. Most people are familiar with the five senses – visual, gustatory, tactile, auditory, and olfactory – which allow us to process information from the world around us. However, in addition to these five 'outward facings' or exteroceptive senses, there are three 'hidden' senses, with which we interpret messages from our internal body. These are the vestibular, proprioception, and interoception systems. Our vestibular system concerns movement and balance and gives us a sense of the spatial orientation of our bodies. The proprioceptive sense provides information about the position, location, orientation, and movement of the body muscles and joints. It also tells us how much muscle force or pressure is required to perform an activity. *Interoception* is the ability to interpret the signals from our internal organs, such as knowing when we are hungry or cold. It also has an important role in emotional regulation, the ability to recognise, respond to, and manage our emotions.

In what follows mentioned are examples of each area, but it is important to remember that many will overlap and cause multiple issues at once; it is impossible to overstate the challenges this can cause. For some, a condition called synaesthesia can cause a sensory overlap, such as where a smell will trigger a taste, or a sound will trigger an image of colours (see Born on a Blue Day by Daniel Tammet). Simply because somebody does not experience this or understand the severity of the issue, or that the child cannot fully explain their experience, doesn't mean these challenges should be ignored, minimised, or allowed to be the cause of discrimination. We accept a tutor may have limited control over the physical environments in which they teach. However, having an empathic acceptance of the environmental impact can make an enormous difference for the individual student experience without favouring anybody.

VISUAL – sight

Potential impact

Lots of different brightly coloured wall displays (very common in nursey or primary education) can be confusing and overwhelming. Large TV display screens or SMART boards can be distracting, and neurodivergent students may experience them as flickering. The amount of people in the space moving around, blocking views, and random movements make focusing and processing difficult. Those with hyperreactive visual sense may experience text pulsating or moving, making reading difficult.

Visually overwhelming rooms can cause nausea and/or headaches. To cope, they may look out of the window or down at their desk. This can be misinterpreted as disinterest or lack of engagement.

Strategies

- Where possible, use lots of natural light from windows or ceiling windows.
- Understand that glass walls can be difficult for someone with proprioception and vestibular issues. Privacy film can be used.
- Do not use fluorescent or LED lights in classrooms. If this is not possible, try not to use them if sufficient natural light is available.
- Make space clutter-free, and provide clear, unobstructed pathways to mitigate potential co-morbid dyspraxia issues.
- Change room to new configurations – create smaller spaces via partitions.
- Avoid making random changes to the room once in use, as some (though not all) autistic people value predictability.
- Allow for appropriate processing time in sessions.

AUDITORY – sound

Potential impact

'Noise bleed', that is, where all the conversations in the room blend into one and thereby become impossible to hear anything. Avoid using rooms with very high ceilings, where sound can be lost. For example, gymnasium. Machines, especially loud, high-pitched, and repetitive – namely, generator outside or an overhead projector. We accept that many classrooms will likely always be noisy environments, but we must endeavour to try to limit this.

Strategies

- Try to limit excessive noise in group study areas with signage.
- Consider moving rooms to quieter venue or more appropriate setting.
- Consider alternative teaching methods other than PowerPoint.
- Limit the cross-over of sounds from one space into another to avoid overload, for example, loud music, video in communal areas.
- Request that distractions be switched off or turned down for the duration of the session.

TACTILE – touch

Potential impact

Touch may cause sensory overload or pain for some. Crowded areas in spaces like corridors or cafeterias can be problematic. However, some people have a sensory need to touch objects as part of their processing system.

- Avoid touching the child/adult where possible. It is common practice for teachers of young children to be tactile, but they may inadvertently be causing distress and anxiety.
- Allow for people to enter room early, if empty, or wait until crowd has moved on.
- Understand some people will touch many items in the room for processing.

OLFACTORY – smell

Potential impact

Smell may be overwhelming and drive people away. Links or associations trigger emotions, especially if negative. Food, food court, restaurant, café, and nearby teaching spaces can be distracting. Monitor smells from other people, which can be poor hygiene or strong perfume/aftershave.

Strategies

- Prevent students eating in the classroom.
- Try to use odourless art materials or cleaning products which leave lingering smells.
- Ensure you can ventilate the space if required.
- Ask personal tutor of any students with poor hygiene to discuss the matter with them.
- Ask students not to use overly strong perfumes, as this can be overwhelming for others.

GUSTATORY – taste

Potential impact

Some people may need to eat at a specific time due to health considerations. Some people will need to eat a specific item as part of a routine or health regime, so if not available, it can be an issue for them.

Strategies

- Allow students to take a break from class in order to eat, for health maintenance purposes.
- Allow a student to leave the space if a smell is triggering gustatory system response – for example, a metallic taste.

VESTIBULAR – balance

Potential impact

Crowds waiting to enter a room can be disorienting and distressing. Cluttered spaces, uneven flooring, staircases, or unsuitable ramps instead of lifts can cause mobility issues. Poor lighting must be addressed. Glass walls to teaching spaces – difficult to judge distance with confusing reflections. Loud sounds in some spaces can impact on orientation.

Strategies

- Accept that the student may be in the space very early, if possible, or last in if not.
- Allow a student/pupil with vestibular difficulties to end their break time slightly earlier to allow for a safer transition back into the classroom.
- Avoid having tables and chairs too close together, as this can encroach on personal space and make aisles too narrow for wheelchair or walker.
- Privacy film can be placed on the glass to minimise confusion and help with depth perception.

Proprioception

Potential impact

All vestibular issues can impact on proprioception. There may be a need to reach out and touch items to 'locate' themselves in space. They may knock into other people. Some bodily movements can appear 'irregular' to others. The person may have the need for a wider 'personal space' than other students. If people dislike being touched by a stranger, this can be interpreted as being inappropriate regardless of the intent, potentially leading to confrontation. This can focus attention on the person, which can be mortifying.

Strategies

- Monitor other student responses, as this can be the root of abuse from bullies at all ages and across settings.
- Consider discreetly offering an individual desk where possible, but avoid isolating them.

- Ensure consistency in terms of use of space, for example, always using the same room.
- Have clearly defined spaces, which allows the person to understand their place within the environment.
- Try not to hold meetings in challenging spaces, such as the canteen, unless requested by the student.

Interoception

Potential impact

Some people do not receive the mental messages about their bodily needs/wants/condition, for example, the urge to urinate/defecate/heavy menstruation. Clearly, this has the potential to be challenging for the child/adult.

Strategies

- Identify quiet rooms or safe spaces where people could retreat/escape to if feeling overwhelmed, to rebalance.
- Develop an 'escape and regulation plan'.
- Temperature controls for the environment to allow change to suit different physical needs.
- Ensure teaching room has easy access to toilet facilities for people who may need fast access to them.
- Do not challenge students who suddenly need to leave a lecture/seminar, as they may have no option other than to leave.
- Show suitable understanding if 'accidents' do happen and they need to leave campus quickly.

All these systems are constantly operating, so preparation for and the journey to university (or school and college setting) could contain a series of negative sensory challenges – meaning, the student could arrive at a session in a highly agitated state. Some may mask their distress, as noted by Pearson and Rose (2021: 53):

> Autistic masking (also referred to in the literature as camouflaging, compensation, or 'adaptive morphing') is the conscious or unconscious suppression of natural responses and adoption of alternatives across a range of domains including social interaction, sensory experience, cognition, movement, and behaviour.

It is not only autistic people who mask; it is also evident in other ND people, arising from being misunderstood and hearing negative comments about the way they behave (Spaeth & Pearson, 2023). Jellinek (2010) states, 'In school alone, a child with ADHD could receive 20,000 corrective or negative comments by the time he or she is aged 10' (p. 12).

Students or pupils may not be able to mask their distress and, in their highly aroused and agitated state, may say something or use a tone that seems inappropriate to some. This should not be internalised by others; it usually is not deliberate or planned on the part of the student impacted (Spaeth & Pearson, 2023). Milton (2012) coined the term 'double-empathy problem', whereby a breakdown in communication or misunderstanding between actors is a result of both failing to understand each other. Communication is a two-way process; hence, the more different the actors are, the more likely it is that misunderstanding will occur. However, because dominant constructions of neurodivergence characterise it as a deficit in communication skills, the ND person is usually unfairly assumed to be the root of the miscommunication (ibid.). This is especially true with younger children, where the categories of childhood and neurodivergence intersect, but sadly carries on through the wider educational sector, where miscommunication due to sensory dysregulation can potentially lead to exclusion.

Having an awareness that the environment can have a deleterious impact on ND students, and taking steps to mitigate them, is a crucial step in creating a safe space within which to learn. This is a fundamental principle of the universal design for learning. (https://udlguidelines.cast.org/engagement/recruiting-interest/threats-distractions), which the MA was underpinned by.

Whilst running the MA in CAS, we utilised and suggested the following approaches:

- Communicate learning outcomes at the outset of each module, and explain how the module content aligns with them.
- Provide exemplars of assignments wherever possible, so students can see what meeting the learning outcomes looks like on specific modules.
- Offer opportunities for both online and in-person sessions.
- Provide formal and informal formative feedback so students can reflect on their own learning and staff can reflect on their teaching and modify it if required.
- Provide maps of how to get from the car park/entrance to teaching spaces, with photographs of the route and room included. This reduces the potential for overload due to fear of the unknown.
- Allow and accept self-soothing behaviours: 'stimming'. Accept the use of objects, such a stim toys or weighted blankets on lap or around shoulders, to reduce anxiety. This in no way disrupts teaching but can help avoid crisis.
- Allow students to move around teaching spaces where possible. Restrictions can cause distress and anxiety, as sitting still for long periods can be painful for some.
- Allow students to sit on the floor instead of at a desk, or remove footwear; we are more receptive to information assimilation when comfortable in ways that best suit us individually.
- Sometimes, students join in-person sessions via an online platform as their learning would be maximised that way.
- For some students who recognise that they sometimes struggle with demands placed upon them, build in more regular supervision sessions.
- If students struggle to remember meetings, set a phone reminder for the next meeting before leaving current session.
- Auto reminders can be set on emails to appear just before a planned meeting.
- Send out reminders via the VLE message system for all students; this will be of benefit for all on many occasions.
- Create short videos, 'bite-size chunks', to highlight the core concepts and assist with information processing, as they can be replayed as often as required.
- Offer the use of recorded feedback to bring a more nuanced response if the learner feels written feedback style is open for misinterpretation. Double-empathy issue.
- Understand that 'engagement' and 'focus' can look different in some people. Looking away can be a way of filtering out extraneous sensory stimuli to help process the session.
- Understand that social anxiety may prevent a student from asking questions, so build in time at the end of sessions for students to ask or for longer supervision or guidance.
- The use of accessible handouts (created in a range of formats, for example, colour background, large font, etc.) for extra context and not just a repeat of what was already presented.
- Image-led PowerPoints for visual learners to anchor information.
- Post slides, readings, and course materials on the virtual learning environment in advance (if possible). This allows for students to reduce anxiety by preparing better.
- Use online seminars as well as formal teaching; relaxed with more opportunity to discuss and assimilate the information or concepts.
- The use of reports instead of essays. This requires the same level of understanding of the topic. This is also a very useful ability to develop for the workplace.
- Oral presentations instead of written work.

Conclusion

In this chapter we have identified some of the barriers that neurodivergent students face in university and, reflecting on our experiences of delivering the MA in critical autism studies, have provided suggestions as to how they may be mitigated. We are not claiming to have all the answers, but we hope we have engendered a safe-enough space in our learning environment that students can tell us when we are not getting it right – and they frequently do – or make suggestions for how we can do things better. Rather than feeling offended, we see it as evidence that students are recognising their needs and taking control of their learning. We believe that this can equally apply to younger children in early years or school and college settings, who can thrive in nurturing and accepting climates rather than in oppressive and environmentally hostile ones. It is understood that teaching staff already carry heavy workloads, and these recommendations may be seen as just another additional responsibility, but although not all the suggestions will be applicable to every setting or subject area, taking some of them, and adapting them to individual educational settings, benefits everyone.

Reflective questions

1. What is your understanding of *neurodiversity* and *neurodivergence* after reading the chapter?
2. Why do you think neurodivergent pupils or students currently experience challenges to studying?
3. What can you do as a practitioner to help improve the experiences of neurodivergent students?
4. What can schools do to prepare neurodivergent learners for higher education?
5. What can universities do at an organisational level to make higher education more accessible for neurodivergent students?

Takeaway activities that the reader can try out in their own setting

- Do an environmental check on your office/teaching spaces/campus thoroughfare/communal spaces. Look for changes that can be made in terms of accessibility and the eight senses that impact on neurodivergent people.
- Audit your teaching resources/assignment guidance and feedback/course administration. Look for changes that can be made to increase usability for neurodivergent learners and staff.
- Commission or undertake contemporary autistic-led/co-produced autism and neurodivergent training.

References

#AttentionUK (n.d.) *Understanding ADHD stigma.* Available at: https://attentionuk.org/frequently-asked-questions/understanding-adhd-stigma/. Accessed: 6th May 2024.

Asasumasu, K. (2015) *PSA from the actual coiner of "neurodivergent"*. Available at: https://sherlocksflataffect.tumblr.com/post/121295972384/psa-from-the-actual-coiner-of-neurodivergent. Accessed: 8th July 2023.

Autism Understood (2024) Situational/selective mutism. *Autism Understood*, 19th January 2024. Available at: https://autismunderstood.co.uk/co-occurring-conditions/selective-mutism/. Accessed: 10th May 2024.

Balasco, L., Provenzano, G., & Bozzi, Y. (2019) Sensory abnormalities in autism spectrum disorders: A focus on the tactile domain, from genetic mouse models to the clinic. *Frontiers in Psychiatry,* 10, p. 1016. Published: 28th January 2020. https://doi.org/10.3389/fpsyt.2019.01016

Ballou, E. P. (2018) What the neurodiversity does – and doesn't – offer. *Thinking Person's Guide to Autism*. Available at: https://thinkingautismguide.com/2018/02/what-neurodiversity-movement-doesand.html. Accessed: 14th December 2023.

Bertilsdotter Rosqvist, H., Hjorth, E., & Nygren, A. (2023) Meeting up in broken word/times: Communication, temporality and pace in neuro-mixed writing. *Medical Humanities*, September, 49(3), pp. 407–415. https://doi.org/10.1136/medhum-2022-012384

Bertilsdotter Rosqvist, H., Hultman, L., Österborg Wiklund, S., Nygren, A., Storm, P., & Sandberg, G. (2023) Naming ourselves, becoming neurodivergent scholars. *Disability & Society*, pp. 1–20. https://doi.org/10.1080/09687599.2023.2271155

Bertilsdotter-Rosqvist, H., Stenning, A., & Chown, N. (2020) *Neurodiversity studies: A new critical paradigm.* London: Routledge.

Bijlenga, D., Tjon-Ka-Jie, J. Y. M., Schuijers, F., & Kooij, J. J. S. (2017) Atypical sensory profiles as core features of adult ADHD, irrespective of autistic symptoms. *European Psychiatry*, 43, pp. 51–57. http://doi.org/10.1016/j.eurpsy.2017.02.481

Bolton, P., & Hubble, S. (2021) *Support for disabled students in higher education in England*. Available at: https://commonslibrary.parliament.uk/research-briefings/cbp-8716/

Cage, E., De Andres, M., & Mahoney, P. (2020) Understanding the factors that affect university completion for autistic people. *Research in Autism Spectrum Disorders*, 72, p. 101519. https://doi.org/10.1016/j.rasd.2020.101519

Cage, E., & Howes, J. (2020) Dropping out and moving on: A qualitative study of autistic people's experiences of university. *Autism*, 24(7), pp. 1664–1675. https://doi.org/10.1177/1362361320918750

Cameron, H., & Billington, T. (2017) 'Just deal with it': Neoliberalism in dyslexic students' talk about dyslexia and learning at university. *Studies in Higher Education*, 42(8), pp. 1358–1372. https://doi.org/10.1080/03075079.2015.1092510

Casanova, M. F., Frye, R. E., Gillberg, C., & Casanova, E. L. (2020) Editorial: Comorbidity and autism spectrum disorder. *Frontiers in Psychiatry*. Published: 20th November 2020. https://doi.org/10.3389/fpsyt.2020.617395

Centre for Disease Control (2024) *Clinical testing and diagnosis for autism spectrum disorder*. 27th February 2024. Available at: https://www.cdc.gov/autism/hcp/diagnosis/index.html#:~:text=Hyper%2D%20or%20hyporeactivity%20to%20sensory,fascination%20with%20lights%20or%20movement. Accessed: 18th May 2024.

Clouder, L., Karakus, M., Cinotti, A., Ferreyra, M. V., Fierros, G. A., & Rojo, P. (2020) Neurodiversity in higher education: A narrative synthesis. *Higher Education*, 80, pp. 757–778. https://doi.org/10.1007/s10734-020-00513-6

Davidson, J., & Orsini, M. (eds) (2013) *Worlds of autism: Across the spectrum of neurological difference*. Minneapolis, MN: University of Minnesota Press.

Department for Work and Pensions (February 2024) *Buckland review of autism employment: Report and recommendations*. Available at: https://www.gov.uk/government/publications/the-buckland-review-of-autism-employment-report-and-recommendations

Edyburn, D. L. (2010) Would you recognise Universal Design for Learning if you saw it? Ten propositions for new directions for the second Decade of UDL. *Learning Disability Quarterly*, 33, pp. 33–41.

Farrant, F., & Owen, E. (2023) How to make your university more neurodiverse friendly. *Times Higher Education*, 7th September 2023. Available at: https://www.timeshighereducation.com/campus/how-make-your-university-more-neurodiverse-friendly

Goodall, C. (2018) 'I felt closed in and like I couldn't breathe': A qualitative study exploring the mainstream educational experiences of autistic young people. *Autism & Developmental Language Impairments*, 3. https://doi.org/10.1177/2396941518804407

Gray, L. (2019) *Educational trauma examples from testing to the school-to-prison pipeline*. Palgrave Macmillan.

Hamilton, L. G., & Petty, S. (2023) Compassionate pedagogy for neurodiversity in higher education: A conceptual analysis. *Frontiers in Psychology*, 16th February;14, p. 1093290. https://doi.org/10.3389/fpsyg.2023.1093290. Erratum in: *Frontiers in Psychology*, 20th February 2024;14, p. 1345256. PMID: 36874864; PMCID: PMC9978378.

Horgan, F., Kenny, N., & Flynn, P. (2023) A systematic review of the experiences of autistic young people enrolled in mainstream second-level (post-primary) schools. *Autism,* Febraury;27(2), pp. 526–538. doi: 10.1177/13623613221105089. Epub 2022 Jun 25. PMID: 35757990.

Irvine, B., & MacLeod, A. (2022) What are the challenges and successes reported by autistic students at university: A literature review. *Good Autism Practice*, 23(1). https://www.researchgate.net/publication/361337091

Jellinek, M. S. (2010) Don't let ADHD crush children's self-esteem. *Clinical Psychiatry News*, 1st May 2010. Available at: https://www.mdedge.com/psychiatry/article/23971/pediatrics/dont-let-adhd-crush-childrens-self-esteem. Accessed: 4th May 2024.

Kamath, M. S., Dahm, C. R., Tucker, J. R., Huang-Pollock, C. L., Etter, N. M., & Neely, K. A. (2020) Sensory profiles in adults with and without ADHD. *Research in Developmental Disabilities*, 104. https://doi.org/10.1016/j.ridd.2020.103696

Keates, N., Martin, F., & Waldock, K. E. (2024) Autistic people's perspectives on functioning labels and associated reasons, and community connectedness. *Journal of Autism Developmental Disorders*, 20th March. https://doi.org/10.1007/s10803-024-06316-3. Epub ahead of print. PMID: 38507152.

Lai, M., Kassee, C., Besney, R., Bonato, S., Hull, L., Mandy, W., Szatmari, P., & Ameis, S. H. (2019) Prevalence of co-occurring mental health diagnoses in the autism population: A systematic review and meta-analysis. *The Lancet Psychiatry*, 6(10), pp. 819–829. https://doi.org/10.1016/S2215-0366(19)30289-5

legislation.gov.uk (2010) *UK Equality Act*. London: The Stationery Office. Available at: https://www.legislation.gov.uk/ukpga/2010/15/contents

Little, C., Pearson, A., & Gimblett, K. (2023) Reasonable adjustment, unfair advantage or optional extra? Teaching staff attitudes towards reasonable adjustments for students with disabilities. *Journal of Perspectives in Applied Academic Practice*, 1(2), pp. 135–146. https://doi.org/10.56433/jpaap.v11i2.546

Mahto, M., Hogan, S. K., & Sniderman, B. (2022) Creating a better work environment for all by embracing neurodiversity. *Deloitte Insights*, 18th January 2022. Available at: https://www2.deloitte.com/us/en/insights/topics/talent/neurodiversity-in-the-workplace.html. Accessed: 2nd May 2024.

Mesa, S., & Hamilton, L. G. (2022) *School transitions for autistic young people in mainstream settings*. Available at: https://ray.yorksj.ac.uk/id/eprint/7063/1/School-transitions-for-autistic-pupils-report.pdf. Accessed: 19th April 2024.

Milton, D. E. M. (2012) On the ontological status of autism: The 'double empathy problem'. *Disability & Society*, 27(6), pp. 883–887. https://doi.org/10.1080/09687599.2012.710008

Milton, D. E. M., Martin, N., & Melham, P. (2017) *Beyond reasonable adjustment: Autistic-friendly spaces and universal design. Autism and intellectual disability in adults*. Volume 1. Pavilion Publishing and Media Ltd.

North East Autism Society (n.d.) *Autistic students most likely to drop out of university: Investigation*. Available at: https://www.ne-as.org.uk/news/autistic-students-most-likely-to-drop-out-of-university-investigation#:~:text=Autistic%20students%20are%20less%20likely,an%20overall%20rate%20of%2029%25. Accessed: 2nd May 2024.

O'Nions, E., Petersen, I., Buckman, J. E., Charlton, R. A., Cooper, C., Corbett, A., Happé, F., Manthorpe, J., Richards, M., Saunders, R., & Zanker, C. (2023) *Autism in England: Investigating underdiagnosis in a population-based cohort*. The Lancet Regional Health Europe.

Pearson, A., & Rose, K. (2021) A conceptual analysis of autistic masking: Understanding the narrative of stigma and the illusion of choice. *Autism in Adulthood*, 3(1). https://doi.org/10.1089/aut.2020.0043

Prato, A., Saia, F., Ferrigno, M., Finocchiaro, V., Barone, R., & Rizzo, R. (2024) Sensory phenomena in children with Tourette syndrome or autism spectrum disorder. *Frontiers in Psychiatry*, 15, p. 1338234. https://doi.org/10.3389/fpsyt.2024.1338234

Sarrett, J. C. (2018) Autism and accommodations in higher education: Insights from the autism community. *Journal of Autism and Developmental Disorders*, 48, pp. 679–693. https://doi.org/10.1007/s10803-017-3353-4

Sedgwick, J. A. (2018) University students with attention deficit hyperactivity disorder (ADHD): A literature review. *Irish Journal of Psychological Medicine*, September;35(3), pp. 221–235. https://doi.org/10.1017/ipm.2017.20. PMID: 30124182.

Sedgwick-Müller, J. A., Müller-Sedgwick, U., Adamou, M., Catani, M., Champ, R., Gudjónsson, G., Hank, D., Pitts, M., Young, S., & Asherson, P. (2022) University students with attention deficit hyperactivity disorder (ADHD): A consensus statement from the UK Adult ADHD Network (UKAAN). *BMC Psychiatry*, 22, p. 292. https://doi.org/10.1186/s12888-022-03898-z.

Spaeth, E., & Pearson, A. (2023) A reflective analysis on how to promote a positive learning experience for neurodivergent students. *Journal of Perspectives in Applied Academic Practice*, 11(2), pp. 109–120. https://doi.org/10.56433/jpaap.v11i2.517

Symonds, H. (2009) Teaching, assessment: You think' learning 'it's not like you think. Pollack, D. (ed) *Neurodiversity in higher education: Positive responses to specific learning differences*. Chichester: John Wiley & Sons.

Tammet, D. (2007) *Born on a blue day*. Hodder Paperbacks.

The Unite Students Applicant Index (2022) Available at: https://www.unitegroup.com/wp-content/uploads/2022/07/Applicant-Index-2022-Final.pdf. Accessed: 10th July 2023.

Walker, N. (2014) *Neurodiversity: Some basic terms and definitions*. Available at: https://neuroqueer.com/neurodiversity-terms-and-definitions/. Accessed: 18th April 2024.

Wood, R. (2020) The wrong kind of noise: Understanding and valuing the communication of autistic children in schools. *Educational Review*, 72(1), pp. 111–130. https://doi.org/10.1080/00131911.2018.1483895

Woods, R., Milton, D., Arnold, L., & Graby, S. (2018) Redefining critical autism studies: A more inclusive interpretation. *Disability & Society*, 33(6), pp. 974–979. https://doi.org/10.1080/09687599.2018.1454380

Conclusion

Clare Woolhouse and Virginia Kay

The examples and case studies shared within the chapters of this book offer suggestions for how innovative research and practice can be conducted with children and the communities they are in. What emerged are three key themes that appear to effectively alter the potential for developing learning opportunities that are experienced as inclusive, which we briefly revisit in what follows.

Children's agency and rights

Within this text, from the very first chapter, by Robinson, concerns are raised about what rights children have and how they can be put into practice. Within educational contexts, reliance is often placed on the importance of internationally recognised guidance, such as the UN Convention on the Rights of the Child (1989), or on national and local policies, but how can this be assured?

Building on the UN's Article 12.1 cited in the introduction to this book, there has been the suggestion that the right for children to actively participate and share their views involves 'ongoing processes, which include information-sharing and dialogue between children and adults based on mutual respect, and in which children can learn how their views and those of adults are taken into account and shape the outcome of such processes' (General Comment No. 12 of the Committee on the Rights of the Child, cited in Duramy & Gal, 2020).

So how can we involve children in this dialogue? Within related literature, there are frequently questions around how adults can establish a child's capacity to understand and access their rights (Dixon & Nussbaum, 2012; Chicken & Tyrie, 2023). This concern is perhaps addressed by Campbell's (1992, p. 5) argument – that the most important aspect is ensuring that any action or decision should be in a child's *best interests* and that these should be protected 'by the imposition of (legal or moral) normative constraints'.

Unfortunately, it has been pointed out that children's agency and voices are mainly absent in UK education policies that affect them (see Harris, 2020). While we support the need for children's rights and interests to be legislated for by experts, this does not negate the need for children's views to be given due attention; indeed, the intention of this text was to reframe how children and young people are experts in their own lives, and their voices could be listened to more actively and effectively. As Jackson points out in Chapter 2, a child's voice may not be verbally communicated, which places the onus on those working with children to find innovative ways to ensure children's needs and desires are recognised and central to policy and practice. Other examples of such innovative approaches are offered in Chapter 4, which details an inclusive student voice programme, with a special focus upon children with a range of communication, interaction, social, sensory, and learning differences whose voices may often go unheard (Goodall & MacKenzie, 2019; Odeh et al., 2021). Chapters 6, 8, 9, and 10 all provide practical examples of how children and young people can be directly involved in collaborative approaches to research and/or redesign practice in order that they can benefit from this involvement and guide future practice. Finally, our own Chapter 7 discusses how visual research methodologies can be used to facilitate the sharing of children's experiences and reflections. Active integration of children's views in any practice that affects them is essential if the places in which they spend so much time during childhood are to adequately reflect their priorities.

Revisiting the concept and practice of inclusion

In reading through the various chapters, it is clear that inclusion can be an indistinct and 'slippery' concept (Hodkinson, 2011, p. 181) that can be difficult to 'get right' (Tajic & Bunar, 2023). Yet at the same time, utilising child-focused, holistic, and individualised approaches can offer routes for creating learning that is experienced as inclusive (Dunne et al., 2018; Sargeant, 2018; Schwab et al., 2018). Approaches that can be utilised whether it is practice to support children's mental health (Chapter 3) or to focus on the abilities of children with autism in school (Chapters 4 and 5), to understand experiences of exclusion (Chapters 6 and 7), or to advance children and young people's involvement in co-produced research (Chapters 8 and 10).

As has been discussed within this text, inclusion is not about supporting a particular group of pupils; rather, there is a need to ensure suitable inclusive approaches are integrated in practice to support all children and young people in education and to challenge systemic inequalities. In the UK, the calls for this have often focused on issues of socio-economic disadvantage and the lack of funding. For example, Andrews et al. (2017) indicate that government financial support over the past ten years and the slow pace of change mean disadvantaged pupils will continue to fall behind their peers in school at least until the second half of the 21st century, a concern also raised by Reay (2018). One possible response considered by Millington (2023) is to enable teachers to feel respected and to have freedom and the power to make more individualised choices about how to support the children they work with. This resonates with concerns raised by Jackson in Chapter 2 about practitioners feeling they are marginalised, even ostracised, when determining the best course of action for supporting an individual child. A view that is echoed by Shevlin and Rose (2022), who argue that there needs to be a commitment to democratic principles, requiring the voices of all individuals to be listened to and respected.

Relationships and communication

One aspect of responding to all relevant voices involved in designing, delivering, or experiencing inclusive education can be to focus on egalitarian, collaborative working, within which transparent, authentic, and honest communications are facilitated. This form of communication can lead to strong and effective relationships being built between children, between children and adults, and between adults – to include teachers, educational support staff, health- and social care practitioners, and parents (for examples, see Bolourian et al., 2021; Messiou, 2019; Mitchell & Sutherland, 2020). Essential factors in this communication include a sense of mutual respect, as, O'Connor et al. (2018, p. 50) argue, there is a need for teachers and parents to build respectful relationships, where 'each partner regards all others with esteem' and where teachers 'communicate care for family through actions and words . . . treating students and families with dignity'.

One of the long-standing challenges with developing good communication has been how professionals from different fields work together, as noted by Jackson in Chapter 2 (see also Ainslie et al., 2010). So alongside respect for families and pupils, there is the need for all professionals to encourage routes of clear communication within a 'transdisciplinary model of collaboration' that offers an integrated, child-centred approach based on individual need (Mortier & Aramburo, 2022, p. 1).

Planning to change policy and practice

In drawing together the themes and experiences shared within the chapters of the book, there have been useful examples that can offer ways to overcome challenges from different settings when working with different groups of learners. Complementing this, each chapter has provided 'takeaway activities' that can be useful to evaluate and rework current policy and practice. As discussed in Chapter 6, this can be done through fictionalised scenarios, or by researching provision with the involvement of children or young people, who can offer innovative approaches (see also Chapters 7, 8, and 10). Involving children at an early stage in planning can be extremely insightful, and we provide in the following an outline of the types of questions or activities practitioners and researchers can consider.

Deciding a focus

- What background information is needed?
- Choose the topic to be addressed, namely, school policy development, experiences of transition, mental health, behaviour, cyberbullying, plastic pollution.
- What is known about this topic? What is missing? What do you need to find out?
- What are the key aspects of this topic to be investigated?
- Who is to be involved in this investigation?
- What might be the issues and difficulties with discussing the topic?

Engaging children

- Undertake a lesson or event with a chosen group to explore a key issue relating to the topic. This could be in one school lesson or across a themed day or week; it could be as part of an informal learning space, such as in a museum or outside with a scout group.
- To plan the event ask:
    - What is the rationale – who, where, when, why?
    - How will the event be put into practice (relevant policy, objectives, and pedagogic strategies to be used, benefits for children)?
    - Do you have an action plan for making it happen in the setting? Who needs to be involved in organising, funding, running day, etc.?
    - Can you use creative activities/develop creative outputs?
    - What will be the process for evaluating what happened at the event?
- Future planning.

Questions to discuss with professional colleagues

- What topics would your staff and pupils be interested in exploring?
- What aspects of the methods discussed in the book could you use?
- How would you use them?
- What questions would you ask to prompt discussion?
- How will this fit in with your curriculum, form time, after-school club, etc.?

. . . and finally

This book has offered a wide range of different case studies, experiences, activities, and projects that have been implemented to enhance the role of children and children's voices in championing positive change. We hope that this will prompt practitioners and students of education studies to reflect upon and question current policies and practice and share their own ideas and experiences more widely.

References

Ainslie, S., Foster, R., Groves, J., Grime, K., Straker, K. and Woolhouse, C. 2010. Making children count: An exploration of the implementation of the every child matters agenda. *Education 3–13*, 38(1), February, pp. 23–38.

Andrews, J., Hutchinson, J. and Robinson, D. 2017. *Closing the Gap? Trends in Educational Attainment and Disadvantage*. Available from: https://epi.org.uk/wpcontent/uploads/2017/08/Closing-the-Gap_EPI.pdf

Bolourian, Y., Losh, A., Hamsho, N., Eisenhower, A. and Blacher, J. 2021. General education teachers' perceptions of autism, inclusive practices, and relationship building strategies. *Journal of Autism and Developmental Disorders*, pp. 1–14.

Campbell, T. 1992. The rights of the minor. In Alston, P., Parker, S. and Seymour, J. (Eds) *Children's Rights and the Law*. Clarendon Press.

Chicken, S. and Tyrie, J. 2023. Can you hear me? Problematising the enactment of UNCRC article 12 in Welsh early years classrooms: Exploring the challenges of "children's voice". *The International Journal of Children's Rights*, 31(2), pp. 301–325.

Dixon, R. and Nussbaum, M. 2012. Children's rights and a capabilities approach: The question of special priority. *97 Cornell Law Review*, p. 549.

Dunne, L., Hallett, F., Kay, V. and Woolhouse, C. 2018. Spaces of inclusion: Investigating place, positioning and perspective within educational settings through photo-elicitation. *International Journal of Inclusive Education*, 22(1), pp. 21–37. Available from: http://www.tandfonline.com/doi/full/10.1080/13603116.2017.1348546

Duramy, B. F. and Gal, T. 2020. Understanding and implementing child participation: Lessons from the Global South. *Children and Youth Services Review*, 119, p. 105645.

Goodall, C. and MacKenzie, A. 2019. What about my voice? Autistic young girls' experiences of mainstream school. *European Journal of Special Needs Education*, 34(4), pp. 499–513.

Harris, N. 2020. *Education, Law and Diversity* (2nd edition). Hart Publishing.

Hodkinson, A. 2011. Inclusion: A defining definition? *Power and Education*, 3(2), pp. 179–185.

Messiou, K. 2019. The missing voices: Students as a catalyst for promoting inclusive education. *International Journal of Inclusive Education*, 23(7–8), pp. 768–781.

Millington, G. 2023. When inclusion leads to exclusion: A consideration of the impact of inclusive policy on school leaders working within a pupil referral unit. *PRISM Casting New Light on Learning, Theory and Practice*, 5(1), pp. 1–15.

Mitchell, D. and Sutherland, D. 2020. *What Really Works in Special and Inclusive Education: Using Evidence-based Teaching Strategies*. Routledge.

Mortier, K. and Aramburo, C. 2022. Collaborative teaming to support quality inclusive education for students with disabilities. *Collaborative Teaming to Support Quality Inclusive Education for Students with Disabilities*. Available from: https://doi.org/10.4324/9781138609877-ree157-1.

O'Connor, S., Azatyan, M. T., Karapetyan, L. and Paylozyan, Z. 2018. The role of families in inclusive education. In *Inclusive Education Strategies: A Textbook*. Institute on Community Integration, University of Minnesota, pp. 39–49.

Odeh, K. B., Jones, N., Pincock, K. and Malachowska, A. 2021. 'I Wish Someone Would Ask Me Questions': The unheard voices of adolescents with disabilities in Jordan. *The European Journal of Development Research*, 33(5), pp. 1328–1348.

Reay, D. 2018. Miseducation: Inequality, education and the working classes. *International Studies in Sociology of Education*, 27(4), pp. 453–456. Available from: https://doi.org/10.1080/09620214.2018.1531229

Sargeant, J. 2018. Towards voice-inclusive practice: Finding the sustainability of participation in realising the child's rights in education. *Children & Society*, 32(4), pp. 314–324.

Schwab, S., Sharma, U. and Loreman, T. 2018. Are we included? Secondary students' perception of inclusion climate in their schools. *Teaching and Teacher Education*, 75, pp. 31–39.

Shevlin, M. and Rose, R. 2022. Respecting the voices of individuals from marginalised communities in research. "Who is listening and who isn't?". *Education Sciences*, 12(5), p. 304.

Tajic, D. and Bunar, N. 2023. Do both 'get it right'? Inclusion of newly arrived migrant students in Swedish primary schools. *International Journal of Inclusive Education*, 27(3), pp. 288–302.

United Nations Convention on the Rights of the Child. 1989. Available from: http://www.ohchr.org/EN/ProfessionalInterest/Pages/CRC.aspx

Index

active learning 48, 69–70, 78, 119
anxiety 27–28, 32, 38, 53, 90, 126–128, 131, 134
autism 45–46, 48, 53–55, 93, 104, 125–126, 128, 134

children's rights 2, 7–10, 13, 29, 77, 139
collaboration 35, 50, 70, 89, 92, 96, 98, 102
communication 3, 8, 12–13, 23, 48–52, 55, 69, 71, 75, 89, 91, 93, 102, 104, 111, 117–119, 120, 126, 133
community 3–4, 13, 23, 30, 48, 50–52, 55, 59, 63–64, 78, 80, 82–84, 90–91, 93, 95, 97–98, 102, 106, 110–111, 115, 118–121
confidence 18–19, 22, 30–31, 34–35, 46, 50, 53–54, 62, 66, 72, 96, 104, 106, 110–111, 116–117, 125, 129
connection 27–32, 34–35, 51, 73, 101, 104, 109, 119
Convention on the Rights of the Child (CRC) 3, 7, 10, 12–13, 25, 29, 45, 47, 50, 59, 65, 69, 77–78, 91–92
Covid-19 1, 24, 77, 102, 111, 115
curriculum 17, 19, 28–29, 50, 64, 66, 70–71, 77, 82, 97, 127–128, 141

Department for Education (DfE) 1, 17–19, 21, 27, 29–30, 45–46, 71, 75, 78, 128
disability 9–10, 20, 45, 49, 60, 89, 101–105, 111–112, 126, 128
discrimination 9–10, 130
dyslexia 59–62, 125

early years education 3, 9, 17–19, 25, 32–33, 70, 79, 135
educational, health and care plans (EHCP) 46, 71, 73–74
empathy/empathic 28–29, 31, 38, 133–134
emotional safety 3, 18, 27–30, 33
engagement 24, 27, 30, 39, 47–48, 51, 53–55, 70, 73–74, 77, 81–82, 84, 90, 93, 102–104, 106, 111, 129–130, 134
environment 3, 7–14, 17–19, 22–23, 30, 32, 34, 46, 48, 50, 55, 61, 63, 70, 78, 83, 89, 93, 97, 104–105, 109, 111–112, 116, 125–126, 129–131, 133–135
ethos 7, 11, 13–14, 17, 20, 50, 52, 64, 74
evaluation 97, 101, 103, 108, 110, 111
exclusion 1, 30, 46, 77–78, 80, 97, 101, 105, 133, 140

gender 1, 126

identity 12, 126
inclusion 1–3, 9, 11–12, 14, 18, 39, 50, 54, 70–71, 77–80, 83, 89, 92, 96, 97, 101–103, 106–107, 111, 125, 128, 140

language 8, 10–11, 20, 23, 29, 35, 49–50, 59, 63–64, 80, 91, 103–105, 111, 118, 120, 126, 129
lifelong learning 79, 89, 101–102, 117
listening 9, 11–14, 17, 19, 21, 24–25, 45, 47, 51, 65, 74–75, 83

marginalisation 9, 78–80, 83, 111
mental health 1, 3, 18, 27, 29–30, 32–35, 39, 50, 74, 84, 89–90, 93–94, 97, 117, 126, 128, 140–141

nurturing 20, 28, 31, 33–34, 47, 135 (caring) 18, 28–29, 32, 75, 105, 111

participation 2, 7, 9–10, 13, 39, 45–52, 71, 78, 90–91, 93, 101–102, 104, 110–112, 116
partnership(s) 17, 21, 48, 59, 61–62, 69, 89–90, 92–93, 97–98, 111, 117, 120
policy 1–3, 9, 17, 22, 26, 30, 45, 59–60, 69, 71, 75, 78, 82–83, 97–98, 116, 120, 139–141
power (empower) 1, 3, 9, 11–13, 31–32, 35–36, 39, 46–49, 51, 54–55, 61, 64–65, 67, 69, 75, 81–82, 90, 92–93, 96–97, 104–105, 111, 116, 118, 128, 140
practical (activities/approaches/insights) 2, 20, 51, 53, 55, 70, 77, 79, 82, 89, 118, 139
primary education/school 22, 27–28, 30–35, 41, 52, 59, 63–64, 66, 69–70, 72–73, 79, 83, 127, 130
professional development 18, 48, 50, 70, 79
pupil 29–30, 64–66, 71–75, 83, 94, 97, 132

race/ethnicity 1, 9–10, 12, 67, 93, 95, 126
reflection(s) 1–3, 20, 24–25, 27–28, 30, 46, 51, 63, 70, 72–73, 81–83, 89–90, 93–94, 97–98, 132, 139
relationship(s) 21–22, 24, 32–34, 47–48, 51, 61, 75, 94, 97, 113
representation 36, 39, 45, 49, 51–52, 90, 111, 121, 126, 129
resilience 3, 18, 27–29, 33
respect(ed/ful) 4, 8, 11–12, 14, 17, 22, 24, 31–32, 45, 49–51, 59–60, 65–67, 69, 91, 96, 104, 109, 118, 126, 139–140
rights *see* children's rights

secondary education 22, 52, 54, 64, 72–73, 79, 81, 83, 89, 93, 95–96, 101, 127
SEND Code of Practice 1, 19, 21, 46, 69, 71–73, 75
space(s) 3–4, 12–13, 19, 21–23, 32, 47, 49, 52, 55, 70, 74, 78, 81, 83, 91–92, 95, 102, 105, 107, 115, 117, 126, 130–135, 141
Special Educational Needs (SEN)/ and Disability (SEND) 1, 17, 20, 46, 60–61, 69, 71, 79, 94

teaching assistant 28, 34, 39–40, 60, 82, 84
time 1, 3, 12–13, 17–18, 20–25, 27, 30, 32, 35, 40, 48–49, 51, 54–55, 63, 72–73, 91, 96–98, 105, 108–110, 112, 117–121, 130, 132, 134, 141

transform (transformation/transformative) 17, 34–35, 47, 52, 83, 111
transition 22, 28, 31, 53–54, 59–60, 73, 83, 101, 127, 132, 141
trust (ed) 13, 27–30, 32–33, 35, 39, 48–49, 54, 63, 83, 93–94, 97

UN Convention *see* Convention on the Rights of the Child (CRC)

voice (pupil/children's) 1–3, 7, 10–13, 18, 21, 23–25, 27–30, 35–36, 38–39, 45–49, 51–56, 64–65, 69, 71, 74–75, 77, 82–83, 89, 92, 96–97, 102, 104, 116–118, 139

For Product Safety Concerns and Information please contact our EU representative GPSR@taylorandfrancis.com
Taylor & Francis Verlag GmbH, Kaufingerstraße 24, 80331 München, Germany

www.ingramcontent.com/pod-product-compliance
Lightning Source LLC
Chambersburg PA
CBHW080909230426
43664CB00017B/2764